POWER SEWING

New Ways to Make Fine Clothes Fast

Sandra Betzina Webster

author of *Fear of Sewing*
and *More Power Sewing*

REVISED EDITION

Practicality Press
New York

I would like to thank my youngest children—Justin, Monique and Shaun—for under-standing the importance of this book and without whose help the book would have been finished far sooner, and my oldest daughter, Kimberly, for helping me set my priorities. I would like to thank my husband, Dan, for the carpooling, grocery shopping and cooking necessary in the book's final stages.

Practicality Press
An imprint of Multi Media Communicators, Inc.
575 Madison Ave., Suite 1006
New York, NY 10022

Illustrations by Tina Cash-Walsh, Amy Maeda and Melanie Graysmith.
Photography by Barbara Thompson.
Cover design by Tina Cash-Walsh.

ISBN 1-880630-13-3

Library of Congress Catalog Card Number: 93-084529

Printed in the United States of America

Table of Contents

Marriage of Pattern and Fabric

More often than not the success of a garment is determined right in the fabric store by the choice of pattern and fabric. If an incompatible choice is made, no amount of meticulous sewing can turn the garment into a success.

Before you begin a new project, think the garment through. Consider your wardrobe needs at the present. Do you need a new coat, a dressy outfit, an outfit for the country, a comfortable but good-looking dress to wear at home? Once you have decided what your needs are, get down to the specifics.

What color do you want? For evening, dramatic colors make you feel more festive. For outdoor activities, earthy tones seem more appropriate. At-home wear is more flexible; let your wild side come out here.

What style do you want: tailored dress, tunic, full sleeves, mandarin collar? Be specific.

Now you are ready for a trip to the fabric store. Try to find what you visualized. Get samples. Look through the pattern books. Try to find one or two patterns that can be combined to get the look you want. Go home with your fabric samples and your pattern numbers and think it over.

What accessories do you have that will work with this outfit? This may influence fabric choice. If new shoes are necessary, you are facing additional cost.

Everyone I know who sews has had failures or, as we sewing teachers sometimes call them, "the dogs." Why do they happen and how can we keep them to a minimum?

For some people, the biggest culprit is fit. The same old fitting problems keep repeating themselves in various degrees, depending on the style. If this is your problem, enroll in a fitting class or pay a dressmaker to tell you how to alter patterns for your figure.

Or the problem may be style. It simply is not flattering. It doesn't look the same on you as it did on the model.

But do you have that model's figure? Be realistic—some styles are only for the very tall and thin. How can you know? Try on a similar style in ready-to-wear and see how flattering it is before you go to all the trouble of making it up.

If possible, before you buy the designer pattern, try on its ready-to-wear counterpart. If you are particularly attracted to a certain designer, try on everything in the collection.

Choose which styles look good on you. Make a note of any style changes you might like to make on your own garment.

Don't make the mistake of thinking that just because the designer ready-to-wear fits you perfectly, the pattern will, too. The designer pattern is a line-for-line copy that is made on the basic pattern used as a size standard by the pattern company.

To be certain of a perfect fit, make up the pattern in muslin or a scrap fabric first.

The problem may be that the fabric and the pattern are not compatible. Usually this is not apparent until after the garment is completed. What went wrong? If you have difficulty combining patterns and fabric, you need to go on a shopping trip. Carefully study what fabrics are used with what styles. What weight works for pants? What weight works in a full skirt?

Demonstrated on *Power Sewing* Video #5: *Construction Difficulties.*

Marriage of Pattern and Fabric

Several well-known designers make up the same designs in ten different fabrics, finally choosing the one that works best for the design. Take advantage of the homework done by the designer and benefit from the results.

The identical fabric is not necessary, but one with similar properties would be the best choice.

I always listen to my inner voice in choosing fabric. If I have the creeping silent thought *this fabric might be too stiff*—it is! Every time I have tried to force a firm fabric into a fluid style, the result has been disastrous.

Study the design details, the trim and buttons. These details often make the difference between a ready-to-wear and a loving-hands-at-home look.

As a sewing instructor, I have seen students use the wrong fabric with a great pattern and come up with disappointing results.

The fabric is too heavy. Full styles call for fabric that drapes well. Gather the fabric in your hand and hang it in front of your body. Is it graceful or bulky? No amount of careful construction can right the initial error in fabric choice.

The fabric is a loose weave and does not hold its shape. A garment made in such fabric will stretch out of shape, making it a perfect candidate for the church rummage sale.

The color is unflattering. This is easily prevented. Take the bolt of fabric over to a mirror. Unwind a few yards of fabric and wrap it around you. Look in the mirror. Does it look OK, good, or spectacular? Nothing less than spectacular should motivate you to take money out of your purse.

The design is overwhelming. Some prints look better on the kitchen table than they do on you. If you find yourself choosing prints that are too big and bold, limit yourself to solids for a while, or a solid with a small, subtle print in it.

Fabric addiction. Do you find yourself saying, "I bought this fabric on sale two years ago, and I simply must do something with it"? Shame on you. You are one of the thousands of "fabricoholics," those who buy fabric without any idea of what they're going to do with it.

Cure yourself of this creativity-stifling disease. Box up all fabrics you bought over three months ago and haul them over to a local charity.

When you have made your decision, choose your interfacing carefully. Button selection should be well thought out: the wrong buttons can ruin the total look.

After the garment has been completed, try it on. Decide what is needed to really pull the look together: perhaps a good belt, some interesting jewelry. Once you've put the whole ensemble together, you will get great enjoyment and satisfaction each time you wear it.

How about the failures where no apparent culprit can be found? Blame the pattern company. Some designs simply are not flattering.

Your only salvation here is always to make a pretest. If the pretest looks frumpy or unflattering, throw out the pattern. A few hours have been wasted, but nothing compared to the time and money you would have put into the completed garment—only to discover the same results.

What to do about the dogs in the closet? Can they be saved? Probably not. Bag them up, give or throw them away, but definitely get rid of them.

Fabric Awareness

Perhaps one of the reasons sewers have failures is that they never get to know the fabric friends. These are fabrics which are ALWAYS A SUCCESS. For cold weather, sew with wool jersey and wool crepe. These fabrics are flattering on the figure, wear well, and travel well. For warm weather, sew with rayon challis, washed silk, and silk crepe de chine. These fabrics offer a good drape as well as a quality look to whatever they are made in.

Have you ever wondered why a busy individual will often sacrifice on garment style to get "serviceable fabric"? Busy life-styles often require a garment to begin service at 7:00 A.M. working double shifts without coffee breaks until 11:00 P.M. A serviceable fabric is one which provides comfort throughout the day in a variety of temperatures, looks crisp and new after years of wear—without shine or sag in seat or elbows—wrinkles little, if any, and has the ability to begin service again without touch-ups after a brief rest overnight.

If your sewing time is limited, it's time to get smart about fabrics by learning to avoid mistakes which cause disappointment in performance. One of the best ways to acquire fabric knowledge is to ask questions as you browse better ready-to-wear. Ask fabric names. Get acquainted with their weave, and feel and drape, so that you will be able to spot the fabric in a fine fabric store. If you do not live in a metropolitan area, you may need to resort to mail order to obtain what you need. If you know the fabric by name, you will be able to request swatches in a limited color range. Requesting swatches by color is considerably more accurate if you send a color sample along. Paint sample cards are excellent if you have access to a local paint store.

Begin your fabric search with these few examples, expanding your knowledge with each discovery.

Cavalry twill is a firmly woven hard surfaced fabric, recognized by a pronounced double twill which can be seen on both sides. Cavalry twills come in wool or cotton, popular in suits, coat and slacks.

Melton is a heavily felted or fulled wool fabric which results in a smooth napped surface. While melton is warm and tailors beautifully, a melton coat may be bulky and heavy to wear.

Covert is a twill weave fabric available in wool or cotton. The fabric itself may look mottled or flecked due to the use of twisted yarns in its production. Covert fabrics resist wrinkles and are often used in rainwear since the fabric responds well to water-repellent treatment.

Broadcloth begins with a fine open twill weave which is fulled, napped, sheared, and combed laying a nap down in one direction. The result in wool broadcloth is a soft, pliable, dressy fabric able to give warmth without weight; the only drawback is that it might attract lint. The result in silk broadcloth is a soft, pliable fabric which is cool and comfortable.

Duvetyn made of wool, silk, cotton, or a combination is a fabric with a silky velvet-like appearance, which gives warmth without weight, and both drapes and tailors well. While beautiful to touch and wear, the fabric spots easily, catches lint, and shows signs of wear.

Boucle, a fabric formed by small loops on the fabric surface, is prone to snags but unbeatable when it comes to texture. Preshrink twice before cutting.

During your fabric research, remember: "Beautiful clothes start with beautiful fabric" or "You can't make a silk purse out of a sow's ear."

Pattern Analysis

Before you actually purchase a pattern, study it carefully. Look at the line drawings that show placement of the seamlines. Are these lines flattering to your body? If you are overweight, any pattern with horizontal seamlines is going to broaden your body and make you look heavier. If you have a large bust or broad shoulders, a wide yoke will accentuate the problem. If you have narrow, sloping shoulders, avoid boat necklines or raglan sleeves, which draw attention to your shoulders. If you have a tummy, pleats and soft gathers will be kinder to your figure than a tailored pant or front yoke.

Study the pattern photograph carefully. Put your hand over the model's face. These beauties look good in anything. Try to imagine your head on that photograph. If you have extra bulges, will they be hidden in this style or brought to the viewer's attention? Have you ever tried on this style in ready-to-wear? Was it flattering? Be realistic. The sewing machine cannot create miracles here.

Look at the neckline and sleeve style carefully. Would this pattern look better on you with another neckline? If so, use a neckline from another pattern as an overlay. How about the sleeves? What do you like or not like about them? These types of things can be changed.

Next, read the pattern description. If the pattern is described as "very loose fitting," you might want to buy one size smaller to eliminate some of the style ease.

Check the jacket or blouse length—will these need to be altered? Also check the skirt length and compare it to your flattering skirt length. Don't forget to alter length before you cut. Check pant and skirt width. Can these be altered easily to your specifications?

Look at the details in this pattern. Are your sewing skills developed enough to tackle this style?

Look at the photograph, again holding your hand over the model's face. Imagine yourself in this outfit. Where are you going to wear this? If you cannot think of an appropriate time or place, maybe this pattern is not for you.

If, after analyzing a pattern in this way, you are still excited about it, make it. This one's going to be a winner.

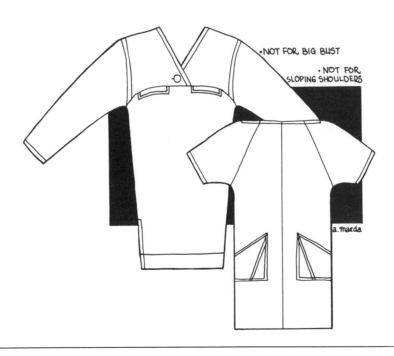

Pretest Your Pattern

Everyone wants to avoid the time spent on a pretest. Here are a couple of shortcuts. Flat-pattern measure the pattern and compare to your measurements plus ease. Flat-pattern measurement is important in problem areas such as tummy and hip.

Pin-fit the tissue to your body. Pin the tissue pattern to you, attaching shoulder seam only. Do not try to pin the side seams—the tissue will tear. A leotard makes a good base for a pin-fit. Pin tissue at center front, center back, and shoulder seams. Ask yourself: Is the neckline too high, too low? Are the shoulders too wide? Is the bodice at high bust area fitting correctly? Would a different size make a difference?

Is there enough room in the sleeve? Check buttonhole and pocket placement. Many pattern alterations may be determined from pin-fitting. Take one last look. Is the style right for you? For people who have difficulty visualizing, this last question may not be answered without making a pretest.

If a pretest is necessary (and it often is), make the pretest in fabric similar to the intended fashion fabric. Muslin rarely gives a feel for the drape of the garment. Here is an opportunity to use up some of your fabric stash or sale fabric.

Mark the pretest piece carefully, indicating waist, center front and center back, darts, buttonholes, buttons, pockets, and existing hemline. Machine-baste pretest with contrasting thread. Press, hand-baste hem up or cut off. Try on. Look carefully for any wrinkles. These point to a fitting problem. Check location of darts, buttonholes, and pockets. Check the shoulders. Would a shoulder pad make a difference? Slip one in. Check fit at bust and hip. Is there enough ease to prevent wrinkles? Is the back wide enough, or too wide? Check the length: skirt, jacket, and sleeves. Now stand back and really be critical. Is this garment worth making? Are you really excited about this, or is it 50-50? Unless you are excited, don't waste your time on this pattern. If you do love the design, make any changes learned from the pretest on the pattern right away.

■ If you simply do not have time to do a pattern pretest (who does these days?) allow for 1 inch seam allowances at the side seams. Given the inconsistency of fit among the pattern companies, wider seam allowances provide a little personal insurance.

Fabric Combinations

Putting stripes, plaids, prints, and solids together in a single garment is a popular fashion trend today, but combining fabrics this way can be tricky.

If this chic look appeals to you, a little observance program can give you a feeling for combining fabrics in an attractive way. First, study the ready-to-wear. How many fabrics are usually combined in one garment? What scale stripe or print is generally used? What is the common element tying the fabrics together?

Usually no fewer than three and no more than five fabrics are combined in one garment. The number is limited by the number of compatible fabrics available and by the need for continuity within the garment itself. Avoid large prints, as they will either dominate the garment or get lost when cut into small pieces. Smaller scale designs work better.

Finding a common element in each of the fabrics is the real trick to making the combination work. A common element can be a single color that repeats itself in each fabric.

If a common color cannot be found, a common design element can pull the fabrics together. A star pattern or a paisley design might appear in several fabrics, for example. You might purchase the same pattern in several colors.

The easiest way to combine fabrics is to use different fabrics for the various pattern pieces. More imaginative is to divide each pattern piece into sections, remembering to add seam allowances at each division so that when the pieces are seamed the combination is the same size as the original pattern piece.

If you are planning a multipieced garment, it is wise to draw a picture of each piece and code each fabric with a different color. After the pieces are cut, it is very easy to get the shapes confused, so pin together all of the pieces that make up each pattern piece. Do this as soon as possible to avoid later confusion.

If you are planning a very detailed garment, it might be wise to buy $\frac{1}{8}$ yard of each fabric and draw two pictures of the garment. Cut up one picture into the desired divisions and cut out fabric pieces to match. Do a paste-up on the second and you will be able to tell how the finished garment is going to look.

Combining textures is another way of adding interest to the garment. Texture not only adds interest but also affects you emotionally. You will find many more excuses to wear a wool challis dress than a linen one, mainly because challis feels so good. Silk makes most women look and feel sexy.

Mixing textures can make an outfit more interesting. A matte jersey skirt with a crepe de chine blouse, for instance, is a very appealing combination.

Combining fabrics can be a real manifestation of the creativity in you.

Fabric Weight Matters

What is the difference between bottom weight and top weight? Bottom-weight fabric is heavy and is used for skirts and pants. A top-weight fabric is lighter and used for blouses.

Have you ever defied these rules? Remember the results. If you use bottom-weight fabric in a blouse, the garment feels stiff and is rarely flattering to the figure. If a top-weight fabric is used for skirts or pants, the result is a wrinkled garment without the proper hang. A top-weight fabric can be used for bottom weight if it is underlined.

Underlining gives support to the outer fabric without bulk.

One particular favorite of mine is 100-percent rayon Bemberg lining. Bemberg is 45 inches wide, sells for about $5 a yard, and is washable by hand. Logantex puts out two Bemberg weights: Ambiance is lightweight, suitable for lining and underlining pants, and Chesterfield is heavier, suitable for lining jackets and coats. Recently I found two fabrics that were perfect companions in color and feeling. I wanted to make a big shirt and pants. Unfortunately, both fabrics were top-weight. I bought the fabric and underlined the pants in the rayon Bemberg. The underlining gave the pants more body and totally eliminated wrinkling.

Underlining is a simple process. Simply cut the underlining to exactly the same size as the outer fabric from the same pattern. If the fabric widths match up, both fabrics can be cut at the same time. Do not underline the pockets and waistband, just the main garment pieces.

Lay the underlining against the wrong side of the garment piece. Pin the two together vertically. Roll one half over toward the other half and see if any extra underlining slides away from the raw edge at the seam allowance. Pin the raw edges together in this position. Repeat the process for the other half. This procedure makes the underlining a tiny bit smaller, perhaps $1/8$ inch or less. The underlining should be slightly smaller, since it is closer to your body. If the outer fabric is quite lightweight, this procedure can be eliminated.

Hand-baste all edges together or, faster still, use dots of SOBO glue within the seam allowance to hold the fabric and underlining together. Hand-baste the two layers together at darts or pleats to keep them from shifting.

Sew darts and pleats through both thicknesses. Proceed in garment construction as though the two layers were one.

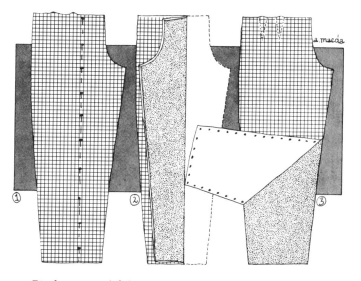

Pin lining and fabric. Pin edges. Apply glue dots.

Preparing The Fabric

Failure to preshrink all elements in the project results in puckered seams, linings which pull at the hem and garments which lack the proper ease to hang correctly. Check the end of the fabric bolt when purchasing the fabric. When returning home, toss machine washable "garments-to-be" fabric in the washing machine. Soak hand-washable "garments-to-be" fabric for 15 minutes in warm water basin. Treat dry-cleanable garments to a steam bath or hot water spritz over the shower curtain. This process should include fusible and sew-in interfacings, underlinings, and linings.

Would you like an easy alternative to paying $4 per yard for preshrinking fabric at the dry cleaners? A local tailor suggests these alternatives: Fill bathroom with steam from hot shower. Turn off shower. Hang fabric over shower rod. Let hang for 6 hours. If water shortage is a concern, fill spray bottle with hot water. Hang fabric over shower pole. Spray fabric lightly with hot water on both sides. Let hang until dry. Accordion pleat fabric in one foot wide pleats. Position fabric on hanger. When you are ready for the fabric, it is ready for you.

Since wool jersey shrinks in both length and width it must be preshrunk. To do this at home, hold iron one inch above fabric surface, letting the steam flow into the fabric. Let fabric dry completely before moving. If you don't have a long table, this process can be done easily on the floor. Always hang velour fabric for 24 hours after preshrinking. A heavy velour can stretch six inches in length.

What about washing silks? Do not hand wash silk fabric that has two or more colors: the colors will run together, giving a muddy appearance. Plain color silk garments wash successfully if the fabric has been preshrunk before being cut out. Wash the fabric by hand in warm water with a little Ivory or protein shampoo.

If the color seems to be leaving the fabric, add 3 tablespoons of vinegar to the wash and rinse water every time you wash it; the vinegar helps set the color. Hang preshrunk silk on a hanger and air-dry. Press silk while it is very damp for wrinkle-free results.

Manufacturers of zippers, stay taping and piping claim products have been preshrunk. If the care of the final garment will be machine washing and drying, preshrinking notions in a basin of warm water and air drying is advised.

How about for those of us who shop for fabric in the morning with plans of sewing in the afternoon? A few options are available: (1) Stop by a dry cleaner and request preshrinking while you wait. If they are not busy, this can be done while you have a cup of coffee or run an errand. Wool crepe should be preshrunk at the dry cleaners. (2) Fill bathroom with steam the second you walk in the door. Dry off shower bar. Toss fabric over shower bar and work on pattern alterations until steam has disappeared and the fabric is dry. (3) Ignore all suggestions about preshrinking; begin cutting immediately and hope for the best. I won't claim I always preshrink, but I can think of a time or two when I wish I had. Considering the time and fabric investment, perhaps preshrinking is not a bad idea.

Know Your Fabrics

How many times have you heard someone say, "That pattern would make a nice skirt in wool crepe or wool challis" or "Wool gabardine makes the best pants—it never wrinkles"?

What are these people talking about? Let's define a few fabric terms, these and others, so you won't be in the dark any longer:

CREPE: The surface of crepe fabric has depth and interest created by using twisted creped yarns in a special weaving process. Both wool and rayon crepe make beautiful bias-cut garments because of their wonderful draping quality.

CREPE DE CHINE: Commonly refers to a silk woven in a plain weave with a twisted warp and tightly twisted filling yarns. The fabric has a very slight crinkle in appearance and is less smooth and heavier in weight than China silk, which is commonly used for jacket linings. Silk crepe de chine makes beautiful blouses and dresses that wrinkle far less than China silk.

CHALLIS: A soft, lightweight plainweave fabric with excellent draping qualities. Challis can be made from cotton, rayon, and wool, but the best from the standpoint of wrinkle resistance and beauty is wool challis.

Imported rayon challis is heavier and more wrinkle-resistant than the American-made rayon challis.

DRILL CLOTH: A strong, long-wearing fabric similar in weight to denim but smoother and of higher quality in appearance. The best drill cloth is 100 percent cotton.

GABARDINE: A twill weave, with a tight, hard surface, that comes in several weights. The diagonal weave is the property that makes this fabric particularly resistant to wrinkling.

JERSEY: A single-knit fabric with purl stitches on the wrong side and plain stitches on the right side. Wool jersey comes in two weights and makes wonderful dresses, skirts, and capes because of its drapable qualities.

MELTON: A heavy woolen coating fabric with a twill weave, which is hidden in the nap. This fabric is soft to the touch and has a nondirectional nap.

WHIPCORD: A fabric resembling gabardine with its twill weave but heavier and stronger. Whipcord is often used for riding clothes.

a. maeda

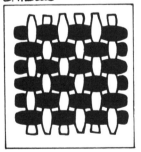

PLAIN WEAVE

TWILL WEAVE

■ If you are allergic to wool, you may be able to wear a garment made of worsted wool. All wool is combed after it is sheared, but worsted wool is combed several times, removing shorter fuzzy hairs. The longer yarns are then twisted for a smooth silk wool.

■ Look for worsted wools described as "Super 120's," "Super 100's," "Super 80's", "cool wool," "high twist" and "double twist." Not only is worsted wool a pleasure to touch, but it is also extremely wrinkle-resistant.

Know Your Fabrics

VIYELLA®: A 50-50 blend of cotton and wool. Viyella® is hand-washable and air-dryable. Most commonly seen in men's shirts, Viyella® makes beautiful blouses and skirts. In many climates, this is a year-round fabric.

ULTRASUEDE® and FACILE®: Two man-made suede products put out by Skinner. These man-made suedes are machine-washable and -dryable. Facile® is the softest and most nearly real suede.

DAMASK: A semi-gloss jacquard-patterned fabric, most commonly used for tablecloths and napkins but recently used in garments. Reversible.

PARACHUTE CLOTH: A lightweight, closewoven, somewhat shiny fabric. Fiber content may vary from silk to nylon. Fabric is strong and excellent for rainwear.

OXFORD: A soft shirting fabric in a close-woven basketweave pattern. Excellent for shirts and shirtwaist dresses.

BROCADE: A highly textured fabric with raised designs in floral or stylized patterns. The silk and cotton fibers are often combined with metallic threads making the fabric appropriate for evening wear. The fabric does not drape well and is suitable for controlled fitted styling.

TUSSAH: Generally refers to the roughest texture in the silk family. Tussah has irregular slubs and tends to take dye in a somewhat irregular fashion as well. Tussah is a crisp fabric which makes up well in conventional pants and straight skirts. Pongee and shantung are lighter weights in the tussah family.

CHARMEUSE: A luxury silk fabric with a soft hand and beautiful drape. The floating yarns give the fabric a soft sheen making it suitable for dressy blouses and luxury lingerie.

PAISLEY: A fabric patterned with curved shapes. The design is abstract in nature ranging from small ¼-inch paisley found in men's ties to 5 inch paisley found in yard goods designed for skirts and dresses.

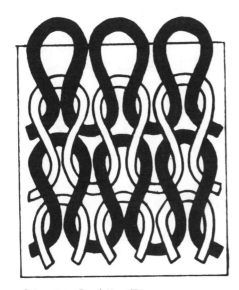

SINGLE KNIT

■ The stitch length used in sewing the garment is determined by the fabric used. The finer the fabric, the finer the stitch.

■ The fabric also determines needle size. Fine fabrics such as silk require a 60/8 size needle. In order to sew-on denim without breaking the stitch, you will need a 100/16 needle.

Standards for a Perfect Fit

To fit a garment perfectly, begin with the high-chest area from underarm to neckline. This area should lie flat with no horizontal wrinkles. The area at the neckline should not only lie flat but feel comfortable.

If a wrap-style or lapeled jacket is worn, the lapels or wrapped front should lie smooth against the body with no gaps.

The shoulder seam should lie at the top of the shoulder, not slanting backward or forward, and end at the joint of the sleeve. Move the arm up and down and you will feel the natural joint of the arm joining the shoulder. This indicates the shoulder point.

Darts should point toward and end behind the apex of the bust, fitting smoothly across the bustline without pulling.

The back of the bodice should fit smoothly without horizontal or vertical wrinkles but with enough ease for comfortable movement.

The sleeve should not bind or wrinkle across the cap or vertically, up and down the sleeve, when the arm is in a relaxed position.

Skirts and pants should fit smoothly over tummy and hips, without tucks or wrinkles at the waistband.

Side seams should be perpendicular to the floor. The skirt or pants backs should fit smoothly over fanny without bagging under the seat. No wrinkles should be visible under the waistband in back.

Fitting can be frustrating and time-consuming. A custom-fitting class at a community college or sewing school is time well spent, since it is very difficult to fit yourself.

Narrow Upper Chest

If you choose a patten size strictly by measurements, the results can be disappointing to the woman who is small in the shoulder area. Often, as women age, shoulders round and the front area from armhole to neck is small in proportion to the rest of the body. Try this alternative for a great fit.

Find a garment you made recently that is too large in the upper chest, and make a vertical fold between the neckline and the shoulder from shoulder to armhole. Fold in enough so the shoulder seam now falls where you want it to. If you have large arms, position the shoulder seam ¼ inch past the ideal shoulder position. This will de-emphasize the arm's fullness.

After you have determined the amount you would like to eliminate in the front upper chest (probably one half to one inch) on each side, you are ready to tackle your next pattern.

Draw a vertical line from the center of the shoulder seam to the bottom of the armhole. Draw a second vertical line next to the first line, leaving the amount of space you would like to eliminate in the next garment you make. Make a horizontal cut in the pattern from the point where the armhole meets the side seam to the intersection of the vertical line drawn from center shoulder to the bottom of the armhole.

This horizontal cut allows you to make a fold in the pattern from armhole to shoulder, without affecting the lower part of the bodice. Redraw armhole curve, blending smaller curve to larger curve.

By decreasing the width of the front shoulder with the horizontal fold, the armhole is now made longer on the front bodice. For the sleeve to fit properly in the front armhole, the width of the horizontal fold must be added to the sleeve front only. For example, if you folded out ½ inch in the upper front bodice, add on ½ inch to the sleeve front only, tapering the addition to zero, five to seven inches down the front sleeve seam. This is added to the sleeve front only.

When joining the front and back bodice pieces at the shoulder you will notice that the front bodice piece is now shorter than the back bodice piece. If the reduction fold on front bodice is ½ inch or less, run an easeline on the back bodice at the shoulder. This accomplishes two things. Shoulder seams are now the same length, and slight fullness is available in the upper back to accommodate a slight roundness in the back. If the reduction fold on the front bodice is more than ½ inch, try a combination of ease and a small shoulder dart on the bodice back.

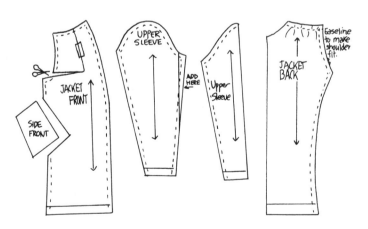

■ When blending cutting lines at armhole, scoop out at armhole curve, blending smaller cutting line to underarm seam.

What Size To Buy

Before you buy a pattern, there are a few things you must know. For starters, pattern sizes do not relate to ready-to-wear sizes at all. To determine pattern size, measurements must be taken. These can be taken right in the fabric store. Ask a clerk to borrow a tape measure.

Ideally, measurements are taken in underwear or over a leotard. If a restroom is available, take upper chest, bust and hip measurements over your under-wear; if not, take measurements in the store over your clothes. Measurements are always taken snugly, allowing no ease. If you are taking measurements over a full skirt or sweater, at least an inch should be subtracted to compensate for the bulk of your clothing.

Patterns fall into two categories, European and America. Burda, Style, and New Look are European patterns. Their sizing runs true to measurement. Stretch and Sew, Kwik Sew, and Folkwear are American patterns which also run true to measurement. Patterns from the above companies are purchased by full bust measurement for a top and hip measurement for a bottom.

American patterns—McCalls, Simplicity, Butterick, and Vogue—run slightly larger in the area from the armhole to the neck (upper chest) than the ones previously mentioned. If you purchase patterns from these companies by the "full" bust measurement you will end up with far too much fabric above the armholes in the upper chest area, resulting in an unflattering, frumpy look. Therefore, when using patterns from these companies, match up your upper chest measurement to the bust measurement on the pattern

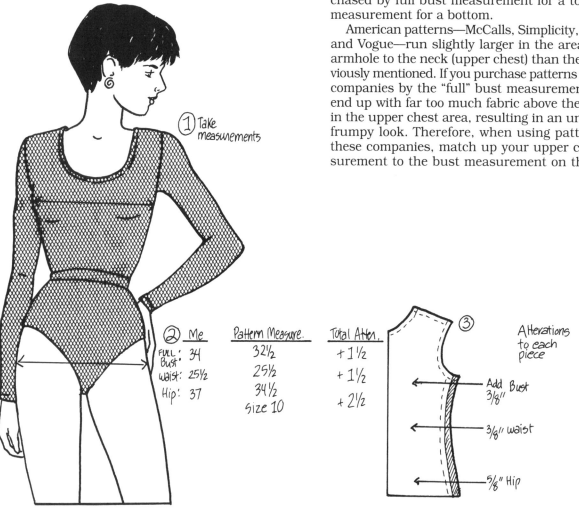

① Take measurements

② Me	Pattern Measure.	Total Alter.
FULL Bust: 34	32½	+ 1½
Waist: 25½	25½	+ 1½
Hip: 37	34½	+ 2½
	Size 10	

③ Alterations to each piece

Add Bust 3/8″

3/8″ waist

5/8″ Hip

18

What Size To Buy

size chart. This measurement is taken high under the arm and flat across the upper chest. Choosing the pattern in this manner gives a good fit in the upper chest, neck, and armhole areas.

A garment which is too large in the upper chest is impossible to correct without taking it apart and totally re-cutting. But a garment can easily be taken in or let out at the side seam from the armhole to the hem.

In the back of the pattern book you will find a chart for determining pattern size. If your measurement falls between sizes, use the larger size if you are full-busted, and the smaller size if you are small-busted.

For all pattern companies, if you are purchasing a pattern for a bottom (skirt, shorts, or pants) buy the pattern size which corresponds to your hip measurement. Unless you are in perfect proportion, the waist size indicated on the same pattern will not be the same as your waist. Do not worry about this, since garment waist can be made larger by letting out or eliminating darts or made smaller by increasing dart size or adding additional darts. The waistband must be increased as well.

If your pattern features both a top and a bottom and you plan to make both, choose the pattern which corresponds to your upper body measurements. Simple adjustments can be made at the side seams to make the bottom fit. Otherwise 90 percent of the people who sew would have to buy two patterns, one for the top and one for the bottom.

If you are 5'5" or under and are interested in a pattern which is described as "very loose fitting," purchase the pattern one size smaller than the size which corresponds to your measurements. This will scale down some of the fullness, creating a better proportion for the shorter figure.

To determine the alterations needed for a dress, for example, measure yourself at the full bust, waist, and hip, and list the measurements in a column under "me" (Illustration 2).

Then list the bust, waist and hip measurements off the back of the pattern envelope (the ones that refer to the size you purchased). Compare the measurements. The difference is the total alteration needed.

To calculate the amount of alteration you will have to make on each pattern piece, divide the total alteration by four. This will be the amount added to each piece at the side seam (Illustration 3). See "Altering Made Simple" page 27.

If you have to add at the hip, add from the hipline all the way down to the hem. In this way, figure problems will not be emphasized.

■ Vogue Designer Patterns seem to be well cut. Could Vogue be using the designers' actual patterns? Good news if they are!

■ Welcome European pattern company Neue Mode into your sewing world. Neue Mode offers exciting styling and runs true to measurement, like Burda. Use Neue Mode patterns as you would Burda: Seam and hem allowances must be added, since they are not included in the pattern.

■ From my experience as both a teacher and an avid sewer, New Look patterns are very flattering on large women but can dwarf a woman 5'3" or under with a small frame.

■ Style patterns, while usually running "true to measurement," can be skimpy occasionally, making you wish you had cut one size larger. By cutting 1-inch seam allowances on the side, seams can be let out, saving the garment from the "unfinished symphony" department.

Smaller Than a Size 8

The small woman has the same problem as the large woman—patterns do not come in her size. Although she may fit into junior and petite sizes, these styles usually do not appeal to or flatter the mature woman.

Although some patterns do come in size 6, they are few and available only by special order. Since a size 8 is readily available, let us learn how to convert a size 8 to a size 6 or 4.

To convert a size 8 pattern to a size 6, draw a line vertically from the shoulder to the hemline and fold out a total of $\frac{1}{2}$ inch (Illustration 1).

To convert a size 8 pattern to a size 4, draw a line vertically from the shoulder to the hemline and fold out a total of 1 inch. This alteration should be done on the front and the back (Illustration 2).

The line is drawn from the shoulder and does not interfere with the neck. Additions for larger hips and waist can be made at the side seams.

Occasionally it is necessary to make an adjustment on the sleeve. Fold out $\frac{1}{4}$ inch to $\frac{1}{2}$ inch vertically from cap to hem and reduce the amount of ease drawn up in the cap. Add $\frac{1}{8}$ inch to the circumference of the armhole (Illustration 3).

When you first attempt this procedure, I strongly suggest that you begin by trying the pattern in scrap fabric. In this manner, you can figure out exactly how much alteration you need for a perfect fit.

Once this is determined, keep a record of it and you can make this adjustment on every size 8.

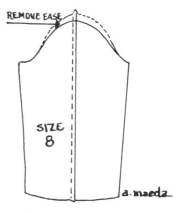

③ IF NEEDED, FOLD OUT 1/4" TO 1/2" AND REMOVE EASE AT CAP AND ADD 1/8" TO BODICE ARMHOLE (FRONT AND BACK).

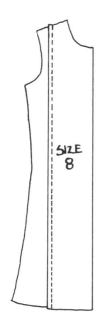 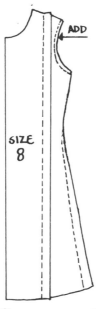

① CONVERT TO SIZE 6. FOLD OUT 1/2" FROM FRONT AND BACK.

② CONVERT TO SIZE 4. FOLD OUT 1". IF NEEDED, ADD TO HIPS AND WAIST.

Bigger Than a Size 16

Just because you are a large woman doesn't mean that you don't want to be fashionable. Unfortunately, patterns available in large sizes are limited both in quantity and in style. Most large women could alter a size 16 pattern and achieve a good fit. Here's how:

A simple way to turn a size 16 into a size 18 is to slit the pattern vertically from the shoulder to the hem and insert tissue measuring $\frac{1}{2}$ inch (Illustration 1).

To turn a size 16 into a size 20, slit the pattern vertically from the shoulder to the hem and insert tissue measuring 1 inch. These alterations must be done on both the front and back pieces.

This alteration does not change the neck. If the shoulder becomes too wide, simply reshape the armhole, taking the addition or part of it off the shoulder at the armhole, tapering to the original by the notches (Illustration 2).

Additions for the tummy and hips can also be made at the side seams.

The sleeve should be analyzed separately. Not all large women have large arms, and some small women do have large arms. If an addition is needed in the sleeve, carefully determine where the extra fullness is needed.

If fullness is needed underarm (from the armhole down), the addition can be made at the underarm seam. If the fullness is not needed from the elbow to the wrist, the addition can be tapered off back to the original at the wrist.

If the addition is also needed in the cap, split the pattern vertically at the center of the sleeve, adding from the cap to the hem. Additions will range from $\frac{1}{2}$ inch to 2 inches, depending on the fullness needed (Illustration 3).

How are you going to get all of this extra fabric eased into the armhole? Instead of running an easeline just between the notches, run the easeline all around the sleeve.

If you have added 2 inches, you may need one or two small darts at the sleeve cap. Custom designers often do this. When pressed well, they will not be noticed (Illustration 4).

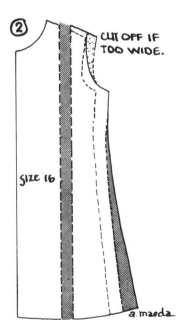

SIZE 16 TO 18. ADD 1/2" TO FRONT AND BACK.

SIZE 16 TO 20. ADD 1" TO FRONT AND BACK. IF NEEDED ADD TO WAIST AND HIPS. CUT OFF IF SHOULDER TOO WIDE.

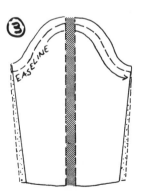

ADD AT SLEEVE CENTER FOR LARGER CAP AND ARM. TAPER SIDES.

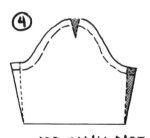

ADD SMALL DART AT SLEEVE CAP, ADD FULLNESS UNDER ARM. TAPER TO 0".

The Oversize Figure

Just because you are a large size doesn't mean you don't care about what's in fashion. Until recent years, large women were relegated to shapeless fashions with little or no fit. Now, since two-thirds of the female population in certain parts of the U.S. are over a size 14, retailers have taken another look at a potential new market.

While the pattern market has responded with an increased number of patterns in the large-size range, sizes in most designer patterns still stop at size 16. What can you do if you crave that Donna Karan suit, but neither the ready-to-wear nor the pattern comes in your size? To begin with, buy the designer pattern in the largest size available (probably a 14 or 16). Next, from the large-size pattern selection, purchase a jacket with a set-in sleeve closest to your size.

If you are small in the upper chest area, as so many women are, you might want to decrease the front upper chest size (see page 17) before you do anything else.

Tape the designer pattern, which we know is too small, on a large piece of paper. Use newspaper if no plain paper is available. Pin out any darts or pleats in this pattern. Now take the large-size pattern which fits closer to your measurements. Pin out any darts or pleats. Trim off excess tissue past the cutting line from this pattern. Overlay the large-size pattern taped to the paper. Match up the neck, shoulders and center front.

You will see immediately that this pattern is larger, not only in the bust, waist, and hip, but in the area above the armhole as well. In my experience in fitting larger women, the area above the armhole is not as large proportionally as the area below the armhole. If you fall into this category, you may want to use the smaller size pattern, the size 16, above the armholes and the large-size pattern as a cutting guide in the area below the armholes. Whatever addition you make at the side seam must also be made to the side of the sleeves as well.

A large body also requires a lower armhole as well. If you are using the smaller size pattern above the armholes, lower the armholes 1 inch on bodice front and back and sleeve as well.

If you own a dress form, you might consider making the Butterick basic 3415 in lycra with a back zipper. Slip it onto the dress form. Using polyester fleece, pad between the lycra cover and the form until the dress form measurements match your own.

If your necklines seem to ride too high in front and too low in back, lower the front neck $\frac{1}{4}$ inch to $\frac{3}{4}$ inch and build up the back neckline. Often these amounts are the same, since the head merely seems to be pivoted slightly forward.

Compare front and back armhole length. To accommodate a fuller back, the back armhole should be $\frac{7}{8}$ inch longer. This alternative is covered in *More Power Sewing* on page 50. The fuller figure needs a straighter back armhole and a more scooped-out front armhole.

Experiment on a pretest to get the look and fit you want. Hopefully this will get you going in the right direction.

Many of the above tips were provided by Marcia Ford, pattern maker from Making it Big, a mail order large-size fashion company. For a free brochure, call 707–795–2324.

(For more tips on the oversized figure see pages 26, 103, 104 in *More Power Sewing*.)

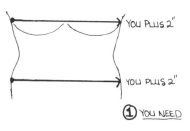

YOU PLUS 2"

YOU PLUS 2"

① YOU NEED

Patterns for Children

Children's pattern sizes correspond fairly closely to ready-to-wear sizes. Take a snug measurement of the child's chest. Match to sizes in pattern catalog. For American patterns, if the child has a slight build, buy one pattern size smaller. If the child has a stocky or heavy build, buy one size larger.

Not all children fit a standard size. For example, a tall, thin child may wear a large size in ready-to-wear just to get the necessary length. In this case a smaller size pattern, altered for length, would fit such a child's small frame better. A chubby child may need a larger-sized pattern scaled down in length. Take child's measurements before pattern shopping.

If you are sewing with an American pattern and your child has a little fanny, try cutting four fronts rather than two fronts and backs.

Choose soft, flexible fabrics which are preshrunk and colorfast. Be careful not to make elastic too tight. Children, like adults, won't wear uncomfortable clothes. If you like European styling, don't overlook Burda children's patterns. Styling is top-notch. Don't forget to add seam allowances (see page 53).

INFANTS - For babies who are not yet walking.

Size	Newborn	Small	Medium	Large
Weight (lbs.)	14	15–20	21–26	27–32
Height (inches)	24	24½–28	28½–32	32½–36

TODDLERS - Measure around breast. Toddler patterns are designed for a figure between a baby and a child. Dresses are shorter than the child's dress and pants have a diaper allowance. Measurements are given in inches.

Size	½	1	2	3	4
Breast	19	20	21	22	23
Waist	19	19½	20	20½	21
Finished dress length	14	15	16	17	18
Approx. heights	28	31	34	37	40

CHILDREN

Size	2	3	4	5	6	6X
Breast	21	22	23	24	25	25½
Waist	20	20½	21	21½	22	22½
Hip	–	–	24	25	26	26½
Back waist length	8½	9	9½	10	10½	10¾
Approx. heights	35	38	41	44	47	48
Finished dress length	18	19	20	22	24	25

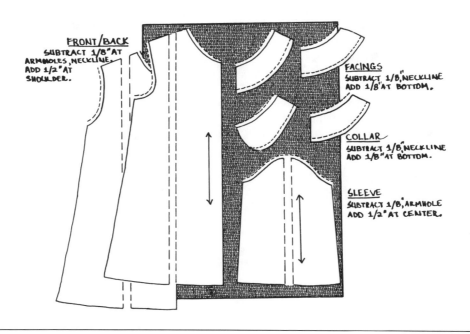

FRONT/BACK
SUBTRACT 1/8" AT ARMHOLES, NECKLINE. ADD 1/2" AT SHOULDER.

FACINGS
SUBTRACT 1/8" NECKLINE ADD 1/8" AT BOTTOM.

COLLAR
SUBTRACT 1/8" NECKLINE ADD 1/8" AT BOTTOM.

SLEEVE
SUBTRACT 1/8" ARMHOLE ADD 1/2" AT CENTER.

Size Options for the Man's Shirt

Making a man's shirt that fits is often difficult. Most men seem to fall between two sizes—perhaps they have broad shoulders and a slim waist or a large neck and small chest. Here is a technique that I have found works.

If the man in question is not perfectly proportioned for one size pattern, buy two sizes. Plan on making your first test shirt in muslin or scrap fabric so that you can work out the kinks in fit.

Start by finding a shirt he already has that fits. Have him try on the shirt and ask him about any changes in fit he would like. Note the neck size and sleeve length.

Measure the width of back yoke of this shirt and the width of the front and back at three specific points: 1 inch underarm, at waist, and at the hip (Illustration 1). Make a note of these measurements. The goal is to alter the shirt pattern to match the shirt that fits.

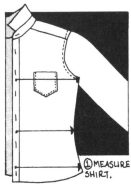

① MEASURE SHIRT.

Open the patterns and take out the yokes, fronts, and backs from each. Measure each one at the same places you measured on the finished shirt. Eliminate the pieces that do not match up closely to the desired measurements.

Working with the remaining pieces, determine what alterations are needed for a good fit. For example, alterations for a shirt for a broad-shouldered, slim-hipped man might look like those in Illustration 2.

Check backs of pattern envelopes for neck size and sleeve length. Choose the collar and neckband closest to the neck size you need.

To make the neck larger, simply trim neck of shirt and add an equal amount to collar and neck-band. To make the neck smaller, simply add to the neck of the shirt and fold out the desired amount on collar and neckband (Illustration 3).

Begin with ⅛-inch additions and subtractions. Measure the new seamline and compare against the measurement of the old seamline to see what adjustments you have made.

Sleeve-length adjustments are easy. Simply compare the desired sleeve length to that indicated on the pattern envelope and adjust on the line indicated on the sleeve pattern.

After you have made a shirt that fits perfectly, make a template in stiff plastic or Pellon®. Lay your template over your new pattern, matching center front and center back. Change new pattern to match old pattern at neckline and shoulder seams. Women's big-shirt patterns can be used for a man's shirt as well. Always using your neckline and shoulder from your well-fitting pattern, each shirt is assured of a perfect fit.

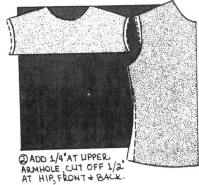

② ADD 1/4" AT UPPER ARMHOLE. CUT OFF 1/2" AT HIP, FRONT & BACK.

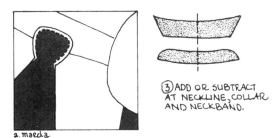

③ ADD OR SUBTRACT AT NECKLINE, COLLAR AND NECKBAND.

a. maeda

■ Extra large men's shirt patterns are available from Kwik Sew and Stretch and Sew.

Sizing Up Pants

A pants pattern should be purchased by the hip size. Waistline alterations can easily be made by decreasing or increasing the size of the dart or eliminating some of the darts entirely. If you have small legs and a small seat, purchase pants patterns one size smaller.

Making pants is one thing, but making pants that fit is quite another. It is very difficult to fit yourself. Help from a friend or someone knowledgeable about fitting is almost essential for a perfect fit. If you are willing to spend the time to get a perfect fitting pair of pants, keep a record of every alteration so that these alterations may be transferred to the tissue pattern.

Measure the leg width of a favorite pair of pants. Compare the width to the width of each leg stated on the pattern. Choose a pattern with a leg width similar to your favorite pair of pants. Wise pattern choice is essential.

Crotch length and crotch depth are completely separate entities. If you are still trying to figure crotch length by sitting on a chair and measuring from waist to chair, give up. Crotch length is impossible to determine accurately by measurements. Trial-and-error gives faster results. If ready-to-wear pants are short in the crotch on you, add an inch at the lengthen-crotch line. If ready-to-wear pants are long in the crotch on you, fold out an inch at the lengthen/shorten line. Your pretest pants will tell you how much more or less you need in crotch length. Keep a record and make this adjustment on all pants patterns.

Front-and-back crotch depth act independently. If you have a large bottom, back-crotch depth will be deeper. If you have a small bottom, back-crotch length will be shallower. The back-crotch seam may also be lowered for a low-slung seat. Front-crotch depth is determined by fullness in front thigh. For a full front thigh, add front depth to accommodate full leg. Any additions or subtractions in pants depth should be completed 7 inches down the inner leg, tapering to zero.

To determine the finished length of the pants, measure your favorite pair of pants from the waist to the finished hemline at the side seam. This determines desired finished length. Compare desired finished length to the finished length stated on the back of the pattern envelope. Remember to add or subtract from finished length on the envelope the amount of any crotch length alteration you may have made. If the pants need to be lengthened or shortened, distribute the alteration throughout the leg so that the style of the pants will not be affected.

Make a pattern marking for knee placement. This can be helpful in lining the knees of pants or on seam placement for leather pants.

After making all of the necessary alterations on the pattern for length, width, and individual figure problems, make a master pattern out of light-weight Pellon®. This can save you many hours of future aggravation.

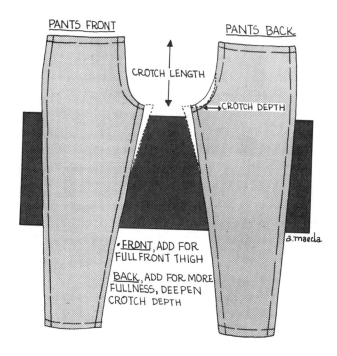

PANTS FRONT   PANTS BACK

CROTCH LENGTH

CROTCH DEPTH

a.maeda

• FRONT, ADD FOR FULL FRONT THIGH

BACK, ADD FOR MORE FULLNESS, DEEPEN CROTCH DEPTH

A Swimsuit That Fits

A swimsuit is the one piece of apparel that most people have difficulty in finding, dreading the shopping quest for that one great-fitting swimsuit out of the hundreds that are available. However, as a home sewer, you can eliminate this trial and error hassle. With an increased number of swimsuit patterns and the wide range of fabrics in the marketplace, the smart sewer can tackle this dilemma with ease.

Most ready-to-wear suits are made of nylon or cotton spandex. Cotton spandex tends to fade faster in the sun, but both fabrics are accessible to the home sewer. The most comfortable suit is one which has vertical as well as horizontal stretch. For fabric and pattern compatibility, make sure that the fabric will stretch the amount suggested on the pattern envelope.

To determine the amount of stretch of a particular fabric, hold four inches of fabric between the thumb and forefinger of each hand and test how far it will stretch. If four inches will stretch to five inches, the fabric has 25% stretch; four inches to 6 inches has 50% stretch; four inches to seven inches has 75% and four inches to eight inches has 100%. Hint: Test both the lengthwise and crosswise grain of the fabric to determine in which direction the greatest amount of stretch lies. The pattern pieces will indicate which direction needs the maximum stretch.

Although most companies have a swimsuit line, Stretch & Sew and Kwik-Sew patterns are my personal favorites. Both of these pattern lines have a large swimsuit selection and feature multi-sized designs that have easy to follow directions for adjusting the fit. To determine the proper size you must take accurate body measurements for full bust, waist and hip. Multi-sized patterns can simplify the fitting process so you need only follow the lines to increase or decrease for the size you need.

Pattern pieces for swimsuits are smaller than the body to compensate for the stretch of the fabric. Stretch & Sew uses an overall body measurement to ensure a proper length fit while Kwik-Sew uses a back waist length and crotch length measurement to achieve proper fit. In a one-piece suit, vertical fit is important both for comfort and to avoid wrinkling. Measure the body in underwear from the center of the right shoulder, under the crotch, and up the back to the center of the left shoulder. You may need help in taking this measurement but it is an important one. Depending upon fabric stretch, your pattern will tell how much to add or subtract to this measurement. If you plan to line your suit, you must add one inch to the overall length to compensate for the play between the lining and the swimsuit fabric. Two way stretch linings are a must.

Swimsuits can be sewn on either a serger or a conventional sewing machine. When using a serger, a three-thread balanced stitch will give the most stretch in the seams. When using a conventional sewing machine stretch the fabric as you sew. That way seams will not "pop" threads when you wear the suit. On a sewing machine, run two rows of straight stitches, two rows of zigzag stitches or one of each. Use a new ballpoint or universal needle during construction to avoid damage to the fabric.

Elastic to finish the arm, leg and neck openings can be cotton swimsuit elastic, rubber, or the new clear elastic and is usually $\frac{3}{8}$ inches wide. Zigzag or serge the elastic to the wrong side of the fabric edge, turn it to the inside and topstitch in place. To topstitch, use a twin needle, zigzag stitch or a multiple zigzag stitch.

The weakest element in the swimsuit is the thread. If you construct your suit using a serger, woolly nylon is the best choice for strength, stretchiness, and texture in the seams next to your body. If using a sewing machine, choose a long staple polyester thread.

To insure a long life for your newest home-sewn creation, rinse your suit in cool water after each wearing to remove chlorine, salts, and lotions. Wash swimsuits in mild detergent, rinse well, and line dry away from the sun to prevent fading.

Now that you have mastered your first suit, let your imagination take over. Your next suit could be color-blocked, piped, painted, appliqued or embellished to make it unique and fit-for-you.

Altering Made Simple

If your pattern is not multi-sized, locate the pattern size you purchased on the size chart. Circle with a felt-tipped pen. You will quickly realize that if you make this pattern "as is," it is not going to fit in certain areas. You are not alone. All sewers need pattern adjustments. Pattern adjustments are easy; they are made at the side seams. Alterations are not made at center front or center back because neckline and shoulder width would be affected. Consider pattern alterations an insurance policy to insure proper fitting. Clothes you love are clothes which fit!

On the chart below, an example is supplied for figuring alterations. Fill in the chart to determine your own alteration.

Chart for Determining Alterations

	Column I Measurements from purchased pattern	Column II Your measurements	Column III Difference– Total Alterations	Column IV Total Alterations÷4 (Amount added to each seam)
Full Bust Your Bust	$32\frac{1}{2}$	$33\frac{1}{2}$	+1	$+\frac{1}{4}$
Waist Your Waist	25	28	+3	$+\frac{3}{4}$
Hip Your Hip	$34\frac{1}{2}$	$38\frac{1}{2}$	+4	+1

Column I: Fill in the pattern measurements for the size pattern you bought.

Column II: Fill in your measurements. Bust measurement indicates your "full" bust.

Column III: Fill in the difference between you and the pattern, calculated by subtracting Column I from Column II.*

Column IV: Fill in the amount added to each area at side seam, calculated by dividing Column III by four.

Make alterations at *side seams*. A curved ruler is helpful in making adjustments. Sometimes it is necessary to tape additional tissue on pattern at the side seams to accommodate pattern adjustments.

If an alteration is necessary at the bust, make a corresponding alteration on the sleeve so that the sleeve and bodice will fit together. The sleeve alteration can be tapered to the elbow so that the sleeve will not end up too wide at the wrist.

---

* Occasionally an individual has a measurement smaller than the pattern. If this is the case, the difference between the pattern and you is in the minus range. Divide by four and subtract this amount in the appropriate area.

All adjustments for the hip are made from the full hip to the hem at the side seam. Connect the full hip addition to the original waistline or the waist addition with the aid of the curved ruler.

If taking backwaist length measurement presents a problem, try the trial-and-error method. If a ready-to-wear garment is usually short-waisted, add an inch to the pattern; if usually long-waisted, subtract an inch. After your first test garment, refine these figures and come up with a standard adjustment that works for you.

The best thing about figuring alterations in this way is that *you only have to do it once*. As long as you continue to use the same pattern size, make the same adjustments even if the style is a full style. If you decide to remove some of the fullness later, feel free to do so. Always make the same alterations and you have the freedom to decide on the look you want. A uniform amount of ease results in a style that works. After machine-basting (long stitch) the garment at the side seams, try the garment on. If you wear shoulder pads, slip them into garment before fitting. At this time, decide where to nip in the garment a little or perhaps sew the whole seam deeper for a closer fit.

Flat-Pattern Measurement and Adjustments

For a perfect fit in a very fitted style, pattern measurement is your answer.

Flat-pattern measurement is the width of the pattern between seamlines, placing a ruler perpendicular to the grainline and through the bust dart on the front.

To flat-pattern-measure the back at the bustline, measure between the seamlines at the place that is the same distance down from the armhole as the place you measured on the front. This measurement is the same one you make when you put a tape measure around your bust, so the ruler must go across the pattern at the same place in the front and the back.

Flat-pattern measurement at the hip is taken at the place on the pattern that corresponds to the fullest place on your hip. For example, if the widest place on your hips is 10 inches down from your waist, find the place on the side seam of your pattern that is 10 inches down from the waist. At this place, put your ruler perpendicular to the grainline and measure the distance between the seamlines. Remember, do not include the seam allowances in the measurements.

After you have flat-pattern-measured the front and the back, add the two measurements together and multiply by two, as the pattern pieces only represent half of the front and half of the back. This gives you the number of inches the pattern actually has, not what the envelope says it has.

After you have determined the flat-pattern measurement, you can now compare this amount to the amount you need, which is your measurement plus a minimum of 2 inches ease for a fitted garment. The difference between the flat-pattern measurement and your measurement plus ease is equal to the alteration.

For example, your hips measure 37 inches. Add 2 inches ease. The amount needed for a comfortable fitted garment would be 39 inches. If you have a flat-pattern measurement of 36 inches, you will need an alteration of plus 3 inches. If your garments tend to be snug across the high hip, flat-pattern-measure 3 inches down from the waist. Compare this measurement to your measurement plus $1\frac{1}{2}$ inches ease.

Bust and hip alterations are done at the side seams. The pattern has two side seams with two seam allowances each. Therefore, the total alteration is divided by four to get the amount added to each side seam. An alteration of 3 inches divided by 4 equals $\frac{3}{4}$ inch, which is the amount added to each side seam.

In a princess style or gored style, multiply by two the number of seams where additions or subtractions will not affect the neckline, and divide this amount into the total alteration. This gives the amount to be changed on each seam.

Alterations at the hip are made from the hip line to the hemline. The addition or subtraction can then be tapered to the waistline. Additional alterations at the waistline may be made by narrowing or eliminating darts for the larger waist or deepening and adding darts for the smaller waist.

Additions or subtractions at the bustline must be made from the bustline to the armhole. The sleeve must then be altered accordingly to fit the new armhole. Taper the addition to the original seamline by the elbow. If sleeve snugness is your problem, flat-pattern-measure the sleeve. Compare this measurement to your arm plus $1\frac{1}{2}$ inches ease.

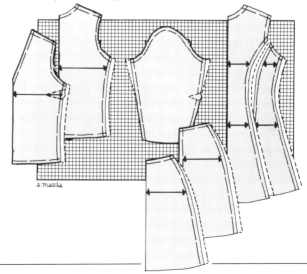

Movement and Design Ease

The concept of ease can be a confusing issue. Two types of ease need to be considered: (a) movement ease—the amount needed to allow movement, and (b) design ease—the amount of ease added by the designer to give the design a certain "look."

If you have become adept at flat-pattern measurement, here are a few guidelines to help you use these measurements. If you took your own measurements and compared them to the pattern, and the measurements were the same, the garment would not fit. Ease must be added to your measurement to allow you to move in the garment. Movement ease varies for different parts of the body: Bust—$2\frac{1}{2}$ inches; waist—1 inch; hip—$2\frac{1}{2}$ inches; front length from neck to waist—$\frac{1}{2}$ inch; back length from neck to waist—$\frac{1}{2}$ inch; arm girth—$1\frac{1}{2}$ inches; thigh—2 inches; knee—2 inches; front-crotch length—$\frac{1}{2}$ inch; back-crotch length—$\frac{3}{4}$ inch. If you are making a fitted garment, add the corresponding movement ease to your measurement. This will give you the minimum amount you need to find when you flat-pattern-measure the pattern in between the seam allowances in the same area.

The difference between the flat-pattern measurement and you, and the movement ease is the amount of alteration needed. Remember, the above formula works for fitted garments only.

Design ease is a totally different ballgame. Design ease varies with each design because it is purely a matter of personal taste. Design ease is the amount of ease added after the movement ease has been added. One designer may add 10 inches at the bust and hip to the bodice to achieve a big shirt where another designer may add 25 inches for a similar look. In a loose, unconstricted style, how do you know how much ease is enough for your particular taste? Your best bet is to measure some of your favorite outfits, or outfits in a store that are flattering to you. This will give you a better idea of how "full" you like your garments.

Read the style description on the back of the pattern envelope. Garments are described as "close-fitting," "fitted," "semi-fitted," "loose-fitting," and "very loose-fitting." For a better idea of the ease in inches allotted in each of these categories, check the "ease chart" in the back of the pattern book. This tells you what to expect in a pattern and helps to eliminate the surprise factor. See chart.

Garments described as "very loose-fitting" are too loose-fitting for many figures. When garments are described as "very loose-fitting," simply buy them one size smaller and make the same pattern adjustments as if you had bought the pattern in your size.

New Vogue and Butterick patterns have the total flat-pattern measurement printed on them for the bust and the hip as well as a bust point. This should simplify things considerably for getting the look you want.

EASE CHART

Fitted, close fitting, loose fitting, semi fitted, very loose fitting…these are terms you'll find in the garment descriptions in the Vogue Patterns Catalog and on our pattern envelopes. They are Vogue's standard for fit and are the terms that tell you exactly what to anticipate when it comes to fitting. Each term indicates a general amount of wearing ease and design ease that is built into the pattern. Ease is the amount of "space" in a garment beyond the body measurements; the specific amount of ease will vary from style to style.

EASE ALLOWANCES*				
		BUST AREA		HIP AREA
		JACKETS	COATS	
SILHOUETTE	DRESSES, BLOUSES, SHIRTS, TOPS, VESTS	LINED OR UNLINED		SKIRTS, PANTS, SHORTS, CULOTTES
CLOSE FITTING	0-2⅞" (0-7.3cm)	not applicable		not applicable
FITTED	3-4" (7.5-10cm)	3¾-4¼" (9.5-10.7cm)	5¼-6¾" (13.3-17cm)	2-3" (5-7.5cm)
SEMI FITTED	4⅛-5" (10.4-12.5cm)	4⅜-5¾" (11.1-14.5cm)	6⅞-8" (17.4-20.5cm)	3⅛-4" (7.9-10cm)
LOOSE FITTING	5⅛-8" (13-20.5cm)	5¾-10" (14.5-25.5cm)	8⅛-12" (20.7-30.5cm)	4⅛-6" (10.4-15cm)
VERY LOOSE FITTING	over 8" (over 20.5cm)	over 10" (over 25.5cm)	over 12" (over 30.5cm)	over 6" (over 15cm)

*Ease allowances given are not applicable for stretchable knit fabrics

Reprinted by permission of Butterick, Inc.

Walking Ease

Stop. Before you cut out that long coat, wrapped skirt or coatdress, pattern additions are necessary if you want the garment to hang properly, not separately near the hemline. Without "walking ease," these garments will hang well as long as you stand perfectly still with your knees together. As soon as you begin to walk, the garment separates since more fabric is needed for action. Without walking ease, the wrap skirt comes unwrapped, the coat shows the garments it covers, and the coatdress pulls apart immodestly.

Walking ease is the amount of fabric required on both sides of the opening of the garment. The amount of walking ease is determined by the length of the garment. For a floor-length garment such as a bathrobe, add 3 inches. For a midcalf-length coat or coatdress without a waist seam, add $2\frac{1}{2}$ inches. For shorter coats: knee length, add $1\frac{1}{4}$ inches; mid-thigh, add $\frac{3}{4}$ inch. For skirts: add $\frac{3}{4}$ inch for knee length; 1 inch for midcalf length.

Walking ease is added either at the center front or the side front. An addition at center front is the most effective since this is nearer the coat opening itself. Of course, if the coat has front detailing such as a lapel or will be made in plaid or stripe, addition must be made at the side front instead.

To make the addition at center front, slash the pattern apart from hem to neckline, spreading the pattern. The greatest amount of spread is at the hemline tapering to zero at approximately the armhole. The addition can taper gradually all the way to the neck, if necessary for the pattern to lie flat. For example, on a midcalf length coat, spread pattern $2\frac{1}{2}$ inches at hemline, tapering to zero as soon as it is possible for the pattern to lie flat (somewhere between the armhole and the neckline.

During layout, the grainline of the coat remains the same, only the front edge of the coat is off grain. Using the pattern as a guide, cut twill tape the length of the front seam. Hand baste to seam to stabilize during facing or trim application.

If the coat has front detailing, such as a lapel or will be made in stripe or plaid, the walking ease addition is made on the side front. Make needed addition along side at hem, tapering to zero by armhole. Add to front only, not back. Walking ease addition is determined by garment length (mentioned earlier).

IMPORTANT—WALKING EASE ADDITION ON COATS IS MADE ONLY ON THE FRONT PIECES. BACK PIECES REMAIN UNALTERED.

You can see how walking ease is the solution for all coatdresses which pull away at knee, straight shirtwaist dresses which strain at the buttons below the hip, wrap skirts which come unwrapped, and straight skirts which button at side or center front, which pull apart after the last button.

On a dress pattern without a waistline seam which wraps or buttons, walking ease amounts are determined by garment length (mentioned earlier) and added in the same manner as the coat technique.

On a skirt pattern, walking ease is added to both sides of the skirt opening. This applies to wrap skirts as well as center front buttoning skirts. If the skirt buttons up one side, walking ease is added to one side front and one side back, the side where the opening will be.

Walking ease amount on a skirt varies between $\frac{3}{4}$ inch to 1 inch depending on length. A knee-length skirt needs $\frac{3}{4}$ inch and a mid-calf skirt needs 1 inch.

Demonstrated on *Power Sewing* Video #5: *Construction Difficulties.*

Walking Ease

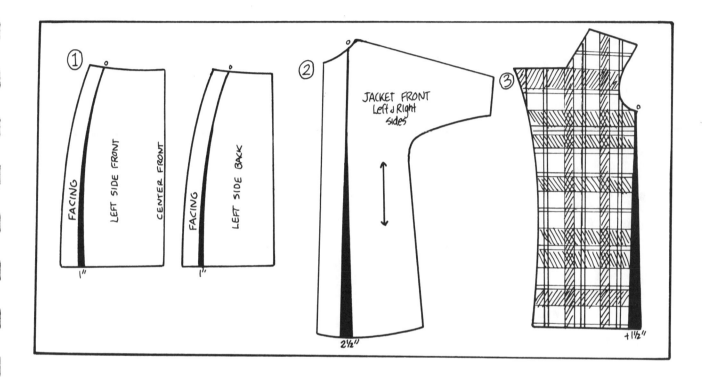

① FACING · LEFT SIDE FRONT · CENTER FRONT · 1"

FACING · LEFT SIDE BACK · 1"

② JACKET FRONT Left & Right sides · 2½"

③ + 1½"

■ If you have a round face and a round body, avoid repeating roundness with curved jacket edges and curved patch pockets. Look for angular detailing such as welt pockets on a slant, pointed rather than rounded lapels, and squared off jacket buttons.

Adding Ease for "Knits Only" Patterns

What exactly does it mean when a pattern says "for knits only"? What if you want to use a "knits only" pattern with a woven fabric? When making a normal pattern designed for non-stretch fabrics in a knit, what adjustments must be made?

Once you know how a pattern for "knits only" varies from a pattern designed for wovens, you will easily be able to make the transition back and forth.

Patterns designed for stretch fabrics rely on the stretch for much of the pattern ease. Therefore, if you wanted to make a "knits only" pattern in a woven fabric, the ease must be added back in.

The total ease difference between "knits only" and regular patterns is about 2 inches. To retrieve this ease, add $\frac{1}{2}$ inch at the side seams of the front and back. Ease is also needed in the sleeve, including the sleeve cap. Add 1 inch parallel to the grainline on the sleeve.

Small adjustments on the neckline and armhole are also necessary to adapt a "knits only" pattern to a woven. Cut off $\frac{1}{8}$ inch from the armhole and the neckline. Remember to adjust neckline and armhole facings also. If the pattern has a collar, add an additional $\frac{1}{4}$ inch to the collar at center back.

When making a normal pattern that is designed for woven fabrics in a knit, the above procedure can be reversed if you like a very fitted look. I seldom take away the ease, since I prefer the easy care of knits without a clingy fit.

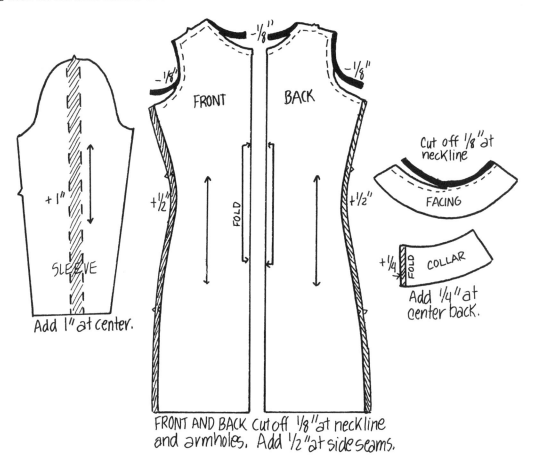

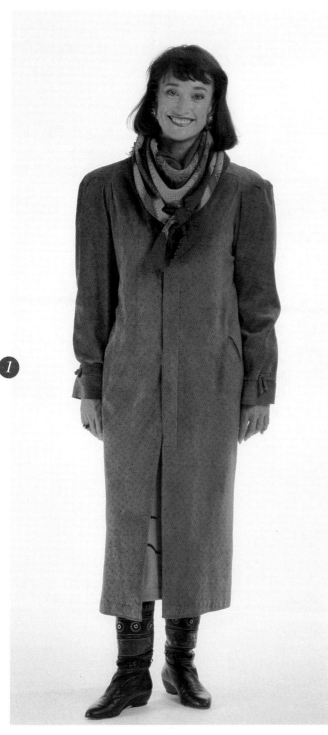

1. **Brown pigsuede coat** is made from Vogue pattern (as is) - no walking ease added. Coat hangs well as long as you stand with feet together. As soon as you begin to walk, coat spreads apart at the front revealing garments beneath (see page 30 for solution to problem).

2. **Brown cashmere coat** is made from a Burda pattern (see page 145 in More Power Sewing for cashmere tips). Walking ease (2 inches) was added at side fronts. Coat hangs well on body, does not reveal garments beneath during movement (see page 30 for technique).

Black melton (see page 87 for melton tips) is made from a Vogue pattern. Walking ease 2 1/2 inches was added at center fronts. Coat hangs straight when standing and does not reveal garments beneath during movement (see page 30 for technique). Leather undercollar and trim added (see page 211). Shoulder seam treatment is an oversized French seam on the outside (see page 195).

Grainline Makes a Difference

1. Grainline parallel to center front:

Most fullness hangs at sides leaving center front and center back flat ... disaster for the full hipped. Extra folds at sides act as arrows pointing to the figure problem (see page 52—pattern reference #1).

2. Grainline parallel to side seam:

Most fullness hangs at center front and center back leaving sides flat. Disaster for the figure with a tummy or protruding back side—makes figure look deep (see page 52—pattern reference #2).

3. Bias grainline:

Fullness is well distributed, but flattering only to the perfect body. Others claim that this cut reveals figure faults. Bias cuts take considerably more fabric and result in uneven hemline after first wearing (see page 52—pattern reference #3).

4. Grainline redrawn in center of pattern piece:

Results in fullness evenly distributed. This cut, flattering to all figures, takes slightly more fabric than #1 and #2, but maintains an even hem after wearing (see page 52 for technique and pattern reference #4).

Striped wool flannel jacket is made from a Burda pattern. Front and side fronts are interfaced with Whisper Weft; facing is interfaced with Suit Shape. Result is a crisper more man-tailored effect. To get professional pressing results, see page 195 in **More Power Sewing**. *Buttons from Worldly Goods— see sources.*

Sitting Ease for Jumpsuits

Jumpsuits are back on the fashion scene, and their prices in ready-to-wear are $100 and upward. A jumpsuit calls for about 3½ yards of fabric, so for less than $50 you can make one that fits perfectly.

One problem in ready-made jumpsuits is the critical fit in the crotch. Both crotch length and back-waist length are important factors to the comfort of a jumpsuit.

To alter a jumpsuit pattern, treat the area above the waist and the area below the waist as two separate entities. If you are long-waisted, you will need to lengthen above the waist. If you are short-waisted, you will need to shorten the pattern above the waist. Simply make the same adjustment that you make on any other bodice and add or shorten at the indicated line on bodice back and front.

The second adjustment you need to make on a jumpsuit is the crotch length. Simply make the same adjustment you normally make when constructing a pair of pants. Do not try to combine above the waist and below the waist alterations because often the curves are thrown off. After these adjustments are made, alter the pattern at the side seams per your usual adjustments.

A blouse can be attached to pants for a jumpsuit. Cut the blouse about 2 inches below the waistline to allow for ease in movement.

Dritz Mighty Snaps are a great solution to the problem of front closings for jumpsuits.

LENGTHEN SHORTEN HERE

BODICE

PANTS

Poor Fitting Necklines

Ill-fitting necklines are not only unattractive but also uncomfortable.

A neckline that is too large and gaping could be caused by using the wrong-sized pattern. Always purchase a pattern by the high-bust size, the measurement taken high under the arm, above the bra strap in back, and above the full bustline in front.

If you are using the correct pattern size and the neckline is still too large, several adjustments can be made. The neckline may be taken in a little ($\frac{1}{8}$ to $\frac{1}{4}$ inch) at the shoulder seam, tapering to the original seamline at the armhole. If $\frac{1}{8}$ inch is taken off the front and back at each side of the shoulder at the neckline, the neckline will be decreased by $\frac{1}{2}$ inch. Be sure to alter the collar accordingly at the dot markings for shoulder seam placement (Illustration 1).

Another alteration technique for a neckline that is too large is to add $\frac{1}{8}$ inch all around the neckline. This makes the neck opening smaller. Collar and facing adjustments are simple for this one. Just add the same amount at the neck edge on the collar and facing as you did on the bodice (Illustration 2).

If the garment is too tight at the neckline, trim off $\frac{1}{8}$ to $\frac{1}{4}$ inch from the neckline before sewing your normal $\frac{5}{8}$-inch seam.

Some necklines may need to be cut down only in the front. Experiment to determine what feels comfortable. Always remember to make the necessary alterations on the collar and facings (Illustration 3).

If you are cutting down the neckline a small amount ($\frac{1}{4}$ inch or less), a similar adjustment can be made on the collar and the facing. A larger alteration requires measurement of the new seamline. Alter the collar at the shoulder dot markings.

If you have problems with poorly fitting necklines, trim off or add on a conservative amount ($\frac{1}{8}$ to $\frac{1}{4}$ inch). Sew a line of staystitching $\frac{5}{8}$ inch from the cut edge and clip at 1-inch intervals to the stitching line. Try on for comfort. Further alterations can now be determined.

Never cut out your collar or facings until you have determined your new neckline. Measure the old neckline from the pattern at the seamline and compare it with your new neckline at the seamline on your garment. Alter the collar and facings accordingly.

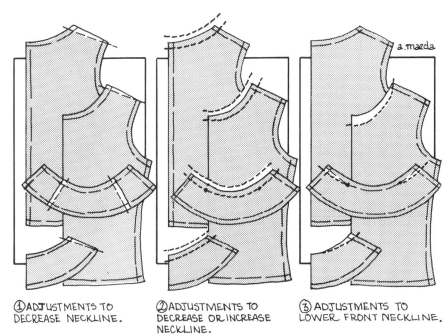

① ADJUSTMENTS TO DECREASE NECKLINE.

② ADJUSTMENTS TO DECREASE OR INCREASE NECKLINE.

③ ADJUSTMENTS TO LOWER FRONT NECKLINE.

a. maeda

Comfort for the Short-Necked

If you have a short neck, many styles not only look funny but are also uncomfortable. The solution is to make the neckband narrower and the neckline lower.

Whenever you lower the neckline, you make the neck opening larger. This must be compensated for in the shoulder seams.

Using a blouse you already have, button the top button (if you can) to determine what exactly is the problem. Is the neck too small? Does the neck need to be lowered in the front or all the way around? To determine all future alterations at the neck, experiment with scrap fabric.

If the neck opening is simply too small, cut off ¼ inch all the way around. Try on and see if more trimming is necessary.

To determine how much to add to the collar, simply measure the old sewing line from the pattern and measure the new. The difference will give you the amount needed on the collar, usually between ½ and ¾ inch.

If the neck simply needs to be lowered, cut down on the neckline and then take in the shoulder seams at the neck, tapering back to the original seamline at the armhole. The size of the actual neckline seam is not affected (Illustration 1).

If you have a short neck, it is an easy task to cut down on the width of the neckband itself.

Working with scrap fabric, fold out between ¼ and ½ inch horizontally on the neckband. Round out the corners affected by the foldout. This alteration does not affect the collar, so no other alteration is necessary. For a standup collar, make the same alteration described for the neckband (Illustration 2).

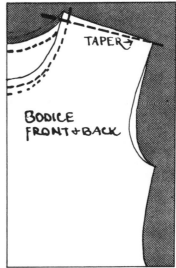

a. maeda

① CUT OFF 1/4" FROM NECKLINE AND SHOULDER; FRONT AND BACK

② FOLD OUT 1/4" AND ROUND OFF CORNERS ON STAND UP COLLAR OR NECKBAND.

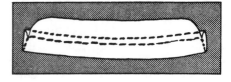

■ Since the neck is positioned differently on everyone, a neckline may need to be lowered in the front and raised in the back. A neckband or collar band can be shortened or lengthened in height.

Uneven or Sloping Shoulders

One common fitting problem that can cause a garment to hang askew is uneven shoulder height. If you notice that your collars do not hang evenly or a diagonal wrinkle hangs from shoulder to hip, you probably have one high and one low shoulder.

To determine the extent of the problem, cut a front and back bodice out of scrap fabric, allowing $1\frac{1}{2}$-inch seams at the shoulder. Mark existing seam lines. Staystitch neckline at $\frac{5}{8}$-inch seamline. Clip to staystitching.

Repin each shoulder until the bodice hangs perfectly straight. This may require releasing some fabric from existing seams or deepening some seams. The seam allowance may vary.

Sloping shoulders will have a deeper seam, and square shoulders a smaller seam, near the armhole.

Check placement of shoulder seam itself. Is it too far to the front or back? Adjust pinning until everything is perfect. Take off the bodice without unpinning either shoulder seam. Study the placement of pins carefully.

If you have square shoulders and additional height is needed near the armhole, remember to add the corresponding amount onto the sleeve cap (Illustration 1). If you have sloping shoulders, lower the armhole the same amount you lowered the shoulder. In this alteration the size of the armhole remains the same, so the sleeve does not need to be altered (Illustration 2).

For one high shoulder, measure the exact amount the seam had to be let out in the front and back to hang properly. Add these amounts together. This amount has to be added to one side of the collar for the collar to hang evenly. Shoulder seam placement is usually indicated on the collar by two dots (Illustration 3).

For one low shoulder, reverse the process. Add the amounts front and back that the seam had to be taken in for correct hang. Subtract this amount by folding out tissue on the corresponding side of the collar. Treat any neck facings the same way (Illustration 4).

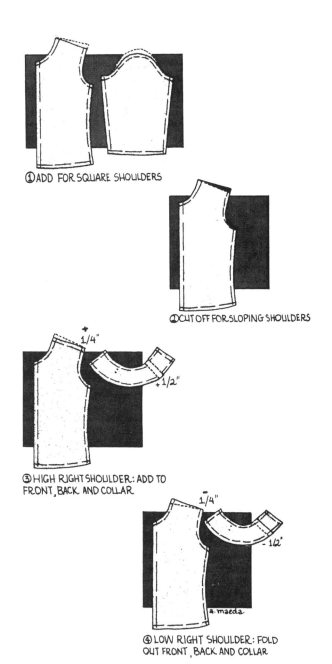

① ADD FOR SQUARE SHOULDERS

② CUT OFF FOR SLOPING SHOULDERS

③ HIGH RIGHT SHOULDER: ADD TO FRONT, BACK AND COLLAR

④ LOW RIGHT SHOULDER: FOLD OUT FRONT, BACK AND COLLAR

Narrow Back

Many people have bodies that are not symmetrical; as a result, their clothes fit in some places but not in others. A perfect example of this problem is the narrow back. Narrow-backed individuals are really one size in front and a smaller size in back. Without proper alteration, their garments will have vertical wrinkles in back.

Make the alteration for narrow back on the pattern before cutting out the garment. Draw two parallel vertical lines on pattern back ½ to ¾ inch apart, from shoulder seam to hemline (Illustration 1). They should be parallel to the grainline.

Fold tissue pattern together between newly drawn lines to decrease width. You will need to experiment by making a dress in scrap fabric first. Determine the amount to be removed from the back by trying the sample garment on and seeing how it looks and feels. Adjust pattern accordingly.

Many individuals have a narrow back through chest and shoulders only. For a two-piece dress, the bodice back is all that needs to be altered. The skirt remains the same. For a one-piece dress, alter back piece as described above, but add the needed width by increasing side seams at the hips in back.

If the back of the pattern has been altered for a narrow back, a small alteration is needed on the front shoulder so that the front and back shoulders match. Measure the amount taken in for the vertical tuck in back. Take the same amount off the front-shoulder width at sleeve seam tapering back to the original cutting line by the front notch (Illustration 2).

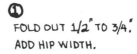

① FOLD OUT ½" TO ¾". ADD HIP WIDTH.

② CUT OFF ½" TO ¾" AT SHOULDER.

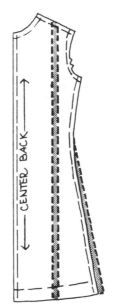

CENTER BACK

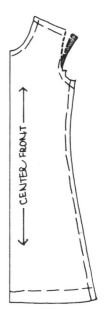

CENTER FRONT

Broad Back

Unfortunately, not all of us have bodies that are divided into perfect halves, front and back. Many individuals are one size in front and one or two sizes larger in back.

Broad back shows in an overfitted appearance in the back and often in sleeves that are ripped out in the seamline from the underarm halfway up the back. The dilemma for ready-to-wear is a difficult one. If you buy a garment that fits in front, the back is too tight. If you buy the garment to fit in back, the front is too loose, resulting in vertical folds. Fortunately, by altering the pattern before you cut out the garment the problems can be eliminated.

Purchase a pattern that fits the front of your body.

The broad-back alteration is done by drawing a line from the shoulder to the bottom of the garment parallel with the grainline. Cut the pattern on this line and add a 1/2-inch or 1-inch piece of paper. Tape in place. A 1/2-inch piece will add 1 inch to the entire back and increase the back by one size. A 1-inch piece will add 2 inches to the entire back, adding two sizes to the back.

When attempting to join the front and back shoulders, the back will be larger, due to the alteration.

To match the back to the front at the shoulderline, make a dart the width of the set-in piece and increase the existing dart or run an easeline across the back within the seamline.

If a great deal is added to the back, a combination of the above methods may be necessary.

For a very fitted garment, flat-pattern measurement will ensure you enough ease in the back. Measure the back of the pattern from notch to notch. Place rubber bands on your arms, pushed up to where the armhole seam would be. Get assistance in measuring across the back in the same areas as the back notches on a pattern. To this measurement add 1 1/4 inch ease. Compare your measurement plus ease to the flat-pattern measurement. The difference is the amount needed in the bodice back.

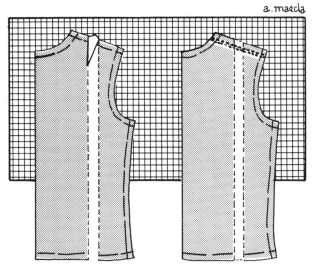

a. maeda

ADD 1/2" TO 1" TO BACK, MAKE SHOULDER DART.

RUN EASELINE ACROSS SHOULDER.

Curved Upper Back

Poor posture or prolonged work over a desk can cause the neck to pitch forward with a certain rounding of the spine near the base of the neck. The resulting fitting problem is usually a neckline that seems too high in front and too low in back.

The appropriate pattern adjustments can make the problem barely noticeable as well as adding greatly to the comfort of the neckline itself. To determine the correct pattern adjustments, make a muslin of Vogue's basic pattern #1004, bodice only. It is only necessary to sew the shoulder and underarm seams. Staystitch the existing neckline at $5/8$ inch. Clip the neckline at $1/2$-inch intervals to the staystitching line. Try on the bodice. Undoubtedly the neck will be uncomfortable. Place your fingers in the front of your neck where the neck joins the clavicle. For a comfortable fit, the neckline should rest right above this bone. With a felt-tip pen, draw on a new front neckline that would rest right above this bone, connecting this line to the original staystitching at the shoulder seam. Clip the fabric down to the new felt-tip line. The front neck of the bodice should be much more comfortable.

Using a hand mirror, stand in front of another mirror so that you can see the back and side back of your neck in the hand mirror. Make a mark in the seam allowance of the back bodice or on your neck itself if the bodice is riding too low. You may need assistance here, but measure the distance from the newly marked seam to the staystitching line in the center back.

Remove the bodice. Sit down with the muslin bodice and front and back pattern pieces in front of you. Tape some extra paper along the back neckline. Draw in a new neckline in back, raised the same distance as that marked on the muslin bodice. Connect the new seamline to the old seamline at shoulder. On the bodice front, measure the amount on the muslin the neckline needs to be dropped for comfort. On your pattern, draw in your new seamline, connecting the new seamline to the old seamline at the shoulder. Since you are lowering the neckline in front and raising the neckline in back, often the actual circumference of the neck remains the same. Check this by measuring both the old and new necklines at the

seamline. Note any differences so that a collar can be altered accordingly.

Remember to make the same adjustments on the facings as you made for the bodice front and back. Because the shoulder is often rounded near the shoulder seam, the traditional dart is inappropriate. Simply cut the back shoulder as is. Do not mark or sew in the back-shoulder darts. Run an easeline along the back shoulder within the seam allowance. Press with steam to ease in the fullness. The elimination of the back-shoulder dart often gives the necessary ease.

If the head is pitched forward quite a bit, a small dart in the neckline on either side of the center back may be necessary. If you use neck darts, be sure to fold these out when measuring your old and new necklines for possible collar adjustments.

The last variable is the center back. If your back is particularly curved, you might want to use a center back seam of 1 inch rather than cutting on the fold. The center back seam can be contoured to suit your curves with the help of a friend.

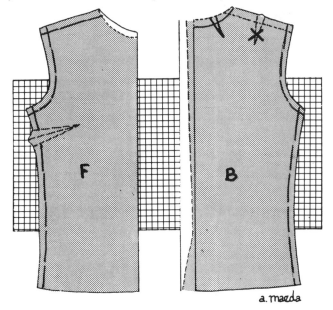

a. maeda

Swayback

Many of us with curvature of the spine, poor posture, or swayback have the problem of excess fabric in the center back.

A jacket tends to pouch out at the waist. A dress with a zipper does not follow the line of the body. A few simple alterations can solve this fitting problem.

If the garment does not have a center back seam, create one by adding a seam allowance at the center back line that was to be placed on a fold. Curve the seam in gradually at the waist to a maximum depth of $\frac{1}{2}$ inch (Illustration 1).

If the garment is not going to be made in a plaid or other pattern that needs to be matched, an additional alteration is possible. Fold the back pattern piece horizontally at the waist, removing a total of $\frac{1}{2}$ inch in the tissue pattern. This alteration is made on the back piece only. When joining back to front, stretch the back piece to match front piece in the waistline area (Illustration 2).

If a zipper is planned for the center back of the dress, lightweight interfacing will control the curve of the zipper. Place a $\frac{1}{2}$-inch strip of lightweight interfacing on the back of the center back seam allowance for the length of the zipper. I use this technique when applying zippers in any lightweight fabric. This eliminates the rippled effect caused by a zipper that is too heavy for the outer fabric (Illustration 3).

One of the most common fitting problems comes from swayback, a posture problem that causes the back of the skirt to droop in the center and the side seams to swing forward.

When a skirt is hanging on grain, the side seams will always be perpendicular to the floor. Swayback causes the skirt to hang off grain, making the side seams swing forward and stretching out the seat of the skirt.

Swayback on pants causes side seam to slant forward, creaseline to twist and seat to stretch out, since pants are actually hanging off grain. For both skirts and pants, the alteration is the same. Cut off $\frac{1}{2}$ to $\frac{3}{4}$ inch at center back waistline, tapering reduction to zero by the side seam. Amount is determined by how much the center back needs to be lifted to permit side seams to hang straight. On pants, it may be necessary to drop crotch curve or add to back inner leg to get enough room to sit comfortably.

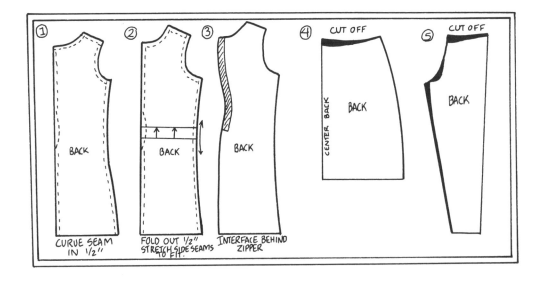

Demonstrated on *Power Sewing* Videos #2: *Pattern Sizing and Alteration* and #3: *Fitting Solutions.*

Repositioning Bust Darts

If a bust dart is too high or too low, the situation is obvious. A high bust dart creates horizontal wrinkles above the bust. A low bust dart creates horizontal wrinkles under the bust. Both are unflattering.

There are two ways to determine the ideal bust dart location. The easiest is to try on a garment with a bust dart and adjust the bodice until the dart feels and looks right. Put a small pin at the point of the bust.

Take off the garment and measure the distance from the pin to the bust point indicated on the garment, which will lie 1 inch back from the point of the dart. This distance will be the amount to raise or lower your bust darts in the future.

Simplicity Patterns gives a wonderful tip for raising and lowering bust darts, which it calls use of a "bust box."

Draw a box around the bust dart on the pattern. Cut out the box and slide it up and down the needed amount. Tape into place. Reconnect cutting lines.

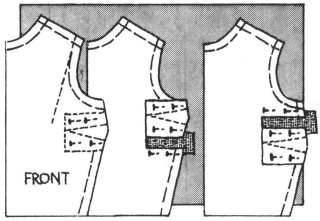

RAISE OR LOWER BUST BOX, PIN IN PLACE.

■ When pinning the pattern to the fabric, place pins only in the seam allowances. This will avoid marks in the fabric.

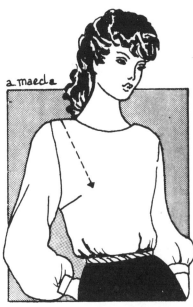

MEASURE SHOULDER TO BUST.

Another method to determine perfect dart location is to measure from the shoulder to the point of the bust. Compare this measurement to that on the pattern.

Demonstrated on *Power Sewing* Video #3: *Fitting Solutions.*

Changing the Size of the Bust Dart

Women with large or small busts have one thing in common: a problem with fitting dress bodices. Adjusting the garment at the side seams often accents rather than alleviates the problem. The small-busted woman often finds horizontal wrinkles that cannot be eliminated by side-seam alterations. The problem lies in the size of the bust dart. The amount of bust room in the bodice is in direct proportion to the size of the bust dart. The larger the dart, the larger the bust needed to fill the bodice.

To decrease the amount of fullness in the bodice, the dart must be made smaller. Most bodice darts originating at the side seam measure between 1/2 and 1 inch. Fold out a 1/2-inch horizontal tuck in the tissue pattern right through the bust dart. This enables the bust dart to be decreased by 1/4 inch on each side of the sewing line without altering the bodice length. Redraw in two new lines for sewing the dart. The dart will be 1/2 inch smaller.

You may need to experiment a little with the amount you decrease your dart. Remember, the horizontal tuck must equal the total amount of dart reduction so that the side seams will match.

In a very full garment, bust darts can often be eliminated completely for the small-busted woman. Then a horizontal tuck in the tissue pattern the width of the bust dart is necessary to eliminate change in the length of the bodice.

The large-busted woman often finds that a bodice may pull away from the armhole or hike up in the front. In a one-piece dress, the problem often manifests itself in a shorter center front even after letting out the side seams.

These problems are caused by a dart that does not give enough fullness for the large bust. Increasing the size of the bust dart adds depth to the bodice.

Horizontally slash the tissue pattern right through the existing dart and add a 3/4-inch paper piece to the pattern. Redraw two new lines for sewing the bust dart. The dart will now be 3/4 inch wider.

You may want to experiment by adding either more or less than 3/4 inch. Remember that the amount of the added tissue equals the total amount of the increased dart. Half of this amount is added to each side. You may also want to experiment with the addition of a second dart rather than increase the existing one.

Through experimentation you will be able to determine the perfect dart width for you. As the dart width varies from pattern to pattern, you may alter the dart size to give yourself just the right amount of bodice fullness.

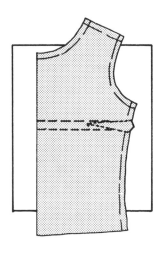

SMALL BUST
FOLD OUT 1/2" AT BUST
REDRAW DART.

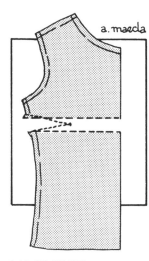

a. maeda

LARGE BUST
SLASH AND SPREAD AT
BUST. REDRAW DART.

Demonstrated on *Power Sewing* Video #3: *Fitting Solutions.*

Protruding Derrière

You will have to make two pattern alterations for a wide and protruding bottom. Adding width at the side seams can take care of a wide seat, but if the bottom also protrudes, the skirt will hike up and wrinkle over the lower back no matter how much width is added (Illustration 1).

The alteration for a protruding bottom must be made horizontally at the center back of the skirt pattern.

First take your measurements. At center back, measure distance from waist to where bottom protrudes most. Make a corresponding mark at the center back of the skirt.

Draw two horizontal lines $\frac{1}{2}$ inch below and $\frac{1}{2}$ inch above the dot from seamline to seamline. Slash along lines and spread the pattern apart, adding $\frac{1}{4}$ inch at each slash at center back, tapering to zero at side seam (Illustration 2).

Using two small slashes like this keeps the pattern from being distorted. Adding the $\frac{1}{4}$ inch at each slash is an average amount; you may need another $\frac{1}{4}$-inch slash in the same area, but start with two slashes—a little goes a long way.

Very often those with a protruding bottom have a bit of a hollow right under the waistline. If this is the case, the center back seam can be contoured a bit to fit the curve in the spine. The darts can also be deepened at the center (Illustration 3).

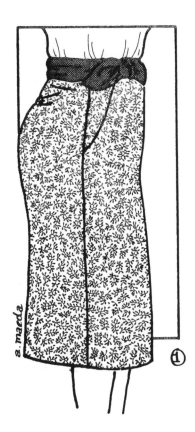

①

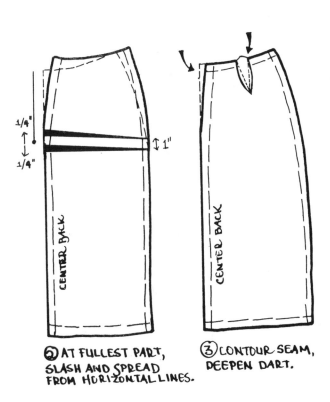

② AT FULLEST PART, SLASH AND SPREAD FROM HORIZONTAL LINES.

③ CONTOUR SEAM, DEEPEN DART.

High Hip

Some women have one hip that is higher than the other, causing their skirts to hang off grain. This shows up as a long, diagonal wrinkle running from the high hip side to the hemline on the other side.

The simplest solution is to add ¼ to ⅝ inch to the top of the skirt at the waistline on the front and back, Experiment to find exactly the right amount for you.

Start by cutting out the skirt with 1-inch seam allowances. Mark seamlines on wrong side. Baste up side seams and baste on waistband at indicated seamline—except on high hip side.

Try dropping the skirt ¼ inch at the waistline above high hip, tapering drop to zero at center front. Try skirt on. If the wrinkle is still visible, drop a little more fabric out of the waistline seam.

A high hip is often accompanied by a larger or smaller hip on one side. After correcting for the high hip, take in side seam on the smaller side until the ease amounts on both sides of the skirt are the same.

Remember, both of these alterations are made on front and back. You might find it easier to use 1-inch seam allowances rather than cutting the adjustments separately.

To determine exactly the differences in the high and low hip, try this: Put a piece of snug elastic around your waist. Attach a tape measure to the end of a yardstick. Place the yardstick on the floor. Measure right and left sides from floor to waist at the side seams. Note the difference.

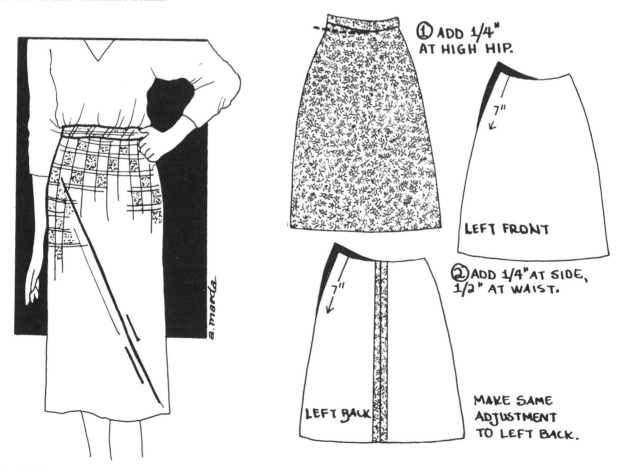

① ADD ¼" AT HIGH HIP.

7"

LEFT FRONT

② ADD ¼" AT SIDE, ½" AT WAIST.

7"

LEFT BACK

MAKE SAME ADJUSTMENT TO LEFT BACK.

a.marda

Smooth Fit Under the Waistband

One of the hardest and most critical areas to fit is the area right under the waist on a skirt. Poor fit can be caused by a pot belly, prominent high hipbones, love handles, or a waistline that drops in the back. If you have fitting problems in this area, the problem may be one or more of these.

If you have quite a bit of fullness (an inch or so) under the waist, an addition is usually necessary at the side seam. Add $\frac{1}{4}$ inch to $\frac{1}{2}$ inch at each side seam (in addition to your usual pattern alterations); that will usually give you enough fabric to be flattering. Add $\frac{1}{4}$ inch at center front, tapering to zero at side seam for tummy (Illustration 1).

To make the skirt fit the waistband, do not dart out this added fabric; an easeline is far preferable. Assemble the skirt. Run one or two easelines around the waistline $\frac{1}{2}$ inch from the cut edge. Press well, using steam with a press-and-lift motion. Do not iron this area or you will iron out the ease created with the easeline. An easeline over the abdomen is a wonderful camouflage for a pot belly.

If you have fullness under the waist in the back, a curved dart is a good solution. Start and end the dart at the same place, but curve the stitching line in toward the fold while stitching. Press this dart over the tailor's ham. Built-in shaping will be clearly visible. Do not sew a curved dart in the front, as this shaping will only emphasize the abdomen (Illustration 2).

If wrinkles form right under the waistband at center back, chances are your waistline drops in the back. Trim $\frac{1}{2}$ to $\frac{1}{4}$ inch from the waistline at the center back, tapering to zero at side seams. This technique lifts the skirt in back, allowing the waistband to follow the natural curve of the body without wrinkles under the waist (Illustration 3).

If your waist curves in quite a bit at center back, this alteration will be helpful: When sewing back seam from hem edge of skirt, sew the seam at $\frac{5}{8}$ inch until 9 inches below waistline edge. Increasing seam width gradually, sew the remainder of the seam at $\frac{3}{4}$ inch. If a zipper is called for, set the zipper in the increased seam allowance (Illustration 4).

Some individuals seem to be one or two sizes smaller in the back than the front. The skirt front may look quite good while the back is a mass of wrinkles. Draw a vertical line parallel to the grainline about halfway across the skirt back. Fold out $\frac{1}{2}$ inch vertically. Now adjust front and back necessary to make the skirt fit over all (Illustration 5).

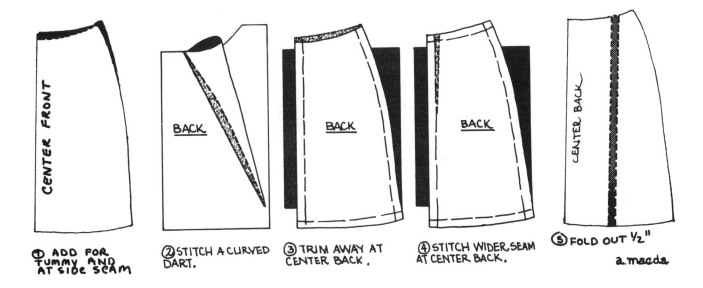

① ADD FOR TUMMY AND AT SIDE SEAM

② STITCH A CURVED DART.

③ TRIM AWAY AT CENTER BACK.

④ STITCH WIDER SEAM AT CENTER BACK.

⑤ FOLD OUT $\frac{1}{2}$"

a. maeda

Camouflaging the Pot Belly

A full skirt can hide a multitude of fitting problems. A straight skirt not only makes one conscious of improper fit but can be quite unflattering.

The most common fitting problem is tightness across the abdomen and high hips, causing wrinkles under the waistband. To correct this problem add $\frac{1}{4}$ to $\frac{1}{2}$ inch at the side seam for 3 to 4 inches, tapering back to the original cutting line 5 inches down on the hip from the waistline. Add to skirt front and backs.

You have now added 1 to 2 inches across the critical fitting area. To fit the excess into the waistband, run an easeline within the seam allowance to the waistline. Press the easeline with steam before joining the skirt to the waistband to avoid the gathered look.

If your skirts tend to hike up in the center front, chances are a small pot belly is causing the problem. This can be corrected by exercise, which most of us hate; eliminating sweets from our everyday life, which seems impossible; or adding on the extra fabric needed to camouflage the problem. For effective camouflage, add $\frac{1}{4}$ inch at the top of the skirt front, tapering to zero at the side seam.

You might also want to experiment with the dart placement. On an individual with a rounded tummy, darts are sometimes more flattering if they are moved 1 inch closer to the side seam. Two small darts are sometimes more flattering than one large one.

In a yoked skirt or pants, the yoke needs to be expanded to give room over the abdomen. Slash the yoke in five places for front pieces. Spread each piece $\frac{1}{4}$ inch. This increase will make the waist larger. Usually the extra at the waist is needed. If not, run an easeline within the seam allowance to draw up the extra width at the waist but still give room over the tummy. Additional height at the center front is also needed on the yoke to prevent the skirt from hiking up.

Add $\frac{1}{4}$ inch at the center front across the waistline in the front tapering to zero by the side seam (Illustration 1).

The circle skirt will also be a problem unless allowance is made for the full tummy. If this alteration is not made, the skirt will hike up in the center front and draw attention to this area which is better disguised. Along the waistline, add between $\frac{1}{2}$ and 1 inch, tapering to zero by the side seam (Illustration 2). This will enable the skirt to fall in a straight line from tummy to hem.

The gored skirt presents yet another problem: the seams swing to the front in an attempt to gain more fabric for the tummy. Both the front and side front pieces must be altered. The amount can range between $\frac{1}{4}$ and 1 inch depending on how much bread you are stockpiling. On the front gore, add $\frac{1}{2}$ inch across the waistline in height and $\frac{1}{2}$ inch at the side of the front piece, tapering to zero at a point 7 inches down.

For the side front piece, add $\frac{1}{2}$ inch along the waist. Add $\frac{1}{2}$ inch on both sides of this side front gore, tapering to zero 7 inches down the sides. In addition, on the side front gore, take a small $\frac{1}{4}$- to $\frac{1}{2}$-inch tuck perpendicular to the grainline at the side that matches up with the next gore unaffected by the tummy, tapering down to zero 7 inches down the side. This method throws the notches a bit out of kilter but enables the skirt to hang properly.

Fabric choice is important in the straight skirt. Fabric that is too bulky, like wide-wale corduroy, will tend to add weight. A fabric that is too thin, such as challis, will be too weak to take stress at the side seams and will pull at the seams.

Avoid fabric that wrinkles easily, because sitting in a straight skirt causes wrinkles. Lightweight wool gabardine is a great choice. Of course, there are many others, but use the properties of lightweight wool gabardine as a guide for fabric selection.

Demonstrated on *Power Sewing* Video #3: *Fitting Solutions.*

Camouflaging the Pot Belly

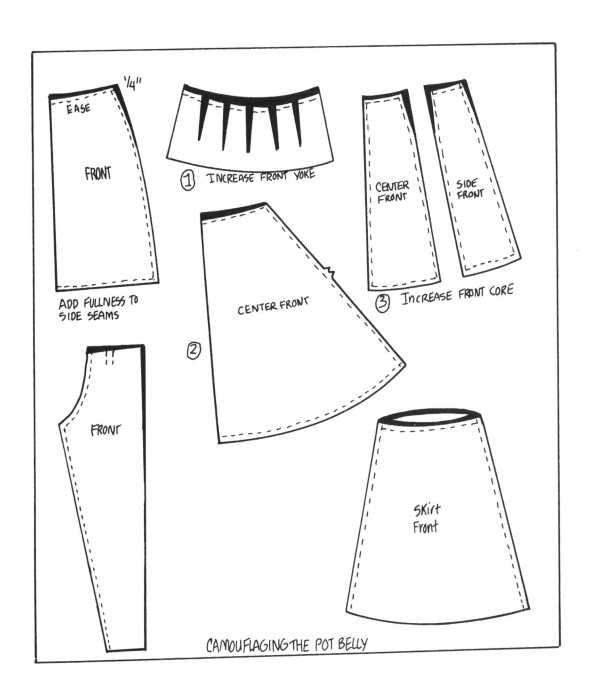

EASE ¼"

FRONT

ADD FULLNESS TO SIDE SEAMS

① INCREASE FRONT YOKE

CENTER FRONT   SIDE FRONT

③ INCREASE FRONT CORE

② CENTER FRONT

FRONT

SKirt Front

CAMOUFLAGING THE POT BELLY

Multi-Sized Patterns

If bodies were in exact proportion, no alteration would ever be made on a pattern. Fitting into a perfect size top and bottom is *extremely rare*. Most people are one size on top and one to two sizes larger on the bottom. Altering the pattern *before* you cut out saves both time and frustration later.

Multi-sized patterns make pattern alterations a snap. If a pattern is multi-sized, this fact is usually indicated on the outside of the pattern envelope. In addition, multi-sized patterns are obvious once the pattern pieces are lying flat. Three or more outside edges are marked on the tissue pieces.

To determine which line to use, refer to the measurement chart on the backside of the pattern envelope or inside on the layout sheet. Find the measurement closest to your bust measurement and circle it along the line which indicates bust. Repeat the process for waist and hip. It is not inconceivable that each of your measurements falls into a different size. No problem. On a piece of paper, make a note of what size your measurement falls in each category—bust, waist and hip. For example, you may measure a size 10 in the bust, size 14 at the waist and size 12 at the hip,

Prepare the pattern as follows, using a colored felt-tip marker. At the bottom of the front and back bodice, trace along the size which corresponds to your back waist measurement. If garment extends beyond waist, lengthen or shorten backwaist length above the waistline. Usually, a lengthen/shorten line is indicated on the pattern. Begin at the neckline, shoulder and bust area, tracing over the pattern size indicated by your bust measurement. Begin crossing over to the next size about 2 inches down from the bottom of the armhole. Aim for the size your measurement falls under at the waist. Stop tracing at the waist. Shift the action down to the bottom of the pattern near the skirt, jacket, blouse or pant hem. Trace over the size line which corresponded to your hip measurement. Trace this line from the hem to the hip (7 to 10 inches away from the waistline depending on how far down the widest spot your hip measures from the waist). At the hip begin crossing over to connect to the size line indicated by your waist. If you have a tummy, don't cross over to waistline size until 2 1/2 inches from the waist at the side seam.

After tracing the main pattern pieces in this manner, continue with the smaller pieces. The armhole of the sleeve will correspond to the size traced on the armhole of the bodice.

If your multi-size pattern comes from Simplicity, McCalls, Vogue, or Butterick, you might want to trace one pattern size smaller in the front upper chest area, specifically on the front bodice armhole and front sleeve cap, the area from shoulder dot to underarm marked by one notch on the sleeve. These patterns tend to run large in the upper chest and will fit better using this method.

After all lines have been traced, cut pattern along these lines. Compare desired length to garment finished length as indicated on the back of the pattern envelope. Shorten or lengthen pattern below the hip to alter. Usually a lengthen/shorten line is indicated on pattern. Smooth out cutting line on side seam. You will now be "cutting to fit." Proceed with lay-out instructions.

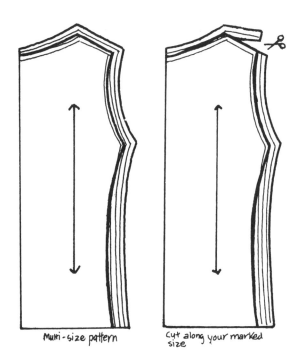

Multi-size pattern

Cut along your marked size

Multi-Sized Patterns

	Your Measurement	Size Closest to Your Measurement	
Bust—Full Bust	Example: 35 You: _____	12 _____	
Waist	Example: 29 You: _____	14 _____	
Back Waist Length	Example: 16 You: _____	½" _____	(lengthen or shorten above waist front and back)
Garment Length	Example:		(lengthen or shorten below waist)

European sizes are listed on top; **American sizes are right underneath:**

34 **8**	36 **10**	38 **12**	40 **14**	42 **16**	44 **18**	46 **20**	48 **22**	50 **24**	52 **26**	54 **28**	56 **extra large sizes**	58
						168 66¼						
80 31½	84 33	88 33¾	92 36¼	96 37¾	100 39½	104 41	110 43½	116 45¾	122 48	128 50½	134 52¾	140 55¼
64 25¼	66 26	70 27¾	74 29¼	78 30¾	82 32½	86 34	92 36¼	98 38¾	104 41	110 43½	116 45¾	122 48
88 34¾	90 35½	94 37	98 38¾	102 40¼	106 41¾	110 43½	115 45¼	120 47¼	125 49¼	130 51¼	136 53½	142 56
40 15¾	40.5 16	10 16¼	10.5 16½	42 16¾	42.5 16¾	43 17	43.5 17¼	44 17¼	44.5 17½	45 17¾	45.5 18	46 18¼

Note for Burda Patterns: Instructions within the pattern are supplied in three languages: German, French and English.

Combining Patterns

Are you one of those hard-to-please customers who like a pattern but would like a different sleeve, a stand-up collar instead of the one shown, or a much fuller skirt?

How much of a pattern can be changed without getting into trouble?

Forget your fears.

The only way you can really get what you want is to combine patterns and cut them up a bit.

As long as you stay with a pattern in the same size, sleeves of the same style armhole are interchangeable. However, you cannot interchange a set-in traditional sleeve with a sleeve from an off-the-shoulder style (Illustration 1).

Collars can be reshaped or restyled as long as the neck edge remains the same (Illustration 2).

Necklines can be changed easily. Cut the pattern from scrap paper or fabric and lay it onto the body (Illustration 2).

Draw on the new neckline with a felt-tip pen. Keep in mind that the finished neck will be ⅝ inch lower all around.

Make a new facing pattern by simply following the shape of the newly cut neck and shoulder. Measure out 3 inches and cut a new facing.

Suppose you would prefer a dolman sleeve to a set-in one. Overlay a dolman sleeve pattern onto the old pattern.

Match shoulder markings as closely as possible, making sure grainlines are parallel. Reshape shoulder and sleeve area (Illustration 3).

Since pattern pictures are often misleading, how do you know if a skirt's fullness is ample or not?

Measure a skirt with the amount of fullness you desire. Compare this measurement to the width of the skirt in inches given on the back of the pattern envelope. Calculate the difference.

Divide the number of additional inches needed by four so an equal number of inches will be added to the right front, left front, right back, and left back.

If, for example, you need 20 additional inches for the desired fullness, add 5 inches per pattern piece.

Decide whether you want the fullness to extend all the way to the waist or stop somewhere short of the waist.

Make slashes in the pattern and spread the pattern no more than 1 inch at the bottom.

Use one of the two slash methods indicated (Illustration 4), depending on how far you want the fullness to extend.

Slash the pattern to within ⅛ inch of the outside cutting line to eliminate wrinkling of the pattern.

This method ensures uniform fullness rather than fullness located at side seams.

Adding seams or style lines on a pattern is also a simple matter. Pin the bodice pattern onto the body and decide on the desired placement of a seam. Draw the seam line on pattern. Unless you want to cut up the master pattern, trace the pattern onto newspaper or pattern paper. Draw in the desired seamline. Mark the pattern with an X on each side of the seamline.

If there is a chance you might get confused in joining the pieces later, write the name on each piece, for example, right bodice, center bodice, left bodice (Illustration 5).

Cut duplicate pattern apart at these markings. When cutting out fabric, remember to add ⅝ inch for seam allowances wherever an X appears. When the seamlines are joined with a ⅝-inch seam, the shape will exactly match the pattern original before the seamlines were added (Illustration 6).

What does this process accomplish? You can pipe the seam in contrasting fabric, or you can use one fabric for the center bodice and a companion fabric for side pieces.

The same theme can be carried through to the skirt.

Combining Patterns

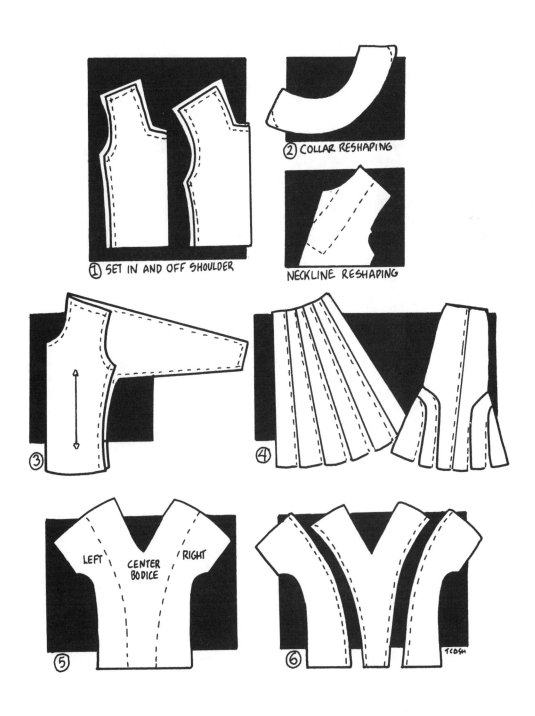

① SET IN AND OFF SHOULDER

② COLLAR RESHAPING

NECKLINE RESHAPING

③

④

⑤ LEFT CENTER BODICE RIGHT

⑥

Grainlines Which Flatter

A skirt you love versus one which hangs in the closet relates to how flattering you feel the skirt is on you. Examine your skirt pattern carefully before you cut. For the skirt to hang well, it may be necessary to change the grainline.

If the grainline is parallel to the center front or if the center front is cut on a fold, although this grainline uses the least fabric, the result is unflattering (Illustration 1). Most of the skirt fullness hangs to the side of the body rather than being evenly distributed, widening the silhouette.

If the grainline is parallel to the side seam, another fabric-saving measure, the fullness hangs in the center of the skirt, leaving the sides flat (Illustration 2). A skirt cut with this grainline is a disaster to the figure with a tummy or a protruding bottom. Undistributed skirt fullness hanging in the center front and center back widens the figure from front to back, accentuating the problem.

While a skirt cut on the bias has a beautiful drape, a bias skirt emphasizes figure bulges, does not retain an even hemline, and consumes the largest amount of fabric (Illustration 3). Therefore, the majority of ready-to-wear uses the following:

The most flattering skirt for all figures is a skirt with the grainline in the middle of each skirt panel (Illustration 4). To change the grainline suggested on the pattern to this more flattering grainline, fold the pattern piece in half lengthwise, matching up the cutting lines on both sides of the pattern piece. The curve along the waistline will not be identical when pattern is folded. With the pattern folded lengthwise, draw a new grainline along this lengthwise fold. This newly traced grainline will now be your guide in layout. Disregard the grainline previously marked on the pattern.

If the old pattern grainline called for the piece to be cut on the fold, it will be necessary to add a seam allowance. Any skirt not cut on the bias with center front or back on the fold is unflattering.

Since a skirt cut with one grainline in the center of the pattern piece requires more fabric than skirts cut with grainlines parallel to center front, back or sides, it is important to determine new fabric amounts before you purchase the fabric. Slip the pattern piece out of the envelope. Measure the width of the skirt piece. After changing the grainline, can this pattern piece be cut double on the fabric you intend to buy or is the piece too wide? If so, you may need four skirt lengths. Trust me—a skirt cut with this grainline is worth the extra fabric investment.

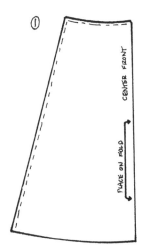
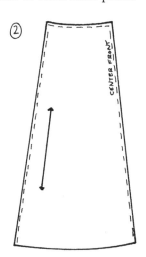
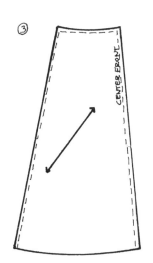
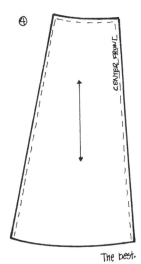

■ Grainline change works with any fabric.

Copy by Measurement

Do you have a favorite ready-to-wear blouse you'd like to copy in another fabric or color? Find a similarly styled pattern in your size to use as a base. Here's how it's done.

Open up the pattern and take out the two main pieces, the front and the back. If the ready-to-wear blouse has no darts, eliminate the vertical darts in both front and back. Provision for elimination of the bust darts must still be made.

Cut the front $\frac{3}{8}$ inch longer than the back and ease the $\frac{3}{8}$ inch extra in a 5-inch area from the underarm seam to a few inches above the waist. You can also add $\frac{1}{4}$ inch in the bust area alone at the side seam, making the seam more curved. If you do this, taper in at the side seams to give a more fitted bodice without the use of darts (Illustration 1).

Check the body of the blouse to see how much ease has been allowed. Measuring the ready-to-wear blouse, you find that it measures $2\frac{1}{2}$ inches larger than your full bust measurement. Measuring the pattern at the same place, you find that the pattern has allowed 4 inches of ease. To eliminate the extra $1\frac{1}{2}$ inches,

divide by four and take off $\frac{3}{8}$ inch at each side seam. You may need to alter only in the bust area if your hips are larger proportionately. Deepen the armhole to return the armhole curve to the same size and shape. A French curve ruler is a great help in this (Illustration 2).

Check the length of the ready-to-wear blouse and compare it to the finished length as stated on the back of the pattern envelope. It may be necessary to lengthen the pattern. If you are long-waisted, do this above the waistline markings.

You might also check the fullness of the sleeve against your ready-to-wear blouse. For a fuller sleeve, slash the pattern and spread the sleeve the desired amount. If you would like to increase your sleeve fullness by 5 inches, make five slits and spread the pieces apart 1 inch. Keep the cap the same shape. Ease of the cap may be cut down by folding out $\frac{1}{4}$ inch horizontally between the notches (Illustration 3).

Compare collar shapes or simply make a sample collar of scrap fabric and see how you like it.

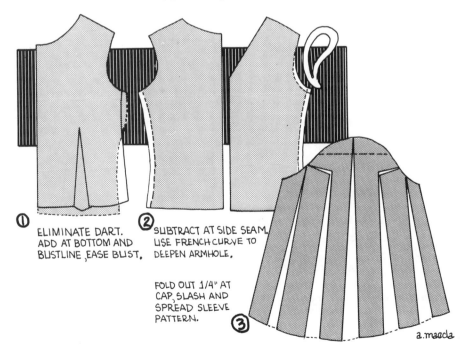

① ELIMINATE DART. ADD AT BOTTOM AND BUSTLINE, EASE BUST.

② SUBTRACT AT SIDE SEAM, USE FRENCH CURVE TO DEEPEN ARMHOLE.

FOLD OUT 1/4" AT CAP, SLASH AND SPREAD SLEEVE PATTERN. ③

a. maeda

Copy Ready-to-Wear by the Rubbing Method

All of us have one or two items in our wardrobe that we would love to have a pattern for. With the help of a new product called pattern tracing cloth you can make a pattern from any ready-to-wear item without taking it apart.

Pattern tracing cloth is a semi-transparent, unwoven nylon cloth printed with dots marking each inch of width and length. For your first copying project, try a simple style without gathers or tucks.

Let's try a simple jacket. Establish a grainline on the jacket. The easiest place to find this is the center front and center back on most jackets (not one cut on the bias, however). Cut a piece of tracing cloth big enough to copy one half of the jacket front with 1-inch seam allowances.

Draw a grainline on the tracing cloth that can be matched up with the grainline established on the jacket. Establish the grainline on the garment by pulling this way and that. The direction in which the fabric is the stronger is the lengthwise grain. This is your reference point. The two grainlines must stay pinned until the seams have been established. Smooth your hand over the tracer to flatten it.

Place pins every inch or so all around, making sure that the tracing cloth lies perfectly flat. Pin the neck, shoulder, and armhole first, pinning right on the seamline. Pin wherever it wants to lie flat naturally.

If the jacket has a dart, save it until last. In the dart area, the tracer will form a dart the same size as the original if you have worked the excess into the dart area.

Copy half of the back in exactly the same manner. Only half of the garment needs to be copied, because the other half is a mirror image.

All seams must meet at right angles for proper assembly. If this is not the case with your garment, it may be a bit stretched. Form right angles at seams on your pattern.

To copy the sleeve, establish grainlines on sleeve and on tracer. Pin grainlines together. Pin around the cap. If the sleeve is gathered, you will have to esti-mate the extra fullness allowed for gathers, usually 1 to 1½ inches. Most flat-cap sleeves measure about ½ inch larger around the cap than around the armhole.

After you have pinned the cap right on the seamline, run three rows of pins down the length of the sleeve, at center, then right and left sides (see Illustration). Using a sleeve board, wrap tracing cloth smoothly around the shape of the sleeve, pinning one side at a time. Mark shoulder.

Before you unpin the tracing cloth from the garment, mark all seamlines with pen or pencil on the tracer. Make additional markings to help you in construction. Draw in the seamlines by connecting your pin markings. If one pin seems particularly out of line, disregard this pin and go with the shape that seems to conform to the garment shape. The garment may be stretched in this particular area. Add 1-inch seam allowances all around.

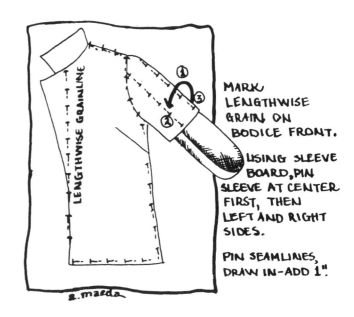

MARK LENGTHWISE GRAIN ON BODICE FRONT.

USING SLEEVE BOARD, PIN SLEEVE AT CENTER FIRST, THEN LEFT AND RIGHT SIDES.

PIN SEAMLINES, DRAW IN—ADD 1".

Copy Your Favorite T-shirt

For summer do you love the look of a sleeveless T-shirt with a full skirt, pants, or shorts, and a big chunky necklace?

If you feel uncomfortable in sleeveless garments, you can always wear this look under an unbuttoned blouse as a color accent. The right neck and armhole shapes are very important for the T-shirt look to be flattering. After experimenting with several patterns and never getting the look quite right, try this technique for the perfect T-shirt: Buy one, copy it, and make five or six in different colors.

At the beginning of the season, try on every T-shirt you can find. Be particular. This prototype needs to be a good one, since you will make several. Buy $5/8$ to $3/4$ yard of good-quality knit for every T-shirt you will make. Try the imported knits, since they are thinner and look a little sexier.

Lay the T-shirt on a piece of paper. Flatten as much as possible. Determine the center front and center back of the shirt by folding in half and placing a pin at the neck and at the hem. Trace the outline of the shirt exactly—tracing only half of the shirt, since you will fold the paper in half to ensure symmetry. To get the shape of the neckline, slip a piece of tracing paper between the shirt and the paper. Trace the shape of the neckline with tracing wheel. After you have traced half of the T-shirt, remove the sheet and fold the paper in half. Cut $5/8$ inch for seam allowance outside your drawn lines (Illustration 1). Make a paper pattern for front and back.

Overlock—or use a stretch stitch if you don't have an overlock machine—all neck and armhole curves. Run an ease stitch within the seam allowance from the armhole notch to the underarm to keep the armhole from gaping. Turn under seam allowances at neck and armholes. Press well. Run two parallel lines of topstitching around neck and armholes or overlock along the folded edge (Illustration 2).

Sew side seams and shoulders. Overlock seams (Illustration 3). Turn up $5/8$ inch at hem. Topstitch with two lines of stitching.

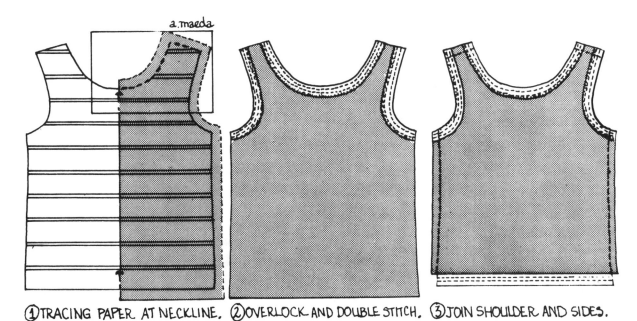

① TRACING PAPER AT NECKLINE. ② OVERLOCK AND DOUBLE STITCH. ③ JOIN SHOULDER AND SIDES.

Where to Alter

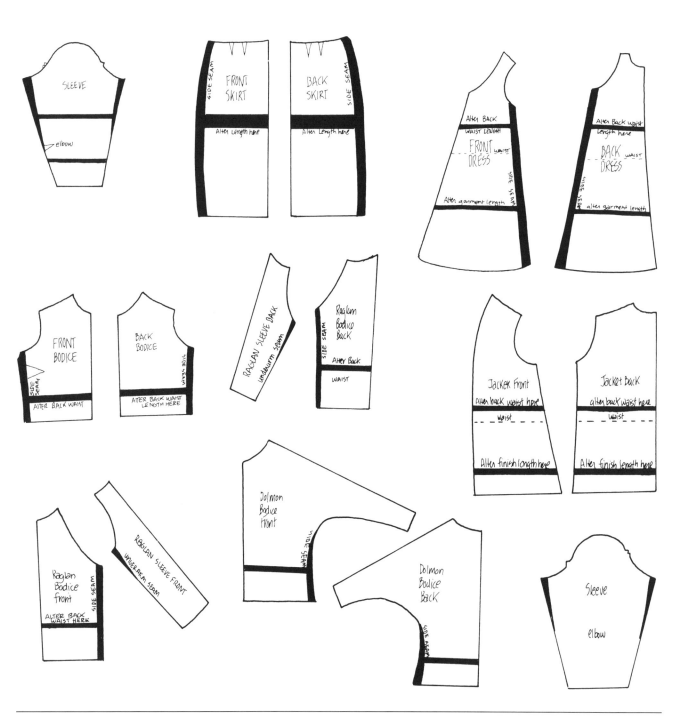

SLEEVE

elbow

FRONT SKIRT

SIDE SEAM

Alter length here

BACK SKIRT

SIDE SEAM

Alter Length here

Alter back waist length

FRONT DRESS

WAIST

SIDE SEAM

Alter garment length

Alter back waist length here

BACK DRESS

WAIST

SIDE SEAM

alter garment length

FRONT BODICE

SIDE SEAM

ALTER BACK WAIST

BACK BODICE

SIDE SEAM

ALTER BACK WAIST LENGTH HERE

RAGLAN SLEEVE BACK

underarm seam

Raglan Bodice Back

SIDE SEAM

Alter Back

WAIST

Jacket Front

Alter back waist here

waist

Alter finish length here

Jacket Back

alter back waist here

waist

Alter finish length here

Raglan Bodice Front

SIDE SEAM

ALTER BACK WAIST HERE

RAGLAN SLEEVE FRONT

underarm seam

Dolmon Bodice Front

SIDE SEAM

Dolmon Bodice Back

SIDE SEAM

Sleeve

elbow

Demonstrated on *Power Sewing* Video #2: *Pattern Sizing and Alteration.*

Independent of Pattern Instructions

When you are constructing a garment, work flat as much as possible. By this I mean hold off as long as possible before you close up the side seams. Sleeves, collars, cuffs, and other details are much easier to insert before the side seams are closed, because once they are sewn up you can no longer lay the garment out flat.

To construct a dress, for example, join the center back and insert the zipper first. Join the shoulder seams. Complete the neckline. As you can see, this takes care of the most difficult items in the garment construction.

Now sew the sleeve to the garment—again, while the garment is still out flat (Illustration 1). Then finish any necessary detail on the bottom of the sleeve. Insert the sleeve vent. To attach a cuff, close the sleeve only as far as the elbow (Illustration 2).

You will find that attaching a cuff is much easier when you are working through a large opening. Now close the side seams at last. Hem the garment and it is finished.

To construct a skirt, the process is similar. Insert the zipper in the center back before attaching it to the front at the side seams.

The secret is to think through garment construction before you begin. Then it is only necessary to refer to the pattern instructions for such details as a tab front or special neckline treatment. After constructing garments this way for a time, you won't need to use the written pattern instructions at all.

① Sew in sleeve to open seams.

② Sew seam up to elbow, set in cuff.

Final Inspection

The most successful home sewers rarely make the pattern the way it comes out of the envelope. For a garment to be successful, changes are usually necessary—sometimes even to save it from the ragbag. Accept the necessity of changing the pattern as part of the home sewing process and your failures will be fewer and fewer.

Here are some of the changes that can make or break the look.

Regardless of how well you know how to alter a pattern for your particular figure, it is mandatory to baste the side seams and try the garment on. Perhaps you need to deepen the seam an additional $1/2$ inch at the waist to give it more shape. Perhaps the skirt needs to be tapered for a slimmer silhouette. Try deepening the underarm seam of a dolman sleeve $1^1/2$ inches to 2 inches to make you look taller and slimmer.

Maybe the sleeve would look better $3/4$-length. Roll sleeves up and check in the mirror. Try tapering a dolman sleeve so that it can be pushed up to $3/4$-length. Perhaps you need to use a sleeve from another pattern. I usually cut one sleeve in scrap fabric and try it out, then I cut the sleeve I want.

Experiment with hem length a bit. Always try a dress on with a belt first; it will be too short if belted later.

Let your eye follow any wrinkles: Perhaps a dart would help, taking up the shoulder seam, resetting the sleeve.

Add design details similar to those found in ready-to-wear. The details often make the difference between an ordinary and an extraordinary outfit.

If you are still not happy with the garment, put it away for 24 hours. Look at it again with a fresh eye when you are not tired. If you still hate it, bag it up and get rid of it. Perhaps the pattern was badly designed to begin with. There's no sense in feeling guilty; move on.

THREAD, NEEDLES AND MÁRKERS

■ A fisherman's bait box provides great storage for a variety of threads. Threads are easy to see and use since the shelves lift out.

■ No one with a waistline larger than 30 inches should be belting at the waist unless the belt is worn inside a jacket where only the buckle shows. Terrific buckles keep the eye off the circumference.

Needle and Thread Considerations

Years ago, while purchasing your pattern and fabric, you picked up a spool of thread and went home. Due to the wide variety of threads now available, thread choice is not so easy, rivaled only by the confusion about which interfacing to buy.

Metler "silk finish"—good quality cotton thread with a smooth shiny finish, and long staple polyesters—Metler metrosene "all purpose," and Gutermann "sew all" make good choices for garment construction. Gutermann "silk" and Tire "silk" threads are capable of making seams almost invisible in a tailoring project when sewing on wool.

Silk thread is a dream for basting as well as the best for wool tailoring. Fine silk thread on the bobbin and regular thread on the top creates a seam capable of sinking into the fabric, creating hardly visible seams. Try Gutermann's "Pure Silk" on the blue spool and Tire's "Machine Twist" by mail order (see Sources). Purchase a separate bobbin case in which you will tighten the tension screw to adjust the flow of bobbin thread until a perfect balanced stitch results. High quality silk thread is available in spun silk with 12 to 15% elasticity, as well as filament silk with 25% elasticity from Tire, making them both suitable for garment construction on silk. Silk thread is great for hand quilting, as well.

Metler "regular machine embroidery" makes a great choice for lighter weight buttonholes or as bobbin thread when using decorative thread on the top of the machine. This thread is also a good choice for machine applique since the fuzz from all cotton thread fills in the spaces.

Sulky "metallic," Sulky "regular," and Madiera create beautiful shiny stitches on top. To pull the top thread slightly to the bottom, thread the bobbin thread through the bobbin finger or move top tension to the minus range. Schmetz 90/14 H is the machine needle most recommended for decorative threads. Blue needles 75/11 HS or 90/14 HS may cause less thread breakage, because they can absorb more heat.

Although metallic thread is capable of giving beautiful results, some experimentation is necessary to prevent thread burrs from occurring behind the eye of the needle. Begin with a 90/14, 100/16 or 110/18 until no burrs develop. Use metallic thread on top, regular thread matching lining in bobbin. If you are still having problems, hand wind metallic thread on the bobbin only, lower top tension and use regular thread on the top. Sew with the wrong side of the garment up.

Rayon thread makes beautiful shiny buttonholes. For best buttonhole results, use an 80/12 HJ needle. For smooth bobbin winding when using rayon thread, pinch thread with fingers between last thread guide and bobbin. Without this technique, tangled, loose bobbins result.

For handwork, purchase a long smocking needle such as Darner #7 and choose from one of many decorative threads. While most sewers know about DMC embroidery thread, Anchor embroidery thread is a long fiber embroidery thread which creates smoother work without the little hairs from short staple thread. All of Anchor's colors are colorfast, which cannot be said of DMC.

For more coverage per stitch, try DMC "Floche" thread or DMC Pearl cotton #5, both good choices for hand saddle stitching featured in ready-to-wear. For hand sewing use a #7 "Between" needle. Floche thread has a soft twist and shreds easily. Therefore, let no portion of the thread be stressed in the eye of the needle too long. Move loose end of thread up as you sew.

To create serger stitches which are both attractive and decorative, try ribbon floss or decorator ribbon in the upper looper.

Perhaps the finest machine thread available is Madiera Tanne 80/2, a perfect top thread when sewing on lace. Use a lightweight embroidery thread on the bobbin for most invisible results. Lightweight Madiera 80/2 lacks strength and breaks easily, limiting its use somewhat to heirloom sewing. If you have been looking for a thread which doesn't twist and knot during hand sewing, Gutermann "Quilting" thread is the hand basting thread of choice. Use it for all of your hand basting to save time and aggravation.

This information was generously supplied by Susan Smith, owner of the Sewing Gallery, a quilter's dream store, in Augusta, Georgia. If you can't find a good selection of thread in your local fabric store, find one which stocks heirloom and quilting supplies. Here thread choices are of utmost importance. You may be

Needle and Thread Considerations

lucky enough to meet an expert on thread, like I did.

For sewing on buttons, try waxed linen thread. Results are permanent.

Once you have used a waxed cotton thread for basting or tailor's tacks, you will want to use no other. Find it in a tailor's supply house.

As more sewers have invested in sergers, thread consumption and thread storage have become more of an issue. Using a three-thread serger, a blouse can consume 65 to 120 yards of thread, a dress 150 to 270 yards, and a skirt 50 to 100 yards. While many sewers previously invested in large, 3,000-yard cones, storage space quickly became an issue. Many sewers are now investing in 275-yard spools of Gutermann Sew-All thread which come in 122 colors. Not only is Gutermann stronger than coned serger thread, it presents far less of a storage problem. A giant cone is capable of making 60 blouses and 60 skirts, but they'll all be in the same color.

Needle life rarely extends beyond one or two garments. Two factors have shortened the life of the needle considerably over the last 20 years: One, fabrics have changed often, using metal dyes, polyester threads, and chemicals for stay-press. Two, the home sewing machine has changed in the last 20 years, requiring precise fitting for a variety of stitches. Since the simplest garment has a minimum of 40,000 stitches, one garment puts a lot of mileage on the needle.

Due to the preciseness of the needle-and-bobbin exchange, needle choice is a major consideration. A ballpoint needle can cut your sewing power in half when you sew on a dense-woven fabric.

For fewer skipped stitches, Schmetz makes the best machine needle. The shaped back of the needle, called the scarf, is longer and more pronounced, permitting a preciseness not found in other needles. All machines of any vintage can use the Schmetz needles. If you own a Bernina in the 800-model series, Schmetz makes a specific "B" needle with a differently shaped scarf. If you are using a needle not designed for your machine, a clicking sound will be heard in the bobbin, European machines should not use the Singer™ Gold Band needle for this reason.

Pay attention to the letter designation as well as the size of the needle. For use on most fabrics as well as silk and silk look-alikes, use the "H" needle. For dense fabric such as denim, corduroy, or ribstock nylon, use the "H-J" needle. For knits and Ultrasuede®, use the "H-S" needle. For lycra only, use the "SUK" needle. For leather, use a wedgepoint "NTW" needle. Since real suede and leather heal themselves after stitching, the wedgepoint needle is appropriate. For manmade suede and leather, use the "H-S" needle to prevent the fabric from tearing at the seam. For topstitching, use the "N" needle, which has a double-size eye that can accommodate the thicker thread you will need.

Choose your needle size carefully: 70/10 is excellent for fine fabrics, silk, silk look-alikes, and fine cottons; 80/12 is perfect for most medium-weight fabrics; 90/14 is a good choice for denim and upholstery fabrics. Larger needles create holes that rarely disappear.

All sewing machine needles have a front groove. It is not necessary to thread the needle through the eye, Simply slide the thread down the front groove and it will go right through the eye.

When purchasing needles for the overlock, always take your owner manuals. Many different needles are available in different lengths. A needle ¼ inch too long can cause big problems with the overlock. These tips were shared by needle-and-thread authority Gale Hazen.

■ Try a 70/10 HJ needle for machine buttonholes. What a difference!

Marking Fabrics

Sewing is similar to putting together a puzzle, only easier since each pattern piece gives you hints. After cutting out the garment, the next step is to transfer the hints given on the pattern to the wrong side of the fabric.

Along the edge of the pattern you will see small triangles (actually diamonds), which indicate where two pieces are joined. Next you will notice dots, arrows, small squares and broken lines. These markings indicate sewing construction. After these are transferred from the pattern to the fabric, the instruction sheet included in the pattern will tell you what to do.

Perhaps the easiest marking method is a tracing carbon and a tracing wheel, which work on the same principle as a typewriter: pressure on carbon transfers the mark to another surface. Caution: use special dressmaker's tracing paper only, please! Since most pattern pieces were cut through double fabric, markings can be transferred to both pieces at once by the following method.

Unpin the pattern only in an area small enough to slip in the tracing paper. Since you probably folded the fabric right sides out before pinning on the pattern, the wrong sides of the fabric are facing each other. Place two pieces of dressmaker's tracing paper, back to back, with colored sides out. Slip these two pieces between the two layers of fabric; the shiny side of the tracing paper faces the wrong side of the fabric. To prevent the pattern tissue from tearing as you run the wheel over the marks, cover the tissue with a thin layer of plastic, such as a plastic bag. A ruler can be helpful when tracing darts and pleats (Illustration 1).

If the tracing paper is not showing clearly on your fabric, you may need to switch to an alternative method of marking with chalk. Remove the tracing paper. Place pins through pattern and fabric, standing up perpendicular to the pattern. Unpin pattern enough to allow you to carefully fold back the pattern and one layer of fabric to expose pin. Mark with chalk the placement of the pin on the wrong side of *both* fabrics (Illustration 2). Air-erasable pens are great for marking pockets and buttonholes onto the right side of the fabric. Marks disappear in 48 hours.

How important are the dots and squares on the pattern? Not important if you don't mind frustration. Transfer anything from the pattern which will make construction easier. Some people even transfer the seamlines, not a bad idea for a first project; later you will know where the seamlines are.

I find small adhesive dots a terrific aid in construction, because they are so easy to see. Before unpinning the pattern from the fabric, wherever you see a dot, square or notch, place an adhesive dot near the seam allowance on the wrong side of the fabric on each cut piece. If the pattern marking is a dot, draw a dot; a square, draw a square; a notch, draw a notch. If the notches are numbered, write the number on the adhesive dot (Illustration 3).

Word of caution: pattern markings are always made

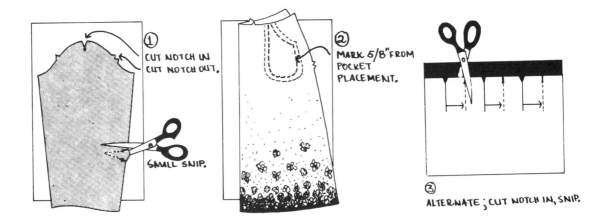

① CUT NOTCH IN
CUT NOTCH OUT.

SMALL SNIP.

② MARK 5/8" FROM POCKET PLACEMENT.

③ ALTERNATE ; CUT NOTCH IN, SNIP.

Marking Fabrics

on the "wrong" side of the fabric. Make sure you've correctly identified the wrong side before you begin the marking process.

To mark a dart, make two snips at the widest part of the dart and put a pin in the fabric to mark the point.

You can also do them by hand, using unknotted double thread. Embroidery thread and dental floss work well.

Pull the needle through pattern and fabric from top to bottom, leaving large loops on both sides (Illustration 4). To remove pattern from fabric, clip thread loops at the pattern top. Pull pattern away from fabric gently, leaving thread markings in place on the fabric.

To separate fabric pieces, pull a single thickness of fabric away gently and clip threads at each point, leaving thread markings on both fabric pieces.

Tracing paper can still be useful for fabric heavy enough not to show the markings. Unfortunately, the marking often tears the pattern. Cover pattern with a plastic bag before marking to prevent this.

Clay chalk is a good marker on the wrong side of the fabric. Waxed chalk is designed to be used on the outside of the fabric, to mark pockets, hems, etc. After the waxed chalk is pressed, it melts into the fabric and disappears. Use white only.

Felt-tip pens come in air- and water-erasable styles. Air-erasable pens become permanent on a small number of fabrics. Water-erasable pens are safer to use. These pens are great for marking buttonholes. When using these markers on the right side, always make a test sample to make sure they will disappear.

Use tracing paper to mark a pocket on the right side of the fabric, tracing a line $5/8$ inch inside the pocket placement marking (Illustration 2). The finished pocket will cover the marks when it is placed on garment. If tracing paper will not show, use waxed chalk.

For pleats, mark the solid line with an in notch and the dotted line with a snip (Illustration 3).

In the case of a tab front, resort to tailor's tacks, especially when using a sheer fabric. Check your sewing machine manual to see if your machine makes tailor tacks.

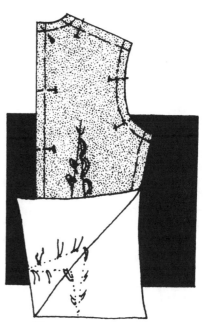

④ TAILOR TACK PATTERN TO LEFT AND RIGHT SIDES.

■ Are you thinking of purchasing a cutting mat? Two 24" x 36" mats are easier to store than one large one. Glass furniture coasters make great fabric weights, says Hazel Boyd, author of *Silks and Satins.*

Personal Marking Code

Are you one of those people who take the pattern in and out of its envelope so many times while making the garment that the pattern often becomes unusable? Do you wonder why the pattern envelope is so small and the pieces keep growing every time they need to re-enter? Okay, let's face it: The reason the pattern goes in and out of the pattern envelope so many times is to refer to the pattern markings. Either you thought the design was such a simple one that you wouldn't need the pattern markings at all, or you can't figure out which marking—of the numerous ones you made—the pattern instructions are talking about.

First of all, you need to come to the realization that pattern markings are important. If they weren't, you wouldn't need to refer to the pattern so often. You may have totally ignored the markings on occasion and winged it, with results that speak for themselves. What you need is a fast way of marking with a personal code you understand.

The notches: If using an overlock machine to finish seams, cutting the notches in or out is pointless. The overlock knife evens out the edges so your markings are lost. Use one color chalk pencil (white) to mark all "NOTCHES." Keep the pencils very sharp so that the markings are clear and precisely in the right spot. On a separate piece of paper, which we will designate your personal code sheet, make a white pencil mark and write the word "NOTCHES" next to it. For your next marking, "BIG DOTS," use the blue chalk pencil. Mark all "BIG DOTS" with the pencil. Write a blue chalk mark on the code sheet and write "BIG DOTS" next to it. Take out a pink chalk pencil and mark all "SMALL DOTS." Write a pink chalk mark on the code sheet and write "SMALL DOTS" next to it. For "SQUARES," use a water-erasable pen or colored wax. Transfer to the code sheet. Don't use the 24-hour air-erasable marking pen for any of these markings unless you are a "fast" sewer and plan to complete the project in one sitting. Use a different color marker for all pattern markings and indicate use on the code sheet.

Put all of the markers you used in a jar or small box and tape your personal marking code on the outside. After you have used this method a few times, you will know the code by heart and will not need to refer to the code sheet.

Before you take off your pattern pieces, place a piece of masking tape or an adhesive dot on the wrong side of all cut-out garment pieces. Write on the adhesive the name of the pattern piece. This will enable you to identify each piece easily and know the right and wrong sides of the fabric. Take off the pattern pieces. Fold them up and put them back into the pattern envelope for the last time, with confidence.

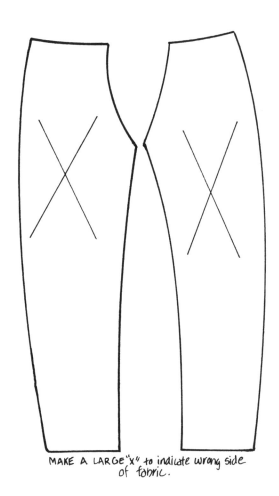

MAKE A LARGE "X" to indicate wrong side of fabric.

LINING, UNDERLINING, INTERFACING, INTERLINING

LINING A VENT - TURN LINING ½" HANDSEW

LINING A JACKET

■ New products come on the market every day. Since some of these products cannot be pressed with high heat, use interfacings which fuse with low heat such as HTC Touch of Gold or a sew-in. Flat fell seams and topstiched details produce the most professional results.

Lining, Underlining, Interfacing, Interlining

What is lining? A lining is an inner garment assembled separately from the rest of the garment. A lining helps protect the shape, reduces wrinkles, prevents clinging, can act as a built-in slip, and finishes the inside of the garment.

What is underlining? Underlining is a second layer of fabric cut exactly the same size as the first. The under and outer layer act as one layer and are sewn in the seams together. An underlining is used to give more shape and support to the outer fabric. Underlining can make a weak fabric strong and prevent over-handling of the fabric. Underlining adds depth to the garment and may act as a hanger for hems and facings so that no handstitching shows on the outside.

What is interfacing? Interfacing is used to provide shape and give character to specific areas of the garment such as collars and cuffs. Interfacing also gives protection in areas of stress such as necklines.

What is interlining? Interlining is a thermal layer of fabric used to underline coats and jackets for warmth. The fabrics most commonly used for interlining are thermal lamb and flannelette. I prefer flannelette, as it is lighter in weight and gives a more supple appearance to the garment.

The same fabrics are often used for lining and underlining, with one exception. Slippery fabric should be avoided for underlining, as it makes the two pieces working together hard to handle. I have been using Soloman's SOBO glue to secure the outer fabric and underlining together during the underlining process. It is a lot faster than hand-basting and provides just enough adhesion to assemble the garment. Place dots of SOBO within the seam allowance. I have tried this on numerous fabrics and found no ill effects.

■ When underlining on lightweight fabrics, I prefer hand basting underlining and garment together. SOBO glue makes seam allowances too stiff for lighter weights.

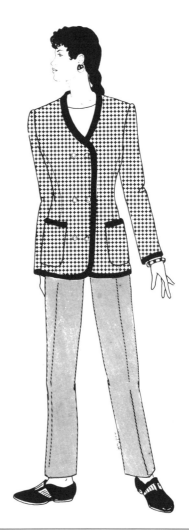

■ Wistful by Springmaid, a cotton polyester batiste, makes an excellent underlining because it doesn't collapse in wearing. Wistful is an excellent substitute if you refuse to pay the price of expensive 100% cotton batiste.

Demonstrated on *Power Sewing* Video #7: *Hassle-Free Designer Jackets.*

Interfacing
Mysteries

If you ask a tailor to estimate the life of a suit he wouldn't hesitate to say 20 years or longer. While a majority of sewing today is production sewing—no pins, no basting—the tailor, a sculptor of fabric, is still in demand. Why? While the hand-tailored suit may last 20 years, a suit with fused interfacings may start showing its age after just four dry cleanings, some sooner. What happened?

Unfortunately, many interfacings are applied incorrectly, resulting in a short term bond, says a local tailor. Although the interfacing appears bonded the glue bead was merely flattened by high heat, without enough time allowed for actual bonding. For success with fusibles follow these steps.

Preshrink fusible interfacing by covering with hot water in a bathtub. Let sit until water cools. Hang over shower rod until dry.

Test intended interfacing on a fabric scrap. If the fabric started with a soft hand, it should finish with a soft hand. If an interfacing makes a fabric stiff and board-like, switch interfacings, or try the same interfacing cut on the bias. Fusible interfacings react differently not only with fiber content but fiber dye as well. A fusible used on blue flannel will react differently on brown flannel.

If you are fusing properly, some shrinkage will result even if both the fashion fabric and the interfacing were preshrunk. While cutting out your garment, allow ½ inch extra length on both the fashion fabric and the interfacing. After fusing, use the piece as a guide for recutting.

If the interfacing curls or bubbles, the fabrics are not shrinking to the same degree. Reduce heat and "differential shrink" will disappear. After testing, pull up a corner of the interfacing. If you can still see the beading, the beads have not yet melted for long-term fusing. While some fusibles require heat, most require heat and moisture. For long-term adhesion use a wet press cloth. Layer the piece to be fused in this manner: Starting at the bottom, place fashion fabric wrong side up, then place layer of fusible interfacing—glue side down—against the wrong side of the fabric. Cover with a wet press cloth (an old pillowcase is perfect). Press with enough heat to melt the glue beads—high medium heat should penetrate all three layers. Allow

6 to 10 seconds for bonding, or until the wet cloth dries. Use a dry iron for consistency.

If you work with a lot of wools, you may want to make yourself a press cloth with a layer of wool and a layer of drill cloth. If you do a lot of fusing you may want to invest in one of the large presses such as the Elnapress. Not only does a large press fuse a large area at once, but it also does the timing for you. After 9 seconds, the press beeps, notifying you it is time to lift the press.

Let fused area dry completely before moving it off of the pressing surface.

Some fabrics cannot bond to fusibles! True. Nonporous fabrics will not let the heat and moisture penetrate, causing "bubble bounce-back." What are your choices? One, use a sew-in interfacing or, two, fuse interfacing to an underlining and underline the garment.

When you bond, slow down a little. After all—what's an extra 30 minutes compared to 20 years of service?

If you decide not to use a fusible interfacing, the SOBO glue technique is almost as fast as fusing. Place dots of Soloman's SOBO glue 1 inch apart within the seam allowance on the wrong side of the fabric. Place interfacing against the glue dots (Illustration 2). Continue with construction as though the two were fused.

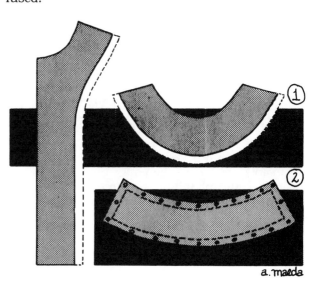

a. maeda

Interfacing Update

Ask most sewing teachers what interfacing to use and they will answer "try a sample." Try a sample of what? Do you know anyone who will go to the fabric store and purchase fifteen different interfacings in ¼ yard lengths just to try a sample? Avid sewers and ready-to-wear professionals usually have two or three interfacings they use all of the time. The following list encompasses the favorites of myself, Gail Hazen, a national lecturer, and Susi Ostlund, a fiber artist and costumer.

Fusible knit tricot is the generic form of Stacy's Easy Knit by Pellon, Fusi Knit by HTC, Knit Fuse by Dritz and French Fuse by Staple. Fusible knit tricot is the interfacing I use most because it gives light support while remaining flexible. This makes it ideal for underlining jacket fronts and side fronts, or entire jackets if the fabric is a handwoven or loose weave, which needs stabilizing. Since these tricots DO SHRINK, it is mandatory to do one of two things. As soon after your purchase, soak entire piece for 15 minutes in a basin of hot water. Hang over shower and let air dry. My friends in the ready-to-wear industry use a 60 inch version of fusible knit tricot. Due to the quantity used, preshrinking is not an option. Therefore, the interfacing is cut on the bias and fused with a fusing machine. For success in using fusible tricot, either preshrink or cut on the bias.

Sof Brush by HTC is the favorite of many in ready-to-wear since it has crosswise give and a soft hand. Soft brush must be fused at a low temperature giving only a temporary bond to assist you as you are sewing. As the garment is worn, the interfacing unbonds giving it the appearance of a sew-in without a "fused" appearance. Sof Brush works well on medium or lightweight fabrics—great for slight support in the neckband on a silk shirt, detailing on challis and support for microfibers.

Touch of Gold by HTC is another low temperature fusible which gives temporary bonding, to assist in sewing, but unbonds in wearing to give the look of a sew-in as opposed to a "fused" appearance. Touch of Gold is suitable for lightweight fabrics, even silk since the resin does not show through to the right side during pressing.

Whisper Weft by Armo while appearing lightweight actually gets stiffer when fused. Whisper Weft is great for lapels and the upper collar in a linen jacket to give crispness.

Armo Weft by Crown is an ideal fusible for tailoring, giving body without stiffness on a wool tailored jacket, giving a nice appearance on lapels and upper collars.

Interfacing Update

Armo Press Soft by Crown, a non-fusible, makes a suitable choice for interfacing upper collar and lapels in silk jackets. Touch of Gold, a temporary fusible is suitable for the same purpose.

Silk organza or a layer of its own fabric is the industry's favorite interfacing on a silk blouse or shirt. Silk organza is especially good after it is prewashed, maintaining its structure but becoming softer.

Kuffner is the interfacing of choice when stiff support is desired, such as on a neckband of a man's shirt or on the facing of high waisted skirts or pants.

Sewin Sheer by HTC is a non-fusible nylon tricot which is both sturdy and supple at the same time. This interfacing works well on textured fabrics which cannot be fused, such as seersucker. Slightly transparent, Sewin Sheer can work well as an interfacing under lace. Nude color makes this ideal for pocket sacks in white skirts or pants, eliminating pocket see-through.

SRF—Stretch Recovery Formula—is a fusible designed for use in knits, since it has the ability to stretch in a neckline as it goes over the head and return back to its original size.

WHERE TO INTERFACE. Interfacing is always needed in pocket flaps or welts and behind pockets to give the fabric support as the pocket is used. Collars and neckbands need interfacing, using a slightly stiffer one for the neckband. Jacket facings and upper collars always need a layer of slightly firmer interfacing than that used in the jacket front, side front, and undercollar—always interfaced to give slight support to the entire front of the jacket. Jacket hems are interfaced with bias pieces of sewin interfacing, attached at hem fold. Any detail on a garment needs some form of interfacing to help it stand out and keep its shape, examples being cuffs and plackets.

■ Always preshrink your fabric before sewing if you are planning to wash garment later. For delicate fabrics, soak fabric in a basin of warm water, then hang it up to dry. For other fabrics, simply treat them the way you would a finished garment in the washer and dryer. While you are at it, preshrink anything else that will go into the garment—cording, zippers, trim, interfacing and elastic. To preshrink twill tape or trim on a card, simply bend the card and submerge card and trim in water. The bent card allows for shrinkage.

Interfacing a Jacket

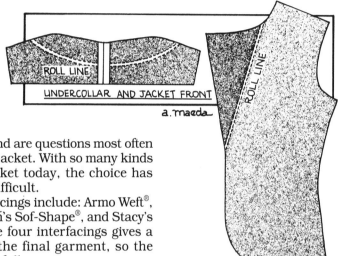

ROLL LINE

UNDERCOLLAR AND JACKET FRONT

a. maeda

ROLL LINE

Where, when, and what kind are questions most often asked about interfacing a jacket. With so many kinds of interfacing on the market today, the choice has become more and more difficult.

Some of the best interfacings include: Armo Weft®, Stacy's Suit Shape®, Pellon's Sof-Shape®, and Stacy's Easy-Knit®. Each of these four interfacings gives a different appearance to the final garment, so the choice must be made carefully.

If the fabric is prone to wrinkle, such as linen or raw silk, or is potentially unstable, as with a loose handwoven fabric, underline the entire body of the garment in Easy-Knit.

Cut the Easy-Knit exactly the same size as the body of the garment. Do not transfer pattern markings onto the garment body or the Easy-Knit until after the Easy-Knit has been fused to the wrong side of the garment body. Easy-Knit is wonderful for this purpose, since it gives soft body to the fabric without imposing itself. Wrinkling is reduced considerably, which is why you might consider fusing Easy-Knit to the entire body of linen or raw-silk pants.

Your next decision for interfacing will be in the look you want to achieve. If you want a crisp look, your next interfacing choice will be Armo Weft or Suit Shape. For a softer look, try Sof-Shape. This interfacing will be used in the entire jacket front as well as the undercollar.

If you have fused Easy-Knit as described earlier, the above suggestions still apply. Interfacing the entire jacket front gives a better final shape to the garment. In addition, fuse a layer of Easy-Knit onto the lapel and upper collar to keep them from stretching and to give additional body.

The correct fusing procedure is important in tailoring to eliminate puckering at later stages. Lay the fusible interfacing onto the wrong side of the garment piece. Using a spray bottle, spray the interfacing lightly with a mist of water. Allow interfacing to sit for two minutes. This permits the interfacing to relax and pre-shrink a bit.

Lay a press cloth over the piece to be interfaced. Spray again with a light mist of water. With a press-and-lift motion, hold the iron onto the press cloth covering the piece to be interfaced for about ten seconds, using an iron temperature compatible with the garment fabric. Do not push the iron around, as this will stretch the interfacing. Test the interfaced piece to make sure the interfacing will not peel off.

If satisfied, using a press cloth, press the interfaced piece from the right side of the fabric. No change of texture should be evident from the right side. Always test press-on interfacing on a scrap before using it to make sure a bubbly look does not result. After all fusing has been completed, transfer pattern markings onto the pieces.

If the pattern indicates a roll-line, this trick can give your collar and lapel roll-line memory: Before fusing, mark the roll-line on the interfacing on the undercollar, collar, and jacket front. Trim away interfacing along this line for $1/8$ inch before fusing.

Working with Hair Canvas

If you are making a tailored wool jacket, the only interfacing you should consider using is hair canvas, which is strong enough to support a lapel. I have seen several jackets ruined because press-on interfacing was used in lapels.

The use of hair canvas does create some special considerations. Although the material gives wonderful support in the lapel, it can make it impossible to achieve sharp edges and corners unless it is eliminated from the seam.

Use the jacket front pattern to cut out the interfacing, extending the interfacing across the front of the jacket into the underarm seam (Illustration 1). This will give added body to the front of the coat. Mark the dart in the hair canvas. Cut a 1¼-inch strip of preshrunk muslin or firm lining fabric, again using the pattern as your guide (Illustration 2). Superimpose the 1¼-inch lining strip onto the hair canvas interfacing. Sew the lining strip onto the hair canvas, ⅞

inch from the edge. Trim the hair canvas to ⅛ inch from the stitching edge.

To sew a dart in hair canvas, use one of these methods. Cut a line down the center of the dart through the lining strip and the hair canvas; overlap the dotted lines marked for seaming. Topstitch into place (Illustration 3). To eliminate hair canvas in dart totally, cut dart out completely, using sewing lines as a cutting guide. Butt-cut edges together, over twill tape. Topstitch onto twill tape. The hair canvas is now ready to be sewn to the garment. Sew hair canvas and lining strip onto the wrong side of the coat with a ⅝-inch seam (Illustration 4).

To use hair canvas on the undercollar, sew the hair canvas to the wrong side of the undercollar at ⅞ inch. Trim off the hair canvas, close to the stitching line (Illustration 5). Proceed to make the collar.

This method allows the hair canvas to give support, eliminating bulk at the seams.

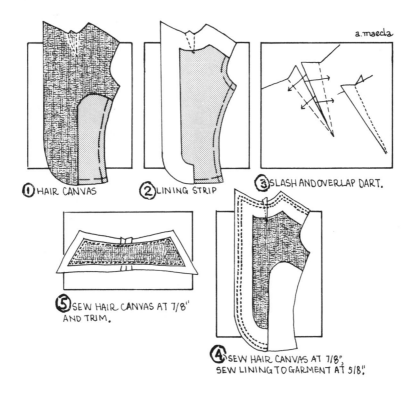

a. maeda

① HAIR CANVAS

② LINING STRIP

③ SLASH AND OVERLAP DART.

⑤ SEW HAIR CANVAS AT 7/8" AND TRIM.

④ SEW HAIR CANVAS AT 7/8", SEW LINING TO GARMENT AT 5/8".

Demonstrated on *Power Sewing* Video #7: *Hassle-Free Designer Jackets.*

Interlining

Interlining is a method of underlining a garment to give warmth without bulk. Often you need the warmth of a heavy winter coat but would prefer the close fit of a coat in lighter weight fabric. Examples might be: a velvet coat for evening, a kimono to wear with pants for an evening wedding, a brocade evening jacket, a lightweight wool in a short jacket. The secret lies in interlining with flannelette or lamb's wool. I prefer flannelette because it is softer and considerably less expensive.

To interline a garment, you must make a choice whether to interline the outer fabric or the lining. If the style is a structured one and the outer fabric could use more body, interline the outer fabric. If the style is a loose style with considerable fullness, interline the lining. If the outer fabric is interlined in a full style, the fabric will become less fluid and the drape will be lost.

Buy ¼ yard more flannelette than you think you need. Wash and dry the flannelette in hot water to preshrink. Press. Cut out flannelette from the garment or lining pattern. Place dots of Soloman's SOBO glue in the seam allowances of the flannelette. Place the wrong side of the flannelette and the wrong side of the outer fabric or lining together. Once the interlining and garment fabric are bonded, continue with garment construction as though the pieces were one.

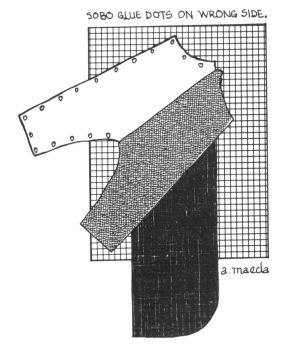

SOBO GLUE DOTS ON WRONG SIDE.

a. maeda

■ If you are reinforcing a shoulder of a very fine fabric, twill tape may be too bulky. Try using the selvage of the same fabric.

■ Silk tweed fabric makes beautiful warm weather jackets only if the fabric is underlined with fusible knit interfacing. Left to its own devices without interfacing, silk tweed will become baggy in sleeve elbows, pockets and seat.

■ Piped seams are not just a great way to show off your sewing skill and creativity; they also add vertical lines. Dig into that button collection and line up rows of contrasting color buttons for another vertical line. Choose piping or buttons; both might be overkill.

Demonstrated on *Power Sewing* Video #7: *Hassle-Free Designer Jackets.*

Underlining with Easy Knit®

Fusible knit Tricot, often referred to as Easy Knit®, is one of the best products on the market with a variety of uses. This interfacing is particularly useful because it gives support without bulk or stiffness.

In addition to common uses of interfacing, Easy Knit® can be used as an underlining to get very professional-looking results.

■ If you are not planning to line a jacket, press a layer of Easy Knit® on the entire sleeve. The sleeve will slip on and off easily and retain its shape.

■ Press a layer of Easy Knit® on the wrong side of a pocket. It will have more body and look crisper.

■ The next time you make a vest, try this: Cut out another vest of Easy Knit® and press it onto the wrong side of the outer vest fabric. Finish the vest with facings only. The vest looks lined, has a nice crisp shape, and takes less than an hour to make (Illustration 1).

■ For a firmer sleeve cap, press on a 2-inch-wide piece of interfacing in the upper sleeve cap (Illustration 2).

■ Because of the splitting process used to cut Skinner's Ultrasuede,® sometimes the fabric may seem somewhat thinner in certain areas. Normally, this is not important unless the thinness happens to come in a place that receives stress, such as the elbow. Reinforce the sleeve at the elbow with a patching of Easy Knit® cut out with pinking shears (Illustration 3). The life of the sleeve can be extended considerably.

■ Fusible knit tricot is the generic form for Stacey's Easy Knit, Fusi Knit by HTC, Knit Fuse by Dritz and French Fuse by Staple.

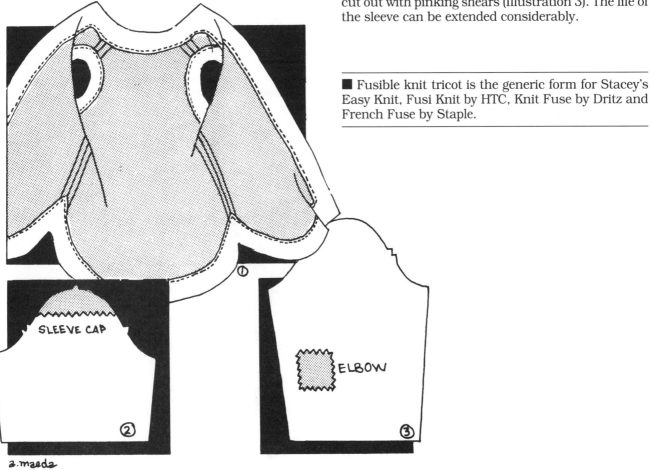

SLEEVE CAP

① ② ③

ELBOW

a. maeda

Underlining Versus Lining a Skirt

Lining and underlining a skirt are two different procedures. The lining, which is free from the garment at the side seams, is attached only at the waistband and, sometimes, at the hemline. A lining can act as a built-in slip, conceal figure faults, and help control ravelling seam allowances if it's attached to the hem at the bottom.

An underlining is treated just like the fashion fabric and gives support to it. Cotton batiste is a good choice for underlining, since it is not slippery. Both lining and underlining eliminate excessive wrinkles in a skirt.

To underline a skirt, cut the underlining exactly the same size as the outer garment. Mark the darts on the underlining fabric. Hand-baste the underlining to the skirt piece on all outside edges to hold the two pieces together until the seams are sewn.

Another method, which eliminates basting, is to place dots of Soloman's SOBO glue within the seam allowance of the garment fabric. Gently lay the underlining fabric onto the glue dots. The two layers are bonded. This works beautifully, saves time, and has never damaged any of the many fabrics I've used it on.

Once the underlining and fashion fabric are attached, they are treated as one fabric in the construction of the skirt. After the skirt is completed, you can zigzag the underlining and skirt seam allowances together for a more finished appearance.

To line a skirt, the lining and the skirt are assembled separately as though you were making two skirts. The lining, however, is cut shorter than the finished length of the skirt.

For a lining that's attached to the skirt bottom, it is necessary to hem the skirt. Press up the hem for the length you want and handstitch a tailor's hem $\frac{1}{2}$ inch from the raw edge.

Placing right sides together, attach the raw edge of the hem of the skirt to the raw edge of the lining. Sew a $\frac{1}{4}$-inch seam.

Pull up the lining and you will see that the wrong side of the lining and the wrong side of the skirt are facing each other. A take-up tuck is formed at the hem for ease in moving and to prevent tearing the lining.

To attach the lining by machine at the zipper, sew the lining seam allowance and the skirt seam allowance together $\frac{1}{4}$ inch from the raw edge. The stitching is invisible and more permanent than hand-tacking.

Machine-baste the lining to the skirt at the waist and apply the waistband in the customary manner.

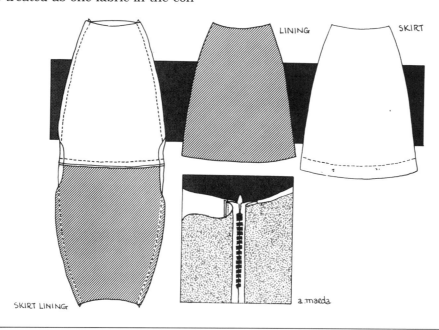

SKIRT LINING   LINING   SKIRT   a. maeda

Attaching a Jacket Lining

There's an easier way to attach a coat or jacket lining than the time-consuming hand method most sewers use.

To begin with, the garment should be completely finished before its lining is inserted. This includes hemming, sewing on buttons and pockets, and giving it a good final pressing. To hand-sew the hem, pin it in place, then turn the top of the hem back $\frac{1}{2}$ inch and sew hem to jacket $\frac{1}{2}$ inch from the raw edge of hem. This leaves $\frac{1}{2}$ inch free at top of hem to machine-stitch the lining to it.

The lining should be cut the length of the coat or jacket minus the hem allowance. Sew the side seams in the lining (but not shoulder seams) and press open. Matching raw edge of lining with finished length of coat, make a notch on both lining and coat front facing $3\frac{1}{2}$ inches from bottom.

To sew lining into coat, place bottom raw edge of lining against raw edge of coat hem, right sides together, letting the lining extend $\frac{5}{8}$ inch past the raw edge of front facing. Sew bottom edge of lining to raw edge of hem with regular-length machine stitches (Illustration 1).

To attach lining to edge of front facing, turn lining around so that right sides are together and the newly cut notches match. A small opening will be left from notch to bottom of lining—this is for the take-up tuck. Sew lining to edge of front facing from notch to shoulder. Do this to both sides (Illustration 2).

Lining is attached to the neck and shoulder facing with small overcast stitches using thread that has been run through beeswax for strength. Use a running stitch to attach lining at armhole.

The sleeve lining is attached separately to enable sleeve and sleeve lining to move together and prevent lining from tearing away at armhole.

To attach sleeve lining to sleeve hem by machine, place right sides together and sew a $\frac{1}{4}$-inch seam. The lining is then brought up to meet the coat lining at the armhole and attached to the lining with the strong overcast stitch used at the neck (Illustration 3).

The take-up tuck is then blind-stitched in place at the bottom corner.

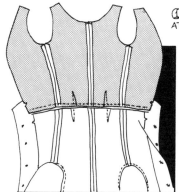

① ATTACH LINING TO JACKET AT HEM, NOTCH AT FRONT FACING.

② SEW LINING TO FRONT FACING, RIGHT SIDES TOGETHER.

③ HAND STITCH LINING AT SHOULDER AND ATTACH SLEEVE TO ARMHOLE.

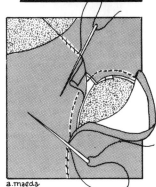

a.maeda

■ Tired of twisted sleeve linings in jackets? On the right side of the lining, mark sleeve front or lining at cap and bottom of sleeve with adhesive dots or masking tape. When pinning in sleeve, correct placement is easily determined. Corrections can be made before the hand-sewing step.

Demonstrated on *Power Sewing* Video #5: *Construction Difficulties.*

Making Your Own Lining Pattern

Many ready-to-wear jackets are unlined—and so are many jacket patterns.

For those of us who prefer a lined jacket, it's a simple matter to make a lining pattern by using the jacket pattern pieces.

Begin by cutting a jacket front and back out of plain paper, to save the jacket pattern for future use. Lay the front facing piece on the jacket front pattern and trace the cutting edge of the facing onto the jacket piece with a felt-tip pen. Remove facing pattern. To allow for a seam allowance, add 1¼ inches to the future lining pattern along the front edge where it will join the facing. Do the same with jacket back and back facing (see Illustration).

Minor additions are also necessary at the shoulder and side seams to keep the lining from tearing from lack of ease. Add ½ inch at the shoulder, tapering to zero at the neck edge; and add ¼ inch at the underarm, tapering to zero at the waist. If shoulder pads are not being used, an addition of ¼ inch is sufficient at the shoulder seam.

You now have pattern pieces for the front and back lining. The sleeve lining pattern can be cut from the sleeve pattern without any adjustment except in length.

The front and back lining and the sleeve lining must be cut shorter than the jacket fronts and backs. They should be cut to the finished length of the jacket: simply cut off from the bottom edge of the lining pattern the depth of the jacket hem.

If a pleat is desired in the back lining, allow 1 inch extra at the center back when cutting out the lining.

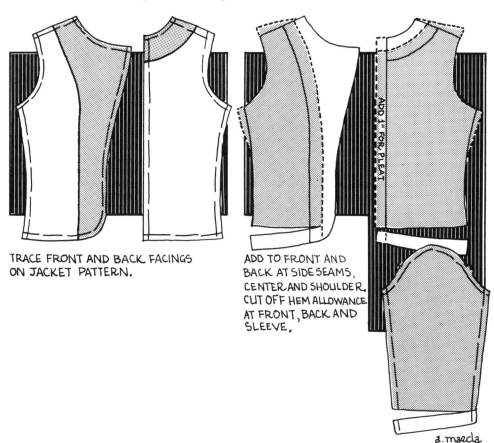

TRACE FRONT AND BACK FACINGS ON JACKET PATTERN.

ADD TO FRONT AND BACK AT SIDE SEAMS, CENTER AND SHOULDER, CUT OFF HEM ALLOWANCE AT FRONT, BACK AND SLEEVE.

a. maeda

SPECIAL FABRICS

Silks

While the idea of sewing on silk is intimidating, silk is actually one of the easiest fabrics to sew with.

Solid color silks are hand washable. For best results hand wash in 1 capful of "angora wash" and warm water. Do not despair when excess dye is released in the water. Set dye in the first washing by using $\frac{1}{4}$ cup of white vinegar and 1 tablespoon of salt in rinse water. Never wring silk when it is wet or fibers will be weakened. Roll up in a towel to squeeze out excess water. To iron, cover ironing board with towel. For wrinkle-free silk, iron on the wrong side until dry. If your silk garment comes from ready-to-wear, dry-clean for safety. The fabric or the interfacing—or both—may not be preshrunk. Do not wash printed silks. Color often runs making the colors muddy.

Silk fades in the sun. If your closet has a window, be careful of garment placement.

When choosing a pattern to use with a fabric in a well defined silk print, simple styling with a cut on sleeve will show off the fabric to the greatest advantage. For plain color silks, any pattern with fullness is suitable. If a silk garment is fitted too snugly, the garment will tear.

If the fabric is a sheer silk, pins will not hold the pattern to the fabric. Cover cutting surface with paper (rolls available at medical supply or office supply stores) or one layer of tissue paper. Pin pattern through the fabric and the paper. For accurate cutting, cut through fabric and paper. Microserrated shears by Gingher cut silk like butter.

What is the proper interfacing to use with silk? Silk organza or another layer of the fashion fabric give the best results. Fusible results are not always predictable in lightweight silks—stick to the sew-ins.

Afraid to use silk thread on silk fabric? Don't be. High quality silk thread is now available from spun silk with 12 to 15% elasticity and filament silk with 25% elasticity. Both threads are good. High quality polyester or cotton is also suitable. Try them to see which one your machine likes best. If you're puzzled about what seam finish to use on silks, better ready-to-wear always features French seams.

To prevent seam puckers in silk, use a fine needle, 60/8 H or 70/10 H—and "taut sewing," slight pressure on fabric from front and back. If this doesn't solve the puckered seam problem on your machine, stitch over strips of adding machine paper. Tear away when seam is complete. Press seams without steam before pressing open. Always use a press and lift motion to avoid stretching the fabric.

When making buttonholes on silk, use extra fine thread or fine embroidery thread and a Schmetz needle 70/10 HJ. Seal cut buttonhole with Fray Check. A little Fray Check goes a long way. Dip toothpick in Fray Check and dab onto buttonhole.

Don't dry clean that hand-painted scarf, if it was painted with Gutta Resist. Lines will be removed in the dry cleaning process. Hand wash in a mild soap or shampoo instead.

If you own a piece of silk charmeuse, but feel it is too dressy for your life-style, throw it into the washing machine and dryer with a pair of jeans. The satiny texture is sanded by abrasion with the jeans, resulting in "sueded silk" great for silk shorts or full pants.

Silk Look-alikes

Although many of the manmade fabrics look and feel like silk on the bolt, the final garment is often disappointing because it simply does not hang like silk.

No matter how much pressing has been done, both the seams and darts have minute wrinkles that do not press out.

Are you using the correct needle? These silk look-alikes need a very fine needle like the Schmetz 70/10 Standard H needle. Do not use a ballpoint needle. This guarantees puckers.

What thread is suitable? Both cotton and polyester work with the same results.

What stitch length? The finer the fabric, the smaller the stitch. On a dial ranging from 0 to 4, set at about 1.2 or 1.5.

If the selvage is stiff, cut it off before cutting out the garment. The fabric will lie better.

Unfortunately, even after getting all of the above conditions right, the seams and darts will still wrinkle if the fabric is cut on the lengthwise grain.

The garment must be cut on the bias or the crosswise grain. A bias cut looks best, but cutting on the crossgrain is the next choice. Seam wrinkling is far less than when cut on the lengthwise grain.

After sewing seams and darts, press the construction details as sewn—closed seams on both sides. When pressing seams open, press with steam on the wrong side and then again on the right side.

Care should be taken not to use too stiff an interfacing. Very often an additional layer of the silk look-alike can be used in the collar in place of interfacing. This gives a softer look to the garment.

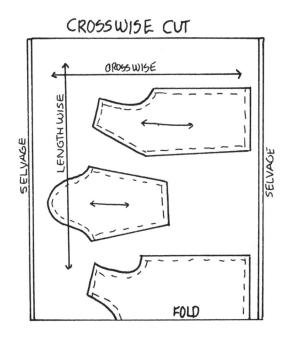

CROSSWISE CUT

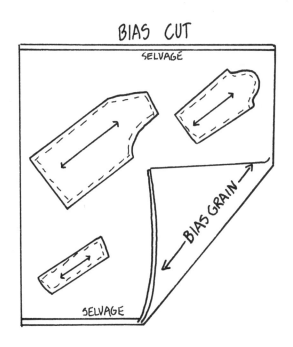

BIAS CUT

Sheers

Even experienced sewers often shy away from sheer silk chiffons, and novices can reap disaster when working with them. Here are a few tips that can help eliminate trouble.

Problems begin when you try to cut out pattern and fabric together; they slip and slide. Pin fabric together double as per layout you are using. Lay tissue paper or an old sheet on the cutting table. Pin the fabric to this. Now pin pattern through all thicknesses. Cut through all layers (Illustration 1).

Don't mark the fabric with a tracing wheel—it makes holes. Use pins, chalk, or tailor tacks.

Before you attempt to sew a seam, a little preparation is necessary. Are you using silk thread? If not, the second-best choice is 100-percent cotton.

Is your sewing machine needle the right size? Size 60/8, or 65/9, or 70/10 are very fine needles that will leave no holes in the fabric and prevent bunching. If you have a problem with skipped stitches on your machine, I'd suggest investing in a Singer Yellow Band™ needle, a patented needle that clears this problem right up. Unfortunately, this needle should not be used on European machines. A brand new Schmetz standard H needle, size 70/9, should be used on the European machines.

Check the throat plate on your machine. The best throat plate to use is one with the single small hole used for straight stitching.

If you do not have this throat plate available, place a piece of tape over the wide zigzag hole. The needle will make a small hole in the tape and simulate the small hole throat plate. This method will prevent the fabric from being pulled down into the bobbin area. Be careful not to cover the feed dog with the tape (Illustration 2).

Try a sample seam on a scrap. If fabric bunches up at the start of the seam, overlap a small piece of cotton fabric onto the sheer. Start sewing on the cotton fabric and continue stitching onto the sheer. Tear away strip afterwards (Illustration 3).

To prevent puckering of seams, use equal pressure from hands on front and back of seam as you sew. But don't stretch the fabric.

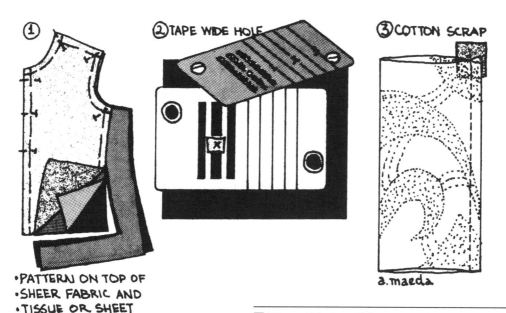

① •PATTERN ON TOP OF •SHEER FABRIC AND •TISSUE OR SHEET

② TAPE WIDE HOLE

③ COTTON SCRAP

a. maeda

■ Sheer fabric will be easier to cut accurately if you hand-baste selvages together

Corduroy and Velveteen

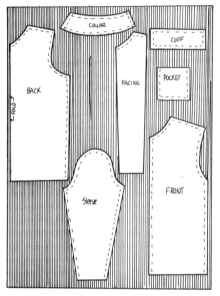

Most sewers do not preshrink corduroy or velveteen before sewing, since they plan to have their garment dry-cleaned. However, the fabric does shrink during the construction pressing if you use steam. This can cause rippled seams and wrinkled lapels. To avoid trouble, simply send the fabric to the dry cleaner to be preshrunk. Corduroy may be washed in mild soap by hand. Turn inside out to run through the dryer.

Since both velveteen and corduroy have a nap, it is mandatory that all pieces be cut going in the same direction, with the nap running down.

When cutting the upper collar, cut off an additional $\frac{1}{16}$ inch around the edges. This will make the upper collar somewhat smaller. This is very important. Most jacket and coat patterns are designed for use with wool. Wool has quite a lot of give, whereas velveteen and corduroy have very little.

By comparing your top collar and undercollar patterns, you will notice a difference of about 1 inch. When the collar is cut of wool, the larger upper collar molds easily over the undercollar.

In velveteen or corduroy, the upper collar cut that size is too big. Since the fabric has little stretch, the excess ends up in wrinkles across the upper collar. By cutting off the $\frac{1}{16}$ inch around the collar, the excess is eliminated. Remember to remark dots $\frac{1}{16}$ inch in on the pattern.

All pressing must be done on the wrong side of the fabric with a needle board against the right side of the fabric.

A needle board is a tough canvas board with closely spaced steel needles protruding. It's essential in tailoring velveteen or corduroy to keep the nap from crushing. Since they're expensive, buy a small one and move it around a lot.

Place needle board on flat surface with needles up. Place right side of velveteen or corduroy against needles. You now can steam-press or use the tailor's clapper to flatten lapels without fear of crushing the nap.

Silk Velvet

If you want a real challenge, have ample time, and want a fabulous outfit, make it up in silk velvet. For evening, there is no fabric quite like this. Silk velvet drapes beautifully, molds to the body, and feels most luxurious. But it must be handled carefully because it is slippery and stretches, and cannot be pressed in the traditional manner.

Most silk velvet comes in a 45-inch width. The selvages must be basted together to prevent slippage when cutting; baste crosswise edges together, too. Pin the pattern to the fabric, sticking the pins in the seam allowances to avoid pin marks.

Silk velvet definitely has a nap, so all pattern pieces must be placed going in the same direction. The nap can be used up or down, depending on the color you prefer. The nap is nicer to wear going down, because it feels so good against the hand.

After pinning the garment together, hand-baste all seams and darts to prevent slipping (Illustration 1). Any fitting of the garment should be done after the hand-basting stage, before permanent stitching. Permanent stitching cannot be removed without leaving very visible marks. Once you sew the seams, that's it. You get no second chance.

For the same reason, all zippers must be put in by hand (Illustration 2). The presser foot on the zipper would make obvious marks.

All pressing must be done on a needleboard with the nap side against the needles. Press lightly on the wrong side with steam. Heavy pressure leaves seam imprints. No pressing can be done on the right side.

Outside facings and collar edges should be basted with silk thread, which is left in until after a professional pressing. Silk thread does not make an imprint during pressing.

Any interfacing or lining used should be cut on the bias if a soft, draped style is desired (Illustration 3). For more control in certain areas, silk organza on the straight grain works well.

Let a skirt hang 24 hours before marking, and mark with a floor hem marker to get an even hem.

Finally, send the garment out to a good cleaner for a professional pressing. The results are fabulous.

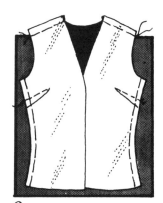

① HAND BASTE; ADJUST FIT, THEN MACHINE STITCH.

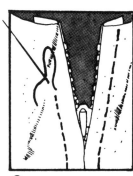

② HAND STITCH ZIPPER.

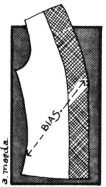

③ LINING AND INTERFACING ON BIAS.

■ You can avoid all slipping and sliding with velvet by simply underlining with prewashed silk organza. Ability to have absolute control of the fabric and an anchor for hand stitches makes underlining well worth this extra step.

Sewing with Knits

If you don't like to iron, cotton knits make a great alternative to cottons and linens. Turning out a knit top in less than two hours is not difficult, but good quality knit fabric is a must. While an imported cotton knit or rayon jersey might be perfect for a wrap top or full circle skirt, this same fabric will be too clingy and revealing for simple T-shirt type patterns. Recovery is a factor which must also be considered. Stretch 6 inches of fabric on the crosswise and see if it returns to 6 inches or remains stretched at 8 inches or more. Fabric without recovery power results in baggy, shapeless garments after a few wearings.

If you are using a cotton knit and truly want a wash-and-wear garment, buy an additional half yard per three yard length. Put the fabric through washer and dryer cycles twice before cutting to insure against future shrinkage.

For machine sewing, use a ballpoint machine needle designated by HS on the package, cotton or polyester thread, and a medium stitch length. Never be in a hurry when sewing with knits. Fast machine sewing causes the top layer to stretch, say numerous knit experts. Moderate to slow machine sewing ensures seams that are not stretched and wavy. If you are using a lightweight knit, a narrow zigzag (.5 width) and a medium length stitch is preferable to a knit stitch. Knit stitches with their back-and-forth motion put too much thread in the seam, resulting in bulky seams that do not lie flat.

The optimum machine for sewing knits is the serger (overlock), since it builds in stretch and simultaneously trims seams. Since knits do not ravel, an overlocked seam gives a nice finish to the inside of the garment. A serger might be a nice gift; in the meantime, a narrow zigzag of medium-length stitches is quite suitable for sewing on knits.

Whether using a serger or a conventional machine, keep the machine speed moderate to prevent stretched and wavy seams. If you notice that, despite your best efforts, your knit is stretching, try placing your finger at the back of the presser foot on a conventional sewing machine or overlock to slow the fabric (Illustration 1). This pressure, which causes slight easing on woven fabrics, merely controls stretching on an unstable knit.

Facings can be eliminated whenever possible in a knit to resemble ready-to-wear. Neckline and armholes are finished by staystitching (a row of stitches through one thickness which prevents stretching) ½ inch from raw edge (Illustration 2). Press under a ⅝ inch seam allowance using the staystitching line as a roll line (Illustration 3). Topstitch into place. Do not stretch these areas as you topstitch. This eliminates bulk and the homesewn look.

Hems, if not done correctly, can also appear wavy and stretched. Finish the raw edge of the hem with an overlock or zigzag stitch. The hem now may be sewn by hand or machine. For every five hand stitches, stretch fabric and thread slightly and knot.

■ To prevent hem from stretching as you topstitch using the double needle, try using hand-wound elastic thread in the bobbin, and even feed foot on top. Push fabric into the needle from the front.

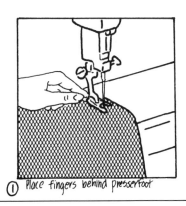
① Place fingers behind presser foot

②

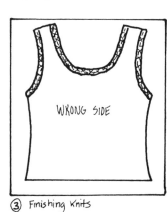
③ Finishing Knits
WRONG SIDE

Sweater Knits

Beautiful sweater knits are available by the yard in both very fine and very bulky knits. Almost any pattern is suitable for a sweater knit. Since many sweater knits have a 75–100% stretch, buying smaller pattern sizes will give you the fit you want in a sweater. If your pattern is designed for a knit, "knits only," buy pattern one size smaller. If your pattern is designed for wovens, buy pattern two sizes smaller. If your pattern is multi-sized, simply trace the smaller size.

Before layout, thoroughly steam machine sweater knit to set the stitches. Cut excess tissue away from the pattern cutting line. This will enable you to get an accurate cut on the knit. Pattern weights are preferable to pins since pins tear pattern tissue when used with bulky knits.

Lay pattern pieces on the fabric directionally, as you would a napped fabric. Handle cut pieces carefully so that they will not stretch out of shape. Stitches will not run unless an extreme amount of stress is applied.

Stabilize shoulder seams, diagonal seams on a wrap bodice and crotch seams with clear stretch elastic. Cut elastic lengths the exact length of the seam, measured from the pattern tissue. Pin elastic in place, easing sweater knit to fit the unstretched elastic.

If the knitted fabric is of the bulky variety, it is a good idea to hand-baste seams before machine sewing. The best seam treatment for sweater knits is a serged seam of the ¾ variety. If your serger is equipped with differential feed, set on "2" to prevent stretched wavy seams. If you do not have this feature, loosen the pressure on the presserfoot. If knit is still stretching slightly, place finger against the back of the presserfoot as you serge. Experiment with a sample seam. If seam is still stretching, stabilize seam edges with Perfect Sew before sewing. This will stabilize and stiffen the edges slightly, eliminating the problem. Stiffness can be removed by hand washing.

Applique and machine embroidery are both possible on sweater knits if area is stabilized with Perfect Sew first.

If some seams are sewn on a conventional machine, dual feed, even feed foot (walking foot), or roller foot is necessary to keep top layer from pushing ahead. If possible, reduce pressure on presserfoot. Use a narrow zigzag .5mm width and a slightly longer stitch (3mm).

Sweater knits are usually finished with ribbing in two-thirds proportion, meaning the length of ribbing is cut two-thirds the length of whatever it will be added to. Stretch ribbing to sweater knit. (See pages 176–178 in *More Power Sewing*.)

If any hand stitching is necessary, stretch thread every fourth or fifth stitch and knot. This builds a little stretch into your hand sewing, eliminating popped stitches.

Sweater knits can also be combined with handwoven fabric as well as synthetic leather and suede with interesting results.

Pressing on sweater knits is very important for professional results. Use lots of steam and finger press every step.

Many of these tips were generously provided by Terri L. Burns. Watch for her book *Sewing and Serging Sweaterknits*, published by Palmer/Pletsch.

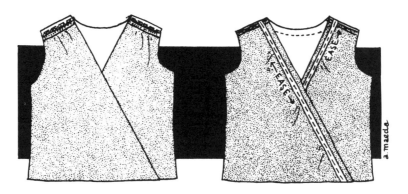

Sweatshirt Fabric

Until recently, the use of sweatshirt fabric was limited to jogging suits and beachwear. Now sweatshirt fabric is widely used in sportswear for tops, shirts, pants, and dresses. The look is loose and comfortable.

What do you need to know about sweatshirt fabric to make it work for you?

First and foremost: You must preshrink the fabric. The fabric shrinks in both length and width. To be certain the preshrinking process is complete, twice wash the fabric in warm water and put it through a medium-heat drying cycle before cutting out.

Avoid washing in hot water unless you are using white. Otherwise, you will experience some color loss. To be on the safe side, I would recommend purchasing 1/4 yard more fabric than the pattern requires, to allow for shrinkage.

Cutting out sweatshirt fabric may present a problem because of the bulk. Pins tend to pop out and tear the pattern. Use of pattern weights is preferable.

Sewing sweatshirt fabric is similar to sewing on other knits except that the stitch length is longer to allow for the bulk of the fabric. Use a size 11 or 12 needle, with a little longer than medium stitch length. Use a stretch stitch or a tiny width zigzag to build some stretch into the seams.

Most hems in ready-to-wear are made simply by turning up a 1-inch hem with an overlocked or zigzagged edge. Topstitch two rows of stitching 1/4 inch apart, 1/4 inch from the folded finished edge of the hem.

Press with steam and pound with the tailor's clapper.

■ Try see-through elastic for a flexible lightweight stabilizer for necks and shoulders on knits.

■ Wipe the scissor blades frequently. Lint accumulates between the blades and prevents smooth cutting.

Water-Resistant and Water-Repellant Fabrics

First, let's discuss the differences between fabrics that are water-resistant and those that are water-proof.

Water-resistant fabrics have been chemically coated to make light rain or snow brush or roll off without penetrating. This means that in a very heavy rain you are going to get wet.

Water-resistant fabrics are used because they drape well and are not bulky or overly warm.

Water resistance is most effective when the fabrics have been treated by the manufacturer. A dry cleaner can put an effective water resistant on most close-woven polyester blends.

For real water repellency, you need either a vinyl- or urethane-coated fabric. The latter is more enjoyable to wear, since it is not stiff.

If the raincoat fabric is slippery and hard to handle, place slippery sides together when you cut it out. Use pattern weights rather than pins, because pins make holes. Use a smooth tracing wheel for marking or, better yet, a washable marking pen for fabric.

Use cotton or polyester thread, depending on which your machine uses best. Vinyl- or urethane-coated fabrics need a size 14 needle with a long stitch (six stitches to the inch).

Pinning seams together is somewhat difficult in these fabrics, so I like to use little clothespins to hold the seams in place while I sew.

For chemically coated, water-resistant fabrics, use a size 11 needle and a regular stitch length (10 to 12 stitches to the inch).

To keep these fabrics from puckering, hold fabric with equal pressure from the front and back as you sew. For vinyl- or urethane-coated fabrics, use a roller or even-feed foot. Topstitch these seams so that they will lie flat.

Be very careful about pressing. Always make a test press on a sample swatch using a warm iron and no steam. Some cannot be pressed at all. Rain-resistant fabrics can be pressed with steam, using a press-cloth on the right side.

Some coats have a zip-in fleece lining—easy enough with the purchase of an extra-long zipper in the slip-cover section.

I find a fleece lining bulky and prefer the method of underlining the lining with cotton flannel (which must be preshrunk). This provides warmth without bulk. Simply cut out identical pieces of cotton flannel and lining, and hand-baste together. Continue construction as though the cotton flannel and lining were bonded.

If you plan to use wooden buttons, paint them on both sides with varnish or clear nail polish. Otherwise, the buttons will turn dark and stain the fabric.

■ A wide variety of water-resistant man-made fibers are now available to the home sewer. If you are looking for a less expensive substitute for water-resistant silk taffeta, check rainwear sources for "Silk O'Hara," a really beautiful rainwear fabric available in a wide variety of colors.

Bulky Wools Lighten Up

Bulky fabrics such as felted wool, boiled wool, double faced wool and melton can be a challenge not only in eliminating bulk in seams but also in creating shape in a fabric which has a mind of its own. This technique can only be used for a non-raveling fabric. After considerable experimentation on a ¼-inch-thick felted fabric, I discovered a technique which eliminates bulk and creates shape simultaneously. Although this technique could be done with a wide zigzag, or a universal "U" stitch, some machines create a beautiful feather stitch, providing a "class act" alternative.

After cutting out the garment, INCLUDING SEAM ALLOWANCES, proceed to CUT BOTH SEAM ALLOWANCES OFF before joining a seam. If you are really brave, cut garment without seam allowances to begin with—easy if using Burda. Although the obvious step is to cut out the garment without seam allowances in the first place, I felt more comfortable cutting them off right before I sew. Use sharp scissors and care in cutting off each seam allowance so that the remaining edges will butt together smoothly. To join garment pieces without seam allowances, butt the two raw edges into each other, allowing the feather stitch to work from side to side, creating a union of the two pieces.

After you experiment on a scrap, you will agree that the results are first-class but the problem of holding the two pieces together while sewing is unresolved. Strips of Scotch tape do not form a strong enough bond. The problem can be solved by pinning a piece of twill tape across the joint, placing a pin on each end of the tape into the fabric.

To hold pieces together, a twill tape bridge every 4 inches or so should be sufficient. Remove pins and twill tape as you sew, right before you come to the bridge.

Surprisingly enough, curved seams can be joined in this manner, including setting in a sleeve. To reinforce the armhole seam, place a piece of narrow bias tape under the seam joint on the wrong side of the garment pieces. Allow the feather stitch to join garment pieces together and onto the bias tape at the same time. This technique works well for seams that receive stress and for weak fabrics which might pull

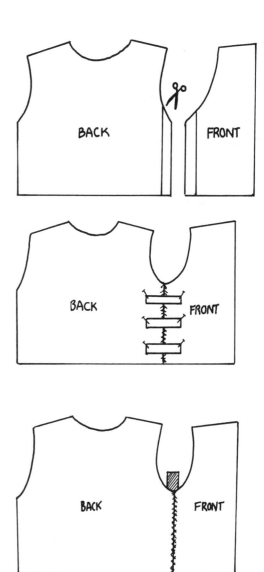

away from the stitching if left to their own devices.

Machine feathering has great possibilities. It is even possible to ease in a fuller side, such as a princess shape. Since this discovery, I have found many applications. This technique produces a beautiful seam alternative in an unlined hood.

Leather

Making a leather garment is not as difficult as many home sewers think. Such lightweight leathers as deerskin, chamois, and cabretta can be sewn on a home sewing machine with a size 14 or 16 leather needle, or a Schmetz 70/10 HJ.

The heavier skins, however, require a special industrial machine designed specifically for leather work.

Since leather has very little give, buy the blouse or jacket pattern one size larger for comfort. Simple, uncluttered styles are easier for your first leather garment. Use a pattern you have tried in another fabric. Removing stitching in leather can be murder and often shows.

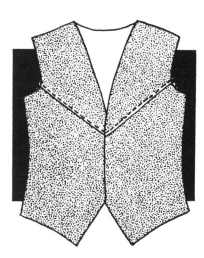

The number of skins required for a particular garment depends very much on the pattern and the size of the skin. Always take your pattern and lay it out on the skins when you shop, or send a copy of your pattern when you order by mail.

Piecing is necessary on almost anything you make in leather. Try to make the piecing seem like part of the garment design. This will take some planning, but the results are worthwhile. Use weights to anchor the pattern to the skin for cutting. Pins leave lasting impressions.

The skins must be cut directionally, as with velvet. The pieces that will take the most stress should be cut out of the center of the skin, as this is the strongest part.

Make copies of all pattern pieces before you begin. You will not be cutting double, and pattern placement on the skin is very important. For a vest, you would have a right front, left front, right back, and left back. On the back skin, circle all skin imperfections in chalk so you can avoid them in pattern placements. Place the pattern pieces on the skin directionally from the top of the skin (the widest part) to the tail. The small pieces of the sides are excellent for belts when pieced.

Use a tracing wheel with no tracing paper to trace the cutting edge of the pattern. Remove the pattern and check to make sure the shape you are cutting out has no defects or color variations. The tracing wheel makes an imprint on the skin; cut along this line.

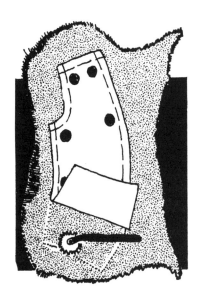

Leather

A shirt will usually take about five skins, a skirt about three or four, pants about five or six, depending on the style. Do not pin the pattern to the skin, as the pins will make holes. Use weights instead. Canned goods are quite adequate for this purpose. Sharp scissors are a must. Taping the skins together before seaming works better than pinning.

Sewing is easy if you purchase an even-feed foot. This is a special foot designed for such problem fabrics as velvet, which tends to creep. The even-feed foot has teeth on the foot, which lock into place with the feed dog, eliminating problems in sewing with leather, suede, and velvet. You can sew leather without an even-feed foot, but you will have to sew quite slowly to control the movement of the top piece of leather. A Teflon® foot is quite effective to control creeping. If possible, use the single-hole throat plate. If not, try your needle all the way to the left.

Sharp needles are a must. Experiment with the stitch length on a scrap to see which looks the best to you. One-hundred-percent polyester thread is the best thread to use on leather.

Leather can be pressed, but only with a very low heat. Do not use steam. Experiment on a sample before pressing the garment itself.

The seams will be flatter and hems will look better if they are glued. Rubber cement or Soloman's SOBO glue will make the seams and hem lie flat, especially if they are later pounded with a heavy padded hammer.

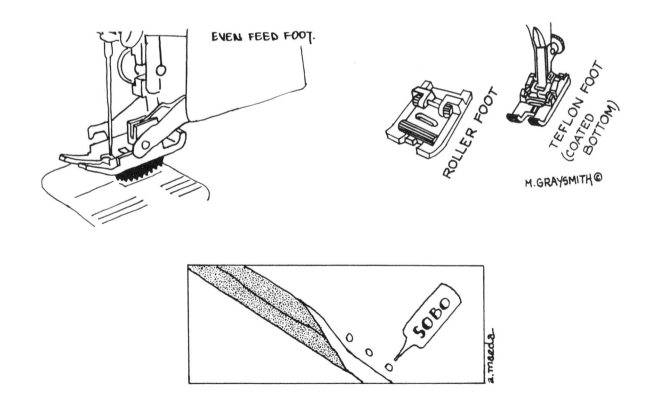

EVEN FEED FOOT.

ROLLER FOOT

TEFLON FOOT (COATED BOTTOM)

M.GRAYSMITH©

SOBO

a.maeda

Handwovens

A well-constructed garment in handwoven fabric can be the most beautiful and interesting piece you own. Choose a pattern with a minimum number of pieces and simple styling to show off your fabric to its best advantage. Always pretest your intended pattern before cutting into your handwoven, so that you can figure yardage requirements precisely and adjust the pattern accordingly. Seam ripping on handwovens can create tragic results by snipping one wrong thread, causing a visible hole.

For accuracy in cutting through single-fabric thickness, use pattern weights rather than pins. Tailor's tacks will be the only markings visible. After cutting, handle the pieces carefully to avoid stretching. Overlock all newly-cut edges (Illustration 1). Reduce presser foot tension to prevent stretching fabric as you serge. Wooly nylon thread on the upper looper makes a soft flexible serged edge.

If an overlock is not available, wrap raw edges with Seams Great and zigzag. Zigzag without Seams Great will cause a stretched edge.

Stay tape is mandatory at the shoulder and neckline seams. Use the pattern as a guide to cut stay tape lengths. Ease the handwoven to fit the stay tape. Do not use stay tape on lengthwise seams or rippled seams will appear after the first wearing.

Fusible interfacing is preferable to nonfusible, since it helps the handwoven retain its shape and prevents ravelling. In more structured styles, consider fusing each garment piece with fusible tricot. Do not fuse any piece where drape is required. When fusing interfacing to handwoven, force the handwoven to the shape of the interfacing. Although they were cut from the same pattern piece, the handwoven will appear larger. Since handwovens have lengthwise stretch and lining fabrics do not, cut linings 1 inch longer than required.

To keep handwoven seams from creeping and stretching, an even-feed foot is a must. Sew seams with a medium-length stitch. Press both seams to one side and topstitch from the right side of the garment (Illustration 2). Press topstitched seam with steam using a press-cloth and pound with a tailor's clapper.

Consider elimination of facing with strips of leather, suede or bias trim (see page 211). Corded loops are preferable to buttonholes (see Illustration 3 and page 150). Buttonholes are possible with the help of an extra piece of fine-woven fabric behind the interfacing to give the buttonhole added support. Corded buttonholes resist stretch and wear better. Rub diluted SOBO on cut buttonhole edges for durability.

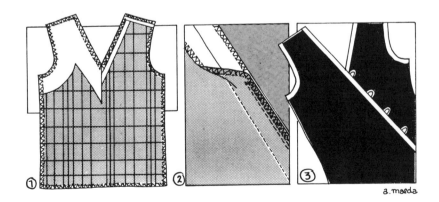

a. maeda

DIFFICULT SEAMS

■ When planning a garment in fragile fabrics—which include handwovens, loose weaves, lambsuede, chiffons, and silks—fit should be perfected in a pretest. Seam repositioning in unstable fabrics results in a garment which looks shopworn before it even goes on a body.

Prevent Shifting Seams

When joining a bodice to a skirt, we like seams to match up perfectly. A true perfectionist will redo a seam several times to get a flawless match; the rest of us will just hope that no one examines the garment too closely. Recently I discovered a foolproof technique for matching seams.

In some lightweight fabrics, sewing over a pin placed perpendicular to the seam will not cause a problem. But as the fabric weight increases, the same technique will cause the thread to drag where the needle encounters the pin.

If you examine your seam closely, you will notice that the stitch length changed at that point. This thread drag weakens the seam, and stress in this area will cause the seam to pop.

Changing the pin placement will eliminate this problem and still prevent the seam from moving during the sewing process. Place the pin parallel to the seam with the pin head facing you an inch from the raw edge of the seam.

As you sew, do not pull out the pin and risk a shift in fabric position. By placing the pin an inch away from the raw edge, you have enough room for the presser foot to pass by without having to remove the pin.

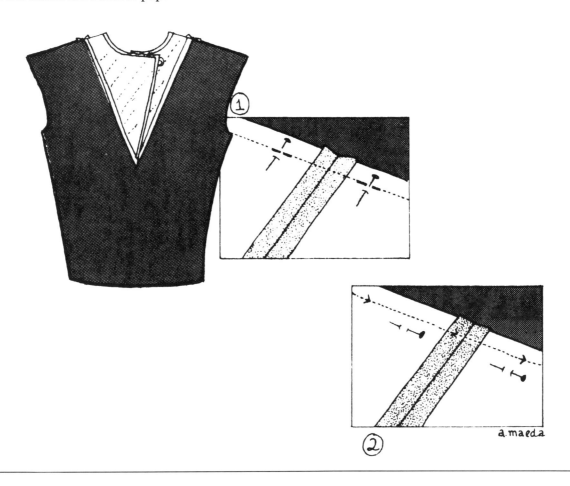

a. maeda

Piecing Fabric

Despite the fact that many of the current styles require large amounts of fabric, the cost of good fabric continues to escalate. You can often save a considerable amount of fabric if you are adept at piecing.

Whenever possible, try to make the pieced seam look like part of the garment's design. If you plainly see that you do not have enough fabric, place the pattern piece on your body and decide where a seam would be the most flattering.

Scarcity of fabric often necessitates piecing on only one side. However, consider piecing on both sides to make the seam look intentional. In this case, you may even decide to pipe or topstitch the seam to make it more visible.

Suppose the garment—such as a circle skirt—does not lend itself to a new seam. Decide where the piecing would be least noticed. For example, a piece in the center back of the skirt along the hem would be very noticeable, but a piece in the back near the side seam would be lost in the folds of the fabric.

The following method has been the easiest and most foolproof for me to execute: Lay the pattern onto the fabric as though you had enough fabric. Pin into place. Cut out the pattern piece, ignoring the missing chunk of fabric. Find a piece of fabric with the same grain as the missing piece. The pieced seam should be a straight seam. Cut off any jagged edges or selvages from all pieces of fabric. With the pattern still pinned to the fabric, unpin only an area small enough to piece the seam. Pin the scrap fabric—larger than you think you need—with right sides together, forming a seam. With the pattern still attached to the main piece, sew and press the new seam. After sewing the new seam, repin the small pattern piece that you folded out of the way. Cut out the rest of the garment, cutting off excess in the piecing.

For me, this has eliminated repiecing because the piece was too small or didn't fit. This technique is also suitable for leather or suede.

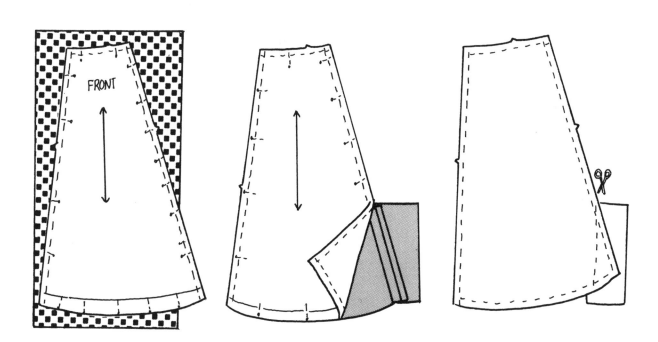

Square Corners

Styling details can look beautiful if they are done correctly. If not, they can cause frustration and leave you with another garment hanging unworn in the closet.

Many patterns cut an angled sleeve to be set in a bodice, an angled cowl neck to be set in a bodice, an angled collar piece to be set in a shawl or notched collar, or a rectangular placket to be set in center front. The angle creates a focal point and must be flawless.

To set a point in a seam easily and smoothly, staystitch ⅝ inch from the cut edge on the "in angle" 1 inch from either side of the point. Slash within one thread of the staystitch line at pivot point only.

To join seams at the point, the slashed piece must be on top while you are sewing. Mark the exact point where the ⅝-inch seamline meets on the "out angle" seam.

Placing right sides together and matching notches, pin angled pieces so that you are able to sew with the slashed piece on top. Match up exactly the dots marking points on both pieces.

Pin only half of the seam to the point. It is necessary to pivot the "in angle" piece to eliminate a pucker. A fully pinned seam will prevent you from pivoting.

Begin sewing with the slashed side up. Exactly at the point, leave the sewing machine needle in the fabric and pivot seam around to conform to the shape. Pin rest of seam and continue sewing.

This technique eliminates any puckers, and the seam goes in easily in any fabric.

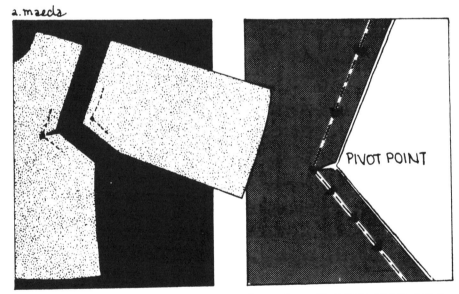

a. maeda

STAYSTITCH AND SLASH BODICE AT PIVOT POINT.

PIVOT POINT

JOIN BODICE TO SLEEVE, LEAVE NEEDLE IN AT SLASH AND PIVOT FABRIC.

Corner with a Seam

A cowl neck joining the V-neck of the bodice at a diagonal seam can be difficult if you don't know the trick of inserting a corner in a seam. Let's simplify the procedure for foolproof results.

Staystitch the lower edge of the cowl neck at $\frac{5}{8}$ inch directionally from neck to shoulder to keep the neck from stretching and to stabilize the point. Use stay tape at the neckline on the bodice to keep the fabric from stretching during the construction process.

Sew the diagonal bodice seam at $\frac{5}{8}$ inch with regular stitch length except for the last 1 inch toward the neck. Switch stitch length to small stitches here, stopping the seam $\frac{5}{8}$ inch from neckline. This will leave the seam open for the last $\frac{5}{8}$ inch and allow you to insert the angular cowl neck with ease and without puckers.

Mark the exact point $\frac{5}{8}$ inch from the raw edges on the cowl neck. With the bodice side up, pin the left side of the bodice to the left side of the cowl neck, right sides together.

Sew the seam from center back to center front, stopping exactly at the point where the seam meets the point on the cowl. Pull the diagonal seam allowance out of the way so that at no time will you be sewing more than two fabric thicknesses near the point.

Use small reinforcing stitches for 1 inch as you near the point. Stop. Now pin the right side in the same manner. Sew from center back to center front as before, stopping exactly at the point. The whole secret to a well-defined point is to allow movement of the seam allowances behind the point.

Press with steam and pound with a tailor's clapper. Topstitch if fabric is bulky.

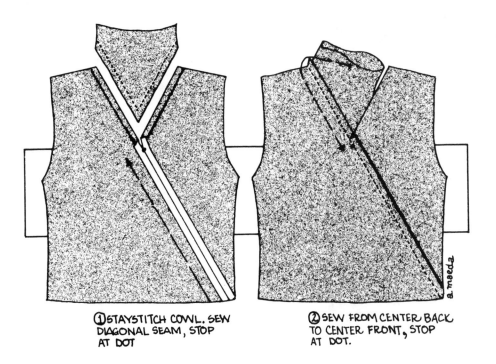

① STAYSTITCH COWL. SEW DIAGONAL SEAM, STOP AT DOT

② SEW FROM CENTER BACK TO CENTER FRONT, STOP AT DOT.

Yoke with Seamed Skirt

Yoked skirts are flattering on most figures. Particularly popular is the V-shaped yoke attached to a front-seamed skirt cut on the bias. Because the yoke is the most prominent feature on the skirt, and the V falls at center front, it is essential that the insertion of the yoke be flawless.

The entire yoke should be interfaced with a lightweight interfacing to give the point support and keep it from stretching.

Sew center front skirt seam from bottom to top using small reinforcing stitches (18 to 20 per inch) for the top inch of the seam. Leave the top $5/8$ inch of the seam open.

On wrong side of yoke, draw two lines $5/8$ inch from bottom edge. Where the lines intersect is the exact center of the yoke (Illustration 1).

Place right side of yoke against right side of skirt, matching center point of yoke with top stitch in skirt center front seam. Pin half of yoke to half of skirt, placing pins on skirt side. Don't try to pin the entire yoke into place or it will be difficult to avoid a tuck in the yoke when stitching.

Sew skirt and yoke together with a $5/8$ inch seam from side of yoke to center front seam of skirt. At this point, lift presserfoot, leaving needle in fabric, and pivot the second half of the yoke around to the second half of skirt front. The fact that the center front seam is open $5/8$ inch from the top enables you to pivot (Illustration 2).

Pin and sew remainder of seam. Press.

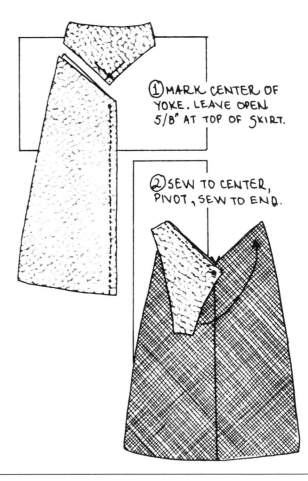

① MARK CENTER OF YOKE. LEAVE OPEN 5/8" AT TOP OF SKIRT.

② SEW TO CENTER, PIVOT, SEW TO END.

Demonstrated on *Power Sewing* Video #5: *Construction Difficulties.*

Sculpted unlined jacket in hand felted fabric is made from a tracing from a vintage jacket (see page 54 for copying ready to wear techniques). Leather trim (see page 211) allows all facings and upper collar to be eliminated.

Bulk reducing techniques for seams and buttonholes can be used for hand felted fabrics, double faced wools and meltons (see page 87 for techniques).

Cobalt blue pigsuede swing coat made from a New Look pattern is piped on all seams with black and white stripe knit cut at right angles to the direction of the stripe (see page 88 for working on leather and suede and page 212 for corded seams). This fun coat shape can be a great maternity cover-up as well as fashion statement. Stirrup pants in stretch wool crepe are made from a Stretch and Sew pattern. Use greatest stretch of fabric around the body. Oversized zipper used for closing (see page 145).

Five lambsuede skins *are used to make this Issey Miyake Vogue pattern overshirt (see pages 88-89 for suede technique). Reverse applique using metallic leather, interfaced striped knit strips and antique buttons create wearable art.*

Curved Seams

Using a pattern with side front and side back seams (princess) can offer the best fit for an individual with a large bust or hips that are large in proportion to the upper torso.

The fit is improved because of the two additional seams available for alterations. The side front seam is shaped to allow for fullness at the bust. Very often the fullness falls in the wrong place, especially if the bust is low.

To ensure yourself a proper fit, whether your bust is large or small, cut a 1-inch seam allowance in the side front seam. Cutting this seam larger will enable you to fit the side front on the body, shaping the seam to fit the bustline, upper chest, waist, and tummy area.

For a perfect fit, pin the side front together, wrong sides out, using the 1-inch seam allowance. Pin the center front and side seams to your undergarments. Let out or take in pinned seam as needed for the body contours.

If you are making a jacket, remember to make identical changes on the lining.

A curved seamline can look very homemade, especially if one seam needs to be eased to the other. The seamline of a princess style in the bustline area is a good example of the difficulty encountered here. To give the amount of ease required for the bust, the side panel is cut larger than the front panel. The pattern requires that the two pieces be eased together. This is no easy task: Not only is one piece larger than the other, but you must ease two opposite curves together, an "in curve" and an "out curve."

Marjorie Arch Burns simplifies this task greatly by treating the "in curve" and the "out curve" separately at first. The out curve is the larger of the two and needs to be made smaller by (1) running a gathering thread and pulling the thread between the notches or (2) a method called "staystitch plus." Staystitch plus is accomplished by pushing on the back of the presserfoot, prohibiting the fabric from flowing through as rapidly as it would like to. Both of the mentioned techniques give a slightly gathered effect. Press the "out curve" lightly over a tailor's ham to eliminate a gathered look.

To make the "in curve" easier to work with, run a line of staystitching ⅝ inch from the edge in the "in" curved area. Slash the seam allowance at 1-inch intervals until the seamline can be pulled into a straight line.

To join the "in" and "out" curves, match the notches and pin the seamline together with the slashed curve on top. The two curves will now fit easily together. If the eased curve seems too small, snip a thread to release some of the gathering. Sew the seam with the slashed curve on top.

Press the seam in the direction it wants to lie, toward the "in curve." Topstitch the seams in place if desired.

On some natural fibers clipping at 1-inch intervals may be unnecessary.

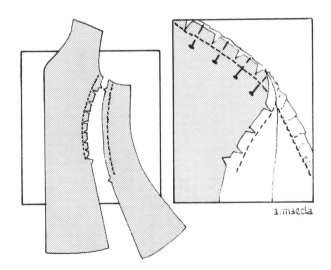

a. maeda

Godets

A godet is a circular or wedge-shaped piece of fabric inserted in a seam to give fullness and add decoration. They are used at the hems of skirts and dresses and in jacket peplums.

To insert a curved godet, it is necessary to clip the garment in a curve for ease of insertion. Run a line of staystitching on the curve of the garment ½ inch from the raw edge. Clip curve every ½ inch up to staystitching line; this allows garment to shape itself around curve of godet (Illustration 1).

Sew in godet with clipped side up, using small reinforcing stitches. Topstitch on right side if desired.

To insert a pointed godet, sew garment seam with small reinforcing stitches for the last ½ inch before the opening. Pin godet into seam with right sides together. Sew from bottom of godet to point. Stop.

Sew other side from bottom to point (Illustration 2). One continuous seam will leave a pucker. Press and pound with tailor's clapper.

a.maeda

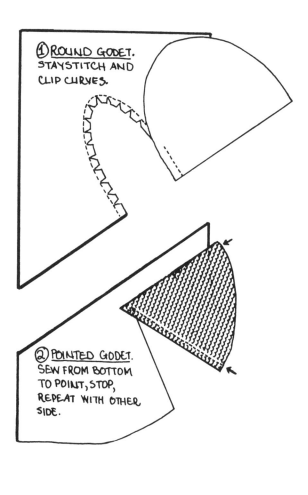

① ROUND GODET. STAYSTITCH AND CLIP CURVES.

② POINTED GODET. SEW FROM BOTTOM TO POINT, STOP, REPEAT WITH OTHER SIDE.

Kimono Sleeve Seams

Simply start from the bottom of the garment and sew right up to the sleeve seam, but not over it.

Complete this process by sewing from the sleeve bottom to the sleeve seam and stop (Illustration 2). Now press the sleeve seam open.

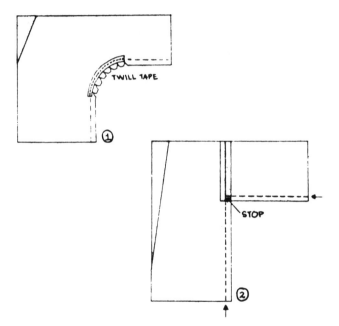

Kimono sleeves can be made in two ways: with a cut-on sleeve or with a sleeve piece added. Both sleeves can pucker under the arm unless a few preventive steps are taken.

The cut-on sleeve is easier to make. To reinforce the underarm seam, sew in a piece of lightweight narrow twill tape or the selvage edge from a lightweight, close-woven fabric. Use small stitches under the arm (18 to 20 stitches per inch). Clip the curve enough so that the seamline can be pulled into a straight line (Illustration I).

The kimono sleeve with a sewn-on piece must be treated differently. The underarm should look angular, not curved. This is accomplished by sewing on the sleeve piece. The underarm seam will be sewn from two directions, stopping at the sleeve seam. Do not sew over this seam or you will create too much bulk.

Reinforcement for the Slit Seam

Slim skirts with slits at the sides, front, or back slip in and out of fashion. Some kimono and jacket patterns also call for slit seams, so knowing how to reinforce a slit can be useful.

A seam with a slit has part of the seam sewn and part of the seam open. If the sewing line is not reinforced, the stitches weaken with normal movement. If the fabric is delicate, it may tear at the point of stress.

Reinforcement of the seam is not difficult. Normal length stitches are used in sewing the seam except for the 1 inch above the spot where the seam opens. Use small reinforcing stitches for 1 inch at this point.

It is also helpful to use a small piece of seam tape or woven lightweight fabric. Simply sew small reinforcing stitches (Illustration) over the small piece of fabric for the 1 inch remaining.

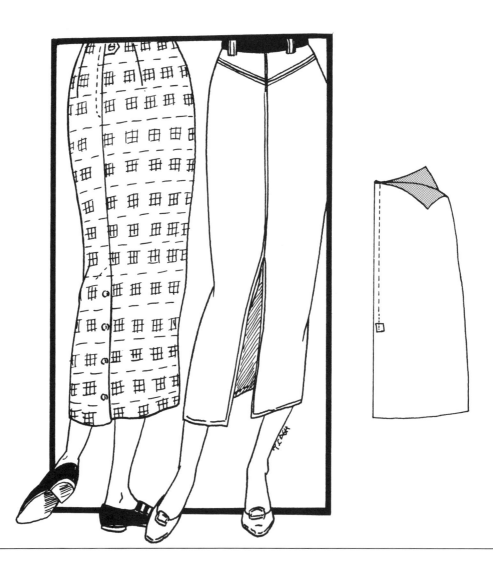

Double Yoke

A good ready-to-wear blouse or shirt will have a double yoke, which gives a finished look on the inside as well as the outside with no visible topstitching. Here is how you can do this with the clothes you sew.

The double-yoke technique can be used with any yoke pattern. Simply cut two yokes rather than one. If you are using heavy fabric, cut the under yoke in a lighter-weight fabric.

With three fabric thicknesses, sandwich lower back between right sides of both back yoke edges. Sew a ⅝-inch seam. Trim seam to ¼ inch. Sew the front right side of the under yoke to the front wrong side of the blouse shoulder only through the two thicknesses.

Place the right side of outer yoke against the right side of blouse by turning the yoke back on itself through the neckline. Sew over the original line of stitching. Repeat the process for the other shoulder.

Turning the yoke back will look strange while you are doing it, but it will give you totally enclosed yoke edges.

An alternative is to turn under the outer yoke seam allowances at the shoulder edge and topstitch into place.

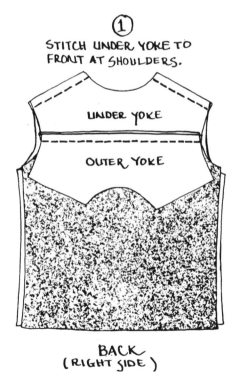

① STITCH UNDER YOKE TO FRONT AT SHOULDERS.

UNDER YOKE

OUTER YOKE

BACK
(RIGHT SIDE)

② TURN BACK SHOULDERS, SEW SEAM FROM INSIDE.

FRONT
(RIGHT SIDE)

Secrets of Bias

Often the question arises—when and how do I use a bias cut?

Very often a bias cut works better than a straight-of-grain cut because the bias cut gives a better drape. This is especially true with a very full skirt. A full-bias skirt will drape gracefully around the legs; the same skirt cut on the straight of grain may appear much too full.

In order to cut a garment on the bias, you will first have to find the bias grainline. Do this by drawing a line on the pattern perpendicular to the lengthwise grainline; this is the crosswise grainline. Draw a line midway between these two lines and you have the bias grainline (Illustration 1). Now lay the pattern on your fabric so that the bias grainline you have drawn (instead of the lengthwise grainline) is parallel to the selvage (Illustration 2).

Certain parts of a garment should always be cut on the bias if that does not interfere with the fabric design. A full sleeve always has softer drape if cut on the bias; cuffs and mandarin collars mold into a smooth circle when cut on the bias.

If, however, you are making a striped shirt, cuffs and collar cut on the bias might be undesirable. In such a case, cut only the undercollar and undercuff on the bias.

Stiff fabrics will usually hang better on the bias. A heavy wool that is too imposing when cut on the straight of grain, for example, takes on a soft drape when cut on the bias.

Do you love the drape of bias but hate the rippled seams and uneven hem? Perhaps these tips from Marcy Tilton of the Sewing Workshop will help.

Always cut 1-inch seam allowances in bias garments. These seam allowances will shrink in the pressing process.

After cutting the garment and before sewing the lengthwise seams, press each piece separately. Moving the iron lengthwise on each piece, stretch the fabric a bit lengthwise as you press.

Pressing before you sew is very important. The ever-changing hemline on a bias garment is caused by stretching, which occurs when the garment is worn or pressed. Pressing before sewing removes quite a bit of the stretch potential (Illustration 3).

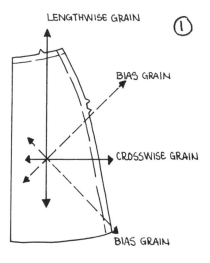

LENGTHWISE GRAIN ①

BIAS GRAIN

CROSSWISE GRAIN

BIAS GRAIN

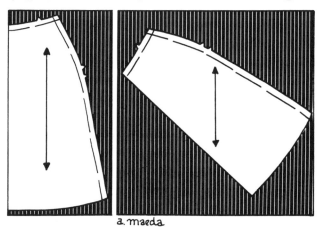

ALIGN LENGTHWISE GRAINLINE WITH FOLD

ALIGN BIAS GRAINLINE WITH FABRIC SELVAGE EDGE ②

a. maeda

Remember to press and stretch at seam areas as well as the body of the garment. Pulling and pressing seams reduces the seam allowance from 1 inch to ¾ inch if the pressing is done correctly.

Sew the lengthwise seams at ¾ inch. To ensure a bit of stretch in the seams, use a narrow zigzag (.5 mm) and a size 2 stitch or 15 stitches to the inch. This narrow zigzag stitch eliminates puckering and ripples at the seams. Press the seams as stitched on both sides. Press seams open (Illustration 4).

Secrets of Bias

Press the entire garment again, stretching a bit as you press. Attach the waistband or bodice and press and stretch lengthwise one more time. These last two pressings will reduce the seam allowances to ⅝ inch. It is not necessary to let the garment hang for 48 hours. Bias stretch has been accomplished in the pressing process.

If you are a real perfectionist, this next step ensures perfection. Baste a thin cord of drapery weights along the bottom of the skirt. Years ago, scrap fabric strips were used for weights. Today, drapery weights in a casing are more convenient. Let skirt hang on a skirt hanger for two to three days. Use a hem marker to mark the hem. Do not be surprised to see differences of 3 to 4 inches in different parts of the garment (Illustration 5).

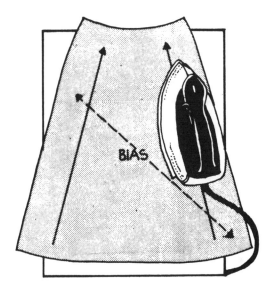

③ PRESS LENGTHWISE.

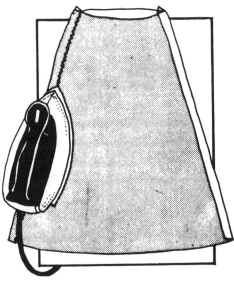

④ PRESS SEAM CLOSED, THEN PRESS OPEN.

⑤

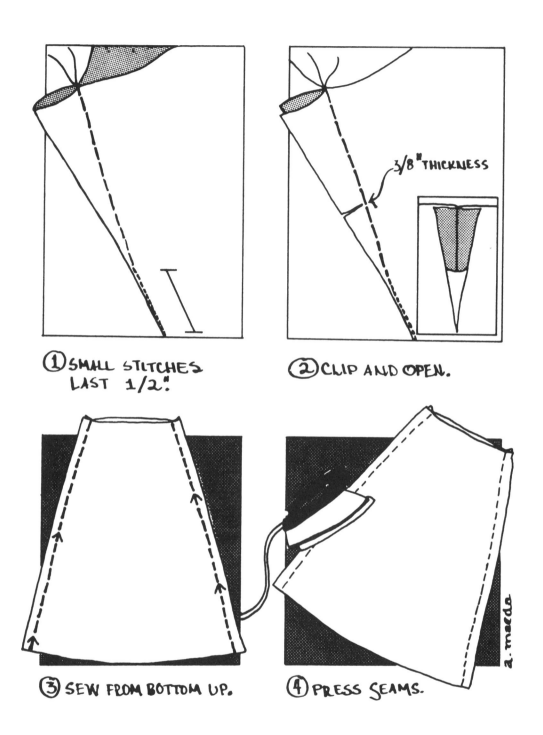

① SMALL STITCHES
   LAST 1/2".

3/8" THICKNESS

② CLIP AND OPEN.

③ SEW FROM BOTTOM UP.

④ PRESS SEAMS.

a. maeda

Demonstrated on *Power Sewing* Video #1: *Fear of Sewing*.

DARTS, GATHERS, PLEATS

■ To eliminate the dimple at the bottom of the dart in fabrics which will not mold, cut a 2 inch square of firm cotton or non-fusible interfacing. Center the dart point in the center of the square. Sew over square as you sew in dart. A small square stabilizes the area, eliminating the dimple.

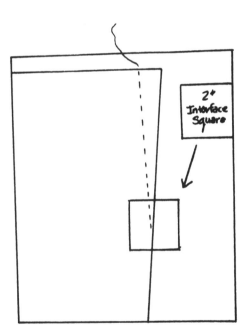

Making Perfect Darts

Many times what gives away a homemade garment is the dart.

For openers, dart placement is very important. To avoid pouched fabric under the front darts of a skirt, move the darts toward the side seam an inch or two so that the darts are near an area of fullness.

The point of a bust dart should not be seen from the front of the garment. The end of the bust dart should be ½ to 1 inch from the apex of the bust. The bust dart may be shortened by merely ending the dart sooner.

Never backstitch at the beginning or end of a dart. Backstitching creates bulk, which prevents the dart from lying flat. It isn't necessary to tie threads at the beginning and end of a dart; it takes too much time, and a machine knot is preferable.

When beginning a dart, pull gently at the fabric 2 to 3 inches from the front of the presserfoot. This prevents the fabric from moving under the presserfoot, causing the machine to sew in place on top of the first stitch. You need to hold the fabric for only a split second, just enough for the sewing machine to take one quick stitch on top of the first.

As soon as you begin sewing a dart, think about ending it. On the last ½ inch of the dart, you should be sewing on practically nothing, just a few threads.

At about ½ inch from the end of the dart, switch the stitch length to a small reinforcing stitch. When you come to the end of the dart, simply run off the end of the dart (Illustration 1). No backstitching or tying threads is necessary.

It is not necessary to clip open darts unless the fabric is extremely heavy. To open a dart, clip only to the point where the dart is ¼ inch wide (Illustration 2).

Darts will lie better if they are pressed over a tailor's ham to block in shape. Avoid this procedure for front darts over the tummy. The molding press makes the tummy more noticeable. Press those darts flat.

A dart that curves in a bit toward the fold provides a better fit if you have fullness over the high hip in back (Illustration 3). The reverse curved dart fits well on an individual with a curved spine (Illustration 4).

a.maeda

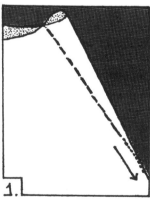

1. SEW SMALL STITCHES NEAR END OF DART.

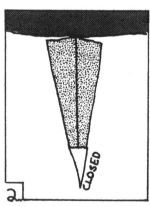

2. SPLIT DART 5/8" FROM END, PRESS OPEN.

3. CURVED DART FOR FULL HIGH HIP.

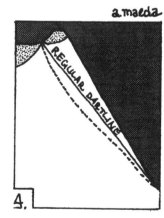

4. DART FOR CURVED SPINE.

Fast Gathering

Anyone who is still pulling two long threads and wrapping them around a pin to gather fabric should know that there is a much easier, less time-consuming method.

Set your machine for the widest possible zigzag and the longest possible stitch. Lay a piece of embroidery floss or smooth bakery string ¼ inch from the raw edge of the fabric.

Zigzag over the string, being careful not to catch the string in the stitching. If you happen to sew on the string, clip the threads (not the string) at this point and continue. To gather, simply pull the string.

One of the problems of attaching a gathered edge to a straight edge (skirt to waistband, ruffle to skirt, sleeve to cuff) is that the gathers tend to bunch together and lump up during the sewing process.

After the desired gathering has been completed and pinned to the straight surface, use masking tape to flatten the gathers into place before sewing. Place the tape ⅞ inch away from the raw edge so that the tape will not get caught during the sewing process.

After joining the gathered surface to the straight surface with a ⅝-inch seam, remove the tape.

Press the gathers (with a press-and-lift motion) before continuing any further. This will flatten the gathers and allow them to hang properly.

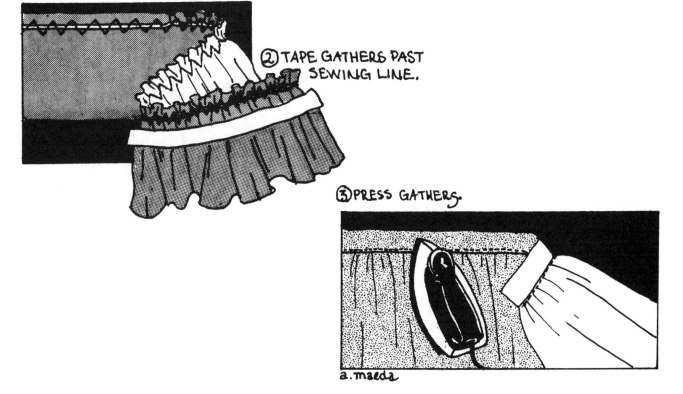

① ZIG ZAG OVER STRING.

② TAPE GATHERS PAST SEWING LINE.

③ PRESS GATHERS.

a. maeda

Gathering for the Perfectionist

For the real perfectionist who wants absolutely even gathers, here's a new technique: Divide the "piece to be gathered" and the "piece to be gathered to" into quarters.

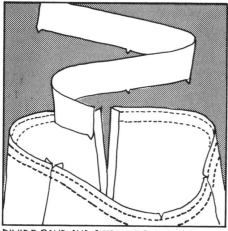

DIVIDE BAND AND SKIRT INTO QUARTERS.

Make clear markings; this will ensure uniform fullness.

Buy the type of heavy-duty thread used in sewing upholstery. The color need not match. Thread it onto the bobbin and insert the bobbin.

Thread your machine with regular thread. With heavy-duty thread on the bobbin and regular-weight thread on the top, sew two lines of long machine basting. Place the first line $3/8$ inch from the cut edge, and the second, $7/8$ inch.

To pull in fullness, pull on the bobbin threads only. The use of heavy-duty thread will eliminate the possibility of thread breakage.

Match up the placement markings on the "piece to be gathered" and the "piece to be gathered to." Pin into place. If you are in the habit of sewing over pins, be sure to use the thinnest pins available. (Sewing over pins is a good habit to break, since it dulls the sewing machine needle.)

After you have adjusted the gathers evenly, you are ready to sew the seam. Sew with the gathered side up so that you can adjust and flatten the area to be gathered as you sew. Sew the seam at $5/8$ inch, which is between the two gathering stitch lines. Before removing the gathering threads, press the recently sewn gathers by merely using a shot of steam over the gathered area. Do not place iron directly on the gathers. Allow gathers to dry before moving to the next section.

Remove the basting stitch sewn at $7/8$ inch from the cut edge. Clip the top thread at several intervals and pull the heavy-duty bobbin thread. It should pull out easily. If no other seaming is necessary, both gathering threads can be removed at this time. If an additional line of stitching is necessary, to secure a waistband for example, remove the basting stitch at $7/8$ inch after this has been completed. This will ensure that the gathers remain perfectly in place until all seams are sewn.

SEW 5/8" SEAM.   a. maeda

Pleats

For a pleated garment to hang properly, it is necessary to allow for enough ease at the hipline. Do not rely on the release of a pleat for the garment to fit properly.

To determine whether a pattern alteration is needed, compare your hip measurement to the measurement on the pattern. The difference equals the alteration needed. Measure the depth of the pleat in the pattern. Determine the number of additional pleats necessary for proper hanging.

If the addition needed is small, an easy way to make up the difference is to sew each pleat a little bit narrower.

For example, if the skirt contains 12 pleats of a 3-inch depth and you need one additional, decrease each pleat by $1/12$ inch.

Use small clips at the top and bottom of the garment to mark the pleat. Baste in the pleatline with contrasting thread. It may be necessary to mark the pleatline with tracing paper on the reverse side of the fabric before basting in contrasting thread.

A quilting foot is not absolutely necessary, but it is certainly helpful. The arm of the quilting foot runs along the sharply creased edge while stitching. If you do not own a quilting foot, place tape on the throat plate to use as a guide.

In very heavy fabric, it is necessary to hem the separate sections of the skirt before sewing the side seams. This is accomplished by leaving the side seams open in the hem area until hemline is determined. The skirt sections are then hemmed separately. Sew the seam through all four layers.

Finish the raw seam edge at the hemline by zigzagging or wrapping with seam binding. This method will prevent bulkiness at the hemline (Illustration 1).

To maintain a sharp pleatline in any fabric, stitch $1/8$ inch along the fold on the wrong side of the pleat from top to bottom. This forces this edge to the underside and keeps the pleats from standing open (Illustration 2).

For pleats in lightweight fabrics it is not necessary to hem the garment sections separately. Press the seam in the hem open and trim the seam to $1/8$ inch. Complete the hem. Clip the seam just above the hemline so that the seam in the skirt lies together. Pinch the right sides of the garment together at the hemline.

Topstitch the back edge of the pleat $1/8$ inch from the seam edge in the hem only (Illustration 3). This will help the pleat to stay in place at the seamline.

Always use silk thread to baste pleats closed.

To give pleats a good press, make a solution of 1 tablespoon of white vinegar and 1 cup of water. Dampen a cheesecloth with this mixture. Placing the cloth over the pleats, press and pound with a tailor's clapper.

Let each pleat dry before moving it off the ironing board.

① On heavy fabric sew seam through all four thicknesses; bind raw edges.

② Edgestitch folds on wrong side.

③ On lightweight fabric, edgestitch along hem fold only on wrong side.

Controlling the Fullness

Many loose styles depend on a belt to control the fullness. If you belt at the waist and would like uniform fullness controlled before the belt is applied, try this trick. Elastic applied correctly not only controls the fullness but helps the hem hang evenly as well.

Try on the dress. Tie a string or piece of elastic around your waist without blousing. Mark your waist at one side seam with a pin. Take off your dress. Turn the dress wrong side out. Transfer the pin at the waist to the wrong side of the dress. Place another pin marking the waist on the other side seam the same distance from the armhole as the first. Decide how much blouson you like (1 inch to 1½ inches). Make a mark 1 inch to 1½ inches lower than original pin marking the waist on each side. On the front draw a line connecting the newly marked points at the side seam (1 inch to 1½ inches) below waist pin markings. In order for the garment to hang correctly in the back, and eliminate a droopy hem, the waistline must be dropped ½ inch in center back. Draw a line across the back, connecting the newly marked points at the side seam 1 inch to 1½ inches below waist pin marking. After this line is drawn, you have a point of reference. Starting at the side seams from this newly drawn line on the back, gently slope the center back down ½ inch.

Now you are ready to apply elastic. If you wish, you may insert a casing to hide the elastic on the inside of the garment. Seams Great® is perfect for casings without bulk. For a quick solution to the problem, cut a piece of ⅛-inch elastic 2 inches smaller than your waist. Using your newly drawn lines as a guide, apply the ⅛-inch elastic with a serpentine or zigzag stitch. To ensure perfection, divide the elastic and the dress into quarters. Fit one quarter of the length of the elastic to one quarter of the dress. Uniform fullness results.

Avoid Gaping Necklines

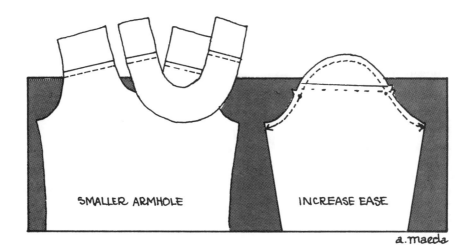

SMALLER ARMHOLE   INCREASE EASE

a. maeda

Scoop and V-necklines return every spring in a variety of silhouettes. They're not only cooler but also make a good frame for important jewelry. Unless you know a few secrets, these necklines can fit poorly, which has nothing to do with bust size.

To prevent open necklines from stretching in the sewing or the pressing process, stay tape must be used. Use the pattern itself to measure the length of stay tape needed. Force the cut neckline of the garment to conform to this size. Accomplish this by pinning the stay tape onto the neckline at 2-inch intervals. If stay tape is not used, a careless sewer can stretch an open neck 1½ inches merely by sewing on the facing. Interface the facing using a lightweight fusible knitted interfacing.

If the individual is short between the shoulder and armhole—apparent by extra fabric sitting away from the body in this area on all garments (including blazers and blouses)—a pattern alteration must be made. Fold out ¼ to ½ inch horizontally on the bodice in the front notch area through the neckline. Make a similar alteration on the facing. This creates a smaller armhole which can create some difficulty easing in the sleeve. To compensate, run an easeline from seam to seam along the cap, not just between the notches or fold out the corresponding amount in the sleeve cap.

■ The only problem with basting is taking out the stitches. Stacy's Stitch Away is a basting thread that dissolves with an iron and a wet press cloth. Use only on fabrics which can take a wet press cloth.

Clean Facings and Understitching

Recently I discovered a way to give a clean finish to the outside edge of facings while interfacing at the same time. This technique gives the support needed at the neckline and under buttonholes while giving a smooth finish to the facing itself—especially nice for an unlined jacket.

Cut the facing and interfacing exactly the same size and shape. Place the facing and interfacing with right sides together. Sew the outside edges with a ¼-inch seam. Clip curve (Illustration 1). Turn right side out and press well. This finish eliminates the need to turn under or zigzag the outside edge of the facing. Now you are ready to join the facing to the garment.

To eliminate bulk and allow the jacket front to hang smoothly when the facing and hem meet, a few steps need to be taken. Join the facing to the garment, trim, and clip seam (Illustration 2).

If understitching is desired, understitch by pulling both seam allowances against the facing. Stitch ⅛ inch from the original seamline, attaching both seam allowances to facing in the same operation.

Do not understitch in hem area. For example, if you are making a rayon crepe dress using a 1½-inch hem, stop understitching 3 inches from raw edge at bottom of garment (Illustration 3).

Although the seam in this area has been trimmed to ¼ inch, open this part of the seam allowance with your fingers. Turn up hem of garment and facing. Line up the seam perfectly (Illustration 4).

Turn the garment over to right side and sew in the well of the seam, by machine or by hand (Illustration 5).

Turn the facing to the inside of the garment and press, using a tailor's clapper to flatten into place. Attach facing to the hem with a loose handstitch (Illustration 6). If stitch is too tight, the garment will not hang smoothly.

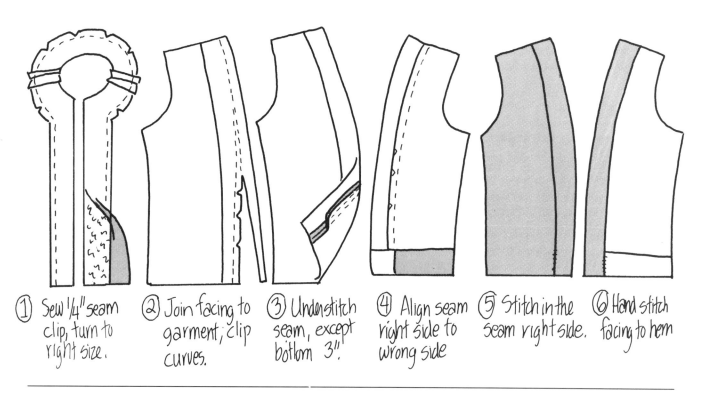

① Sew ¼" seam clip, turn to right size.

② Join facing to garment; clip curves.

③ Understitch seam, except bottom 3".

④ Align seam right side to wrong side

⑤ Stitch in the seam right side.

⑥ Hand stitch facing to hem

Facings in the Forefront

The unexpected detail never fails to attract the attention of potential buyers. Sportswear manufacturers continually amaze me with new ways of doing the obvious. Programmed to think of facings turned to the inside of the garment, we stop to examine the opposite: facings turned to the outside of the garment.

Since the facing now becomes a style detail, and therefore more visible, the outside edge of the facing must be finished in an attractive manner. This can be accomplished in one of two ways: the Hong Kong finish or the overlock finish. If you own an overlock machine, the overlocked edge gives a sporty touch with little effort. Adjust your machine so that the overlock stitches are very close together. If your overlock machine has a narrow plate, the marrow or overedge finish (commonly seen as edging on napkins) might be preferable (Illustration 1).

①OVERLOCK AND MARROW.

If you do not own an overlock, experiment with some of your decorative stitches to get a nice edging. Keep in mind that the edging must be a very clean finish with no ravelling edges visible. This may or may not be possible with your home sewing machine.

The other choice for finishing the outside edge, the Hong Kong finish, can be preferable if you find a companion fabric that draws attention to the shape of the facing itself. Cut a strip of true-bias fabric 2 inches wide and long enough to go around the outside edge of the facing. Piece if necessary. Place the right side of the bias against the right side of the facing. Sew a ¼-inch seam. This seam can be trimmed to ⅛ inch if you like the look better. Wrapping the raw edges of the newly sewn seam, bring the bias strip toward the wrong side of the facing (Illustration 2). A tight wrap looks the best. From the right side of the facing, sew the bias strip into place by sewing in well of seam. Press.

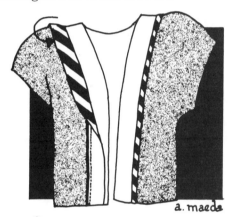

②HONG KONG FINISH.

a. maeda

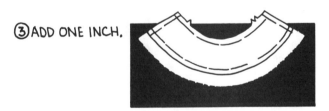

③ADD ONE INCH.

Attach the facings in the opposite manner you are accustomed to; place the right side of the facing against the wrong side of the garment. Seam, trim, and press seam. Bring facing to the outside of the garment. Press and pound with a tailor's clapper. Attach the facing to the garment at the shoulder by sewing in the well of the seam with a handstitch for a more quality look. If the facing pattern seems a bit narrow, simply cut the outside edge of the facing 1 inch wider. Cut the facing wider whether it is turned to the inside or the outside (Illustration 3).

Eliminating Facings

If you look at the necklines and armholes of sleeveless garments in ready-to-wear, you will notice an absence of facings. You can eliminate facings in your garments also with the use of bias strips.

Cut a strip of bias 2 inches wide and long enough to go around the neckline amply. If true bias is not possible, a piece of fabric well off-grain will usually work as well.

Overlock one long side of the bias strip. Pin the strip to the neckline with right sides together. Sew the ends of bias strip together when you have determined how much you need to go around the neck (Illustration 1).

Make sure this strip is about ¼ inch smaller than the neckline. Stretch the strip a little to fit the neck. Making the bias just a little bit smaller makes the neckline conform to the curve of the body.

Sew the bias strip to the neckline with a ⅝-inch seam. Trim seam to ¼ inch. Clip curve at ½-inch intervals. Press the bias away from the seam over a tailor's ham (Illustration 2).

Wrap the bias strip around the neckline seam allowance, enclosing the raw edges. Pin in the well of the seam. The overlocked edge will hang about ½ inch lower than the neckline seam. Sew in place by sewing in the well of the seam. This is a very common finish for knits and lightweight fabrics (Illustration 3).

If you do not mind handwork and prefer a finish that looks the same on the inside and outside, try this technique. Cut a 2-inch bias strip. Press under ½ inch on long side. Sew bias in a circle.

Sew bias strip and neckline with right sides together using a ⅝-inch seam. Trim seam to ¼ inch and clip at ½-inch intervals.

Wrap bias strip around neckline seam, and pin folded edge of bias right to the stitching at the neckline seam. Sew folded bias strip to neckline seam by hand on the wrong side of the garment. This finish is often used on silk garments (Illustration 4).

The final step in either of these finishes is to press and pound with a tailor's clapper. These are beautiful finishes that can show creativity as well. I often use a companion fabric—real suede or leather—as the finishing strip, rather than the same fabric.

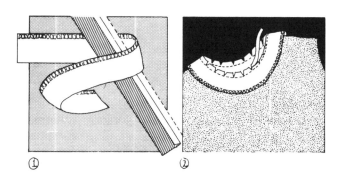
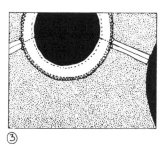
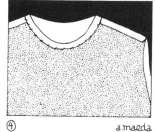

① ② ③ ④ a.maeda

Overlock, then clip curves, trim excess.

Sew edge into well of seam, attach bias strip to wrong side.

Demonstrated on *Power Sewing* Video #12: *Handwoven and Quilted Garments.*

Anchor with Fusible Web

Would you like to know a way to anchor the facing to the body of the jacket without handstitching? This technique is one of the last steps in jacket construction, after the final construction pressing but right before hemming the bottom edge.

After stitching jacket and facing along outside edge, trim and grade seams. Cut a ¼-inch strip of fusible web and dot-press this strip along the facing seam allowance, against the side that will eventually face against the inside of the jacket.

Touch the iron gently along this strip about every 6 inches, just enough to hold the strip in place against the facing seam allowance until the jacket is turned right side out.

After turning the jacket right side out, press the jacket on the right side with a damp presscloth. During the process, the heat of the iron will melt the fusible web, thus bonding the facing and the jacket slightly and invisibly, just enough to keep it from moving.

For invisible results, use this technique on textured medium- to heavy-weight fabrics and Ultrasuede®.

Fusible Web

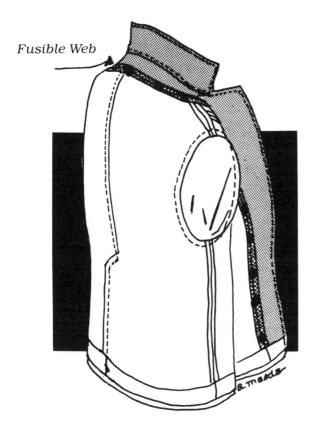

■ Sewing exact ⅝-inch seam allowances is mandatory on the shoulders of the bodice and the facings. If this is not done, the collar and neckline simply do not fit right.

Anchoring the Facing by Machine

How many times have you hand-tacked a facing at the back zipper or under the arm, only to find that your handstitches come out in the first washing?

In areas of stress, handtacks do not hold up as well as these two machine-tacking techniques. Both are invisible and last the life of the garment.

If the facing is located in the underarm or similar area, first trim the facing and garment seam allowances, then trim out the additional triangles in the underarm area to eliminate bulk (Illustration 1).

Pin the facing to the garment in the desired position. Stitch through both the garment and the facing in the well of the seam with an inch of machine stitches.

Sew this row of stitches with the garment right side up so if you happen to miss a seam well, it will be on the facing, not the garment (Illustration 2).

For a neckline facing at the shoulder or at a back zipper, an even more invisible technique is used.

Place the facing in the desired finished position and lift up the garment and the facing so that your fingers are holding the two seam allowances (that of the garment and that of the facing) together.

Sew the two seam allowances together about ¼ inch from the raw edge and up toward the neckline as close to the seam as possible (Illustration 3).

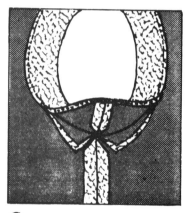

① TRIM SEAMS AT ARMHOLE TO ELIMINATE BULK.

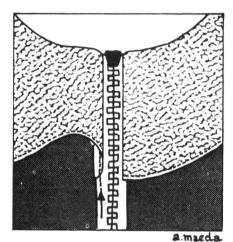

a.maeda

③ SEW FACING TO SEAM UP TO NECKLINE.

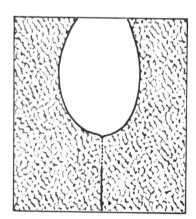

② STITCH IN WELL OF SEAM, ON RIGHT SIDE.

Perfect V Necklines

Skill and knowledge combine in making a perfect V neck without stretching it out of shape. Silk organza is a good interfacing to use with silk. Cut the organza on the bias and baste to the wrong side of the facing.

Sew the shoulder seams of the blouse and the facings. Press open.

It is easier to sew the neck while working flat. Sew the side seams after the neckline has been completed.

Stretching at the neckline can be avoided with the use of twill tape or selvage in this area. Twill tape is a little heavy to use with silk, so instead cut off about 25 inches of selvage from your silk to be used here.

Place the facing and blouse with right sides together. Pin and baste into place your narrow strip of selvage right on the intended $5/8$-inch seamline, stopping 1 inch from the point of the V. Mark the exact point of the V on the facing.

Bobbie Carr gives these additional hints: To help the neck conform to the body shape, deepen the neckline seam by $1/8$ inch from 1 inch above the point, tapering to the original seamline 2 inches from the shoulder (Illustration 1). If you have a large bust, a V neckline can be filled in a bit to conceal the fuller bust. Simply curve the seamline $1/8$ inch toward the seam allowance sewing the seam at $1/2$ inch from about 2 inches above the V point to 3 inches from the shoulder seam.

Using small stitches, sew the neckline through the narrow selvage. The selvage stops an inch away from the point to eliminate bulk when the facing is turned to the inside (Illustration 2). Hand-walk the machine two stitches at the point of the V to give the fabric room to turn (Illustration 3).

Slash the seamline to the point, cutting within one thread of the stitching line. Trim seam allowances to $1/4$ inch. Clip curve.

Understitch neckline except for 1 inch on either side of point. Do not understitch facing near the point to eliminate bulk. Press and pound with a tailor's clapper. Topstitch for a more tailored look, if desired.

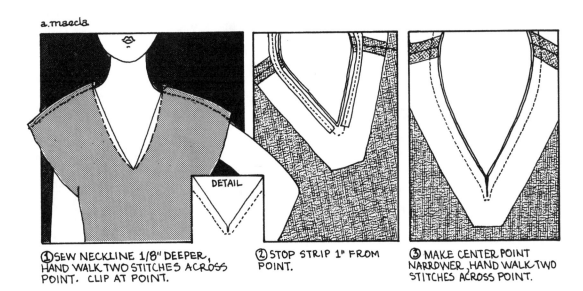

a. maeda

① SEW NECKLINE 1/8" DEEPER, HAND WALK TWO STITCHES ACROSS POINT. CLIP AT POINT.

DETAIL

② STOP STRIP 1" FROM POINT.

③ MAKE CENTER POINT NARROWER, HAND WALK TWO STITCHES ACROSS POINT.

V Neckline Inset

If you have ever tried to inset separate strips to form a V neck, you are aware of the problem that occurs at the place where the strips join the V of the dress. Recently I saw a technique demonstrated by a master in the sewing field, Marjorie Arch Burns, which was not only easy but gave beautiful results.

If the pattern calls for a ⅝-inch seam allowance at the neck, cut it down to ¼ inch. Mark the center front of the dress with a basted thread for 3 to 4 inches.

② STITCH STRIP FROM SHOULDER TO CENTER FRONT (ON WRONG SIDE).

① TRIM NECK SEAM DOWN TO 1/4". BASTE IN A CENTER FRONT LINE.

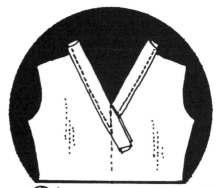

③ STITCH STRIPS TOGETHER AT CENTER FRONT (WRONG SIDE).

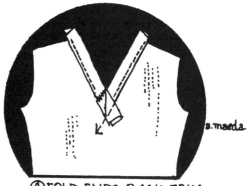

a.maeda

④ FOLD ENDS BACK, TRIM EXCESS, HAND-TACK IN PLACE.

Neckline and Sleeve Placket

There's no doubt about it—a tab front done incorrectly can ruin a blouse, dress, or man's sport shirt. On the other hand, if done correctly, and pucker-free, a tab front can fool the best eye into thinking this is a ready-to-wear number.

If using silk, do not interface the entire tab piece. Use a very lightweight interfacing, not a press-on, and hand-baste it to the wrong side of the tab. If using lightweight cotton or slightly heavier fabric, it is perfectly acceptable to interface the entire tab with a lightweight fusible interfacing. Fold in $5/8$-inch seam allowances on lengthwise edges and hand-baste into place.

Place RIGHT side of tab piece against WRONG side of garment, matching tab placement lines exactly. If you are not careful here, the tab will not end up in the center front of the garment.

Sew tab to garment along stitching lines as indicated on pattern, using small stitches (18 to 20 per inch). Hand-walk machine at corners for two stitches to eliminate puckering when the tab is turned.

Cut opening through tab and garment and cut very close into corners, within one stitch. You do not need to worry about cutting too close, since you have sewn this section with small stitches. Cutting close to the stitching line is very important for a perfectly smooth tab. Press newly cut edges away from opening toward tab.

Turn tab to outside of garment through newly cut opening. Slash for easier turning at the corner. Fold side without the point into place, bringing folded edge just over the stitching. Machine-sew into place.

To complete tab, fold other side into place the same way. When completing triangle at bottom, don't feel you have to use the indicated marking on the pattern; the fabric bulk should determine best foldline for the garment. Using your eye, fold fabric and baste into place.

Bring all tab ends to outside of garment at bottom edge of tab and trim unnecessary bulk. Topstitch triangle into place.

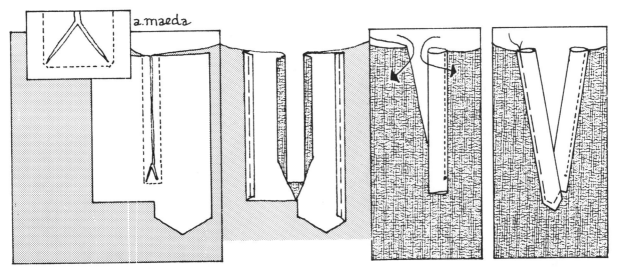

WRONG SIDE OF GARMENT

RIGHT SIDE OF GARMENT

Traditional Collars

If your collars are not as perfect or professional as you might like, try these tips:

To cushion the upper collar from seam imprints during pressing, interface the top collar on garments, not the undercollar as the pattern often suggests. On jackets and coats, interface both upper and undercollar. If you are using a press-on interfacing product, try on a scrap fabric first to make certain a press-on product is workable with your fabric. Non-porous fabrics resist steam, causing the steam to back up under the interfacing with bubbly puckering results. If press-on interfacing is incompatible, use a sew-in interfacing as a substitute. Trim interfacing out of collar points.

Adhering to the turn of the cloth principle, trim off $\frac{1}{8}$ inch around outside collar edges—not the neck edge. Slight trimming of the undercollar enables the undercollar to fit smoothly beneath the top collar eliminating collar points which stick out. If separate upper and undercollar pieces were used, the undercollar is already cut smaller. Do not trim again. Stretch undercollar outside edge slightly to fit outside edge of interfaced top collar. Pin in place.

If you have difficulty determining a $\frac{5}{8}$ inch seam allowance when the fabric is under the needle, mark $\frac{5}{8}$ inch seam allowances for 1 inch on either side of the collar points. Simple marking can determine exact collar points, enabling you to sew two collar ends which are identical. With the undercollar side up, sew the two collar pieces together, allowing the presser-foot to slightly stretch the trimmed undercollar while stitching to conform to the shape of the upper collar. Standard stitch length can be used to join outside collar edges except for 1 inch on either side of the collar points. Smaller stitches will prevent raveling during close trimming of collar points.

When collar points are reached, handwalk the machine diagonally two small stitches before turning the corner. Handwalking enables you to turn out finer points. Press seam open. Grade collar seam, trimming the upper collar seam allowance to $\frac{3}{8}$ inch and the undercollar seam allowance to $\frac{1}{4}$ inch. Grade and trim diagonally at corners, bringing trimming even closer to the seam in these areas. Close trimming results in a more pointed collar.

Turn collar right side out, using a point turner to extend points. In some fabrics even a point turner will not enable you to turn out a truly fine point. Try this: Use a needle and unknotted thread. Insert thread through the stitching line at the end of the point. Pull both ends of the thread simultaneously to create a far sharper collar point than was previously possible.

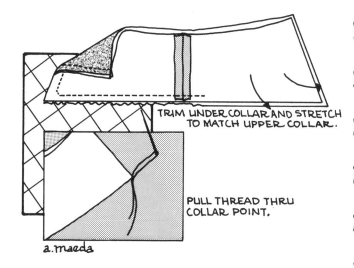

TRIM UNDER COLLAR AND STRETCH TO MATCH UPPER COLLAR.

PULL THREAD THRU COLLAR POINT.

a. maeda

■ For accuracy, always hand-baste garments on a flat surface, not in your hands.

Stand-Up Collar

Applying a stand-up collar can be the easiest collar application if you know the trick of eliminating the bulk at the ends of the collar. Mark the placement dots on the collar carefully—these are important for proper fit. It is usually necessary to stretch the collar to fit the neckline at the shoulder seam. This technique allows the collar to hug the neck and eliminates the problem of the collar standing away from the neckline.

Interface both collar pieces, the outside collar with lightweight interfacing. The weight of the interfacing for the undercollar depends on the look you want. Interfacing will ensure that both collars remain the same size as you are working on them. The front facings have been completed. Trim off ⅛ inch from the outside (not the neck) edge of the undercollar. This will eliminate undercollar wrinkling after the stand-up collar is completed. If you do not like hand-sewing, start with the undercollar application first. The top collar may then be handstitched into place. Do not sew the upper and undercollar together first.

With one collar layer only, pin the undercollar and the garment neckline together, matching notches and placement dots. It is usually necessary to clip the neckline at 1-inch intervals up to the staystitching to allow the neckline to relax and conform to the straight edge of the collar. Sew the seam. Pin undercollar and upper collar together, stretching the trimmed undercollar edges to fit the upper collar (Illustration 1).

In order for the garment and collar edges to match up perfectly, use the garment edge as a guide for sewing the ends of the stand-up collar. Begin joining the upper and undercollar together at the center back, sewing one half of the collar at a time. Continue the seam along the long collar edge down the ends of the collar, sewing two threads past the garment front. The extra two threads give the collar room to turn right side out, allowing it to match up perfectly with the front of the garment. Continue sewing the second half of the collar in the same manner (Illustration 2).

Trim and grade seams, being careful not to trim the neckline seam too close which would make it difficult to hide the raw edges. Turn under long seam of the outer collar. Pin into place, covering original seam. Pinning is best accomplished over a tailor's ham. Press and pound with a tailor's clapper. If you prefer no topstitching to show, start the collar application with the upper collar.

This same principle can help you in finishing the ends of the waistband.

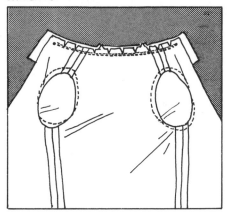

a. maeda

① STAYSTITCH, CLIP NECKLINE, SEW.

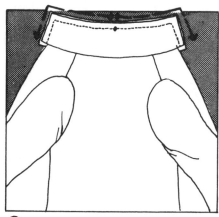

② JOIN COLLAR FROM CENTER BACK TO FRONT

Easy Neckband Application

Try this method of applying a collar with a neckband—this technique is fast and simple, and eliminates the small bulge usually unavoidable at the ends of the neckband.

Start by interfacing, sewing, clipping, and pressing the collar without the neckband. All collar edges are finished except for the neck edge.

Staystitch shirt neckline ⅝ inch from edge and clip neckline curve at 1-inch intervals (Illustration 1).

The neckband is made of two pieces: an outer and an inner neckband. Interface outer neckband completely. To eliminate wrinkling of inner neckband, trim off ¹⁄₁₆ inch from outer edge (not the neck edge) of inner neckband piece. Press a ½-inch strip of press-on interfacing along neck edge seam allowance (Illustration 2).

For easier application, clip neck edge of collar at 1-inch intervals. This permits collar to mold more easily to shape of neckband. To join collar and neck-band, place upper collar against right side of inner neckband and undercollar against right side of outer neckband. Collar is sandwiched between inner and outer neckband pieces. Stitch seam, stopping a few stitches beyond ends of collar. Do not sew ends of neckband (Illustration 3). This trick eliminates bulge on end of neckband.

Attach neckband to blouse by placing right side of inner neckband against wrong side of blouse. Stitch and trim seam to ¼ inch (Illustration 4).

Placing right sides together, sew ends of neckband, stitching ¹⁄₁₆ inch beyond edge of blouse. Trim seam to ¼ inch (Illustration 5).

To complete neckband, turn under outer neckband seam allowance ⅝ inch and topstitch into place. The ½-inch strip of pressed interfacing makes for accuracy. This last step is sometimes easier if you wrap the neckband around your tailor's ham and pin outer neckband into place on ham.

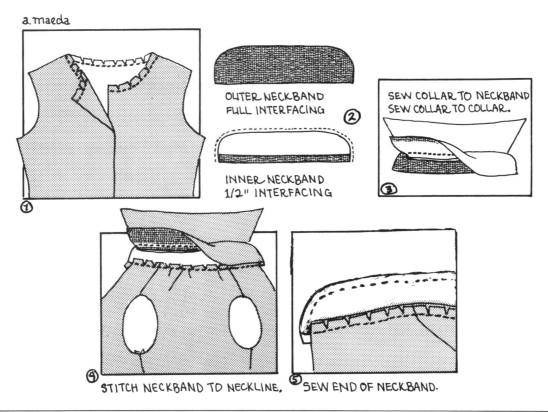

a. maeda

①

OUTER NECKBAND FULL INTERFACING ②
INNER NECKBAND 1/2" INTERFACING

SEW COLLAR TO NECKBAND SEW COLLAR TO COLLAR. ③

④ STITCH NECKBAND TO NECKLINE.

⑤ SEW END OF NECKBAND.

Crisp Tailored Collars

If you prefer a very crisp look in a blazer-type collar rather than a soft roll in the back of the collar, try this technique.

Using the undercollar pattern, cut interfacing to match the undercollar shape. Your choice of interfacing depends on your outer fabric. Hair canvas makes a good choice for wool flannel. Stacy's Veriform® is a good choice for corduroy or raw silk.

Cut an extra piece of underfacing to the moon shape indicated on the undercollar from the roll line to the neck edge (Illustration 1). This extra piece will give a little more firmness to the back of the collar.

Make snips ⅝ inch from center back, cutting line on interfacing pieces (Illustration 2). These snips indicate seamlines. Never interface seams in the traditional manner. Always overlap seams, matching indicated seamlines.

Zigzag interfacing at seamline by overlapping at snips. Trim away excess interfacing. Trim away ¾ inch from all outside interfacing edges to avoid bulk. Clip off corners of interfacing. Seam undercollar of jacket in the traditional way. Press open seam allowances.

Place prepared interfacing onto the wrong side of the undercollar. Lay the additional moon-shape piece of interfacing over the collar interfacing, forming a third layer from the roll-line to the neck edge. Hand-baste interfacing in place.

Machine pad-stitch the interfacing to the undercollar from roll-line to the outside collar edge at ¼-inch intervals parallel to the roll-line.

From the roll-line to the neckline seam, machine pad-stitch at ¼-inch intervals perpendicular to the roll-line. Work from the center back out in this small area (Illustration 3). Shape and press over the tailor's ham. The undercollar is now ready to join the jacket.

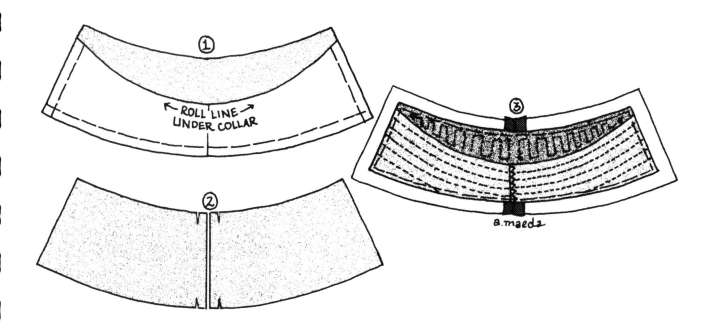

ROLL LINE
UNDER COLLAR

a.maeda

123

Soft Roll Tailored Collar

Making a collar in a heavy coat or jacket fabric is different from regular collar construction.

To begin with, most patterns for tailored garments include two separate pattern pieces for the collar: a top collar and an undercollar. The top collar is cut in one piece on the straight of the grain, while the undercollar and its interfacing must be cut on the bias and in two separate pieces to give a better roll.

If your pattern includes only one pattern piece for both collars, it will be necessary to make a few changes.

To make a bias undercollar pattern, draw a line perpendicular to the lengthwise grainline on the collar pattern. This line is the crosswise grain. Draw a line diagonally between lengthwise and crosswise grainlines. This is the bias. Since undercollar and interfacing are cut in two pieces, add a ⅝-inch seam allowance at center back.

The interfacing and the undercollar are both cut on the bias. Place the interfacing pieces on the wrong sides of the undercollar pieces and join them by sewing ⅞ inch from all edges. Trim off interfacing close to stitching line to eliminate bulk.

Seam center back of undercollar. Trim off the points at the ends of the seam and topstitch ⅛ inch from the seam itself. This helps keep the seam flat. Trim seam to ¼ inch.

If you look closely at the interfacing on the back of the undercollar, you will notice visible crosswise and lengthwise threads. Your collar will roll better if you stitch through all thicknesses in a pattern like that shown in the illustration. Be sure to stitch with the crosswise or lengthwise threads. Do not stitch diagonally—this interferes with the collar roll.

If your pattern supplied two separate pieces for the top and undercollar, the undercollar piece has already been cut smaller. If you made your own undercollar pattern as indicated above, trim ⅛ inch off all undercollar edges except for neck edge.

Lay undercollar on top collar, right sides together. Stretch undercollar to meet size of top collar. Sew edges with small reinforcing stitches (18 to 20 per inch). Press seam open and trim top collar seam allowance to ⅜ inch and undercollar seam allowance to ¼ inch. This will layer edges and eliminate bulk.

Turn collar right side out; press and pound with a tailor's clapper.

Fold under neck edge along roll-line if indicated on pattern, or fold under ⅝ inch if no roll-line is given on pattern. Wrap collar around a tailor's ham and mold into shape with steam. Allow to dry before taking off ham.

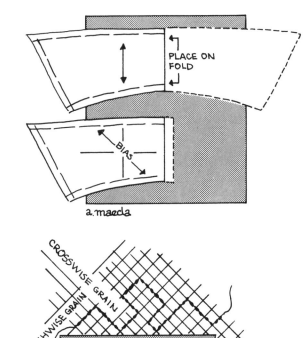

a. maeda

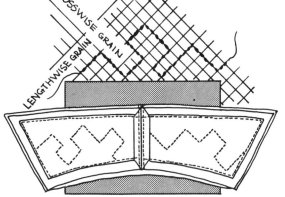

STRETCH UNDERCOLLAR TO FIT
TOP COLLAR AND SEW TOGETHER.

Top Collar Roll

Have you ever wondered if there is an easy way to construct a jacket so that the collar will lie perfectly flat and cover the neckline seam? Read on.

Join the back and front facings and upper collar together. Press well. Join undercollar to jacket. Press and mold collar roll-line. Press seams open.

Placing wrong sides together, lay upper collar (and facings) and undercollar (and jacket) together.

Pin the seam joining the upper collar and the back facing to the seam that joins the undercollar and the jacket.

Pin accurately from shoulder to shoulder (see illustration). If you own a dress form, hang the pinned jacket on the dress form.

The upper collar, in its attempt to go up to the roll-line and over the back of the collar, often does not seem quite big enough.

Depending on the weight of the material, the undercollar will seem $\frac{1}{8}$ to $\frac{3}{8}$ inch larger at the center back.

With a sharp, soft lead pencil, mark the outer edge of the upper collar onto the wrong side of the undercollar. Unpin the pieces.

To join the upper and undercollar, allowance must be made for the fact that the upper collar was not big enough to meet the undercollar.

Do not cut off the excess on the undercollar. Pin the upper and undercollars together, matching the seamline of the upper collar with the pencil marking on the undercollar. Sew the under and upper collar seam, $\frac{5}{8}$ inch away from the outside edge of the undercollar.

If you had cut off the excess from the undercollar and then seamed the upper and the undercollar together, the collar would be too short to cover the neckline seam.

Try this technique and you will be convinced. The results are outstanding.

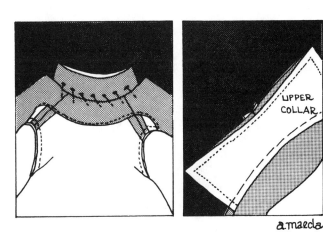

a.maeda

Jacket Lapels Made Easy

Every season the fashion houses bring out some variation of the classic blazer with tailored lapels.

Lapel construction is one area in sewing where perfection and accuracy are required and reward you with beautiful results. If you are in a hurry, the garment will suffer. Set aside ample undisturbed time and follow this procedure.

First, make sure that all pattern markings are accurately done and clearly visible—no shortcuts here.

Cut the undercollar and the collar interfacing on the bias. This will give the collar a better roll at the neckline. Join the upper collar and the interfaced undercollar along the outside edge (not at the ends) with small, reinforcing stitches.

Press seam open. Trim the seam of the upper collar to 1/4 inch and the undercollar seam to 1/8 inch.

Staggering the width of the seam allowances eliminates bulk. Turn the collar right side out and press well. Pound the outside edge with a tailor's clapper.

Staystitch the neckline of the jacket and clip the seam allowance at 1-inch intervals. Join the back facings to the front facings at the shoulder. Sew the jacket fronts to jacket backs at shoulders. Sew the front facings to jacket fronts, stopping at the large dot, which is where the jacket joins the lapel (Illustration 1).

With right sides together, pin the upper collar to the jacket facings, matching markings. Sew in one continuous seam, from one large dot to the next. Do not close the ends of the collar yet (Illustration 2).

② JOIN UPPER COLLAR TO FACING ONLY.

With right sides together, pin the undercollar to the jacket, matching markings. Sew the undercollar to jacket from one large dot to the next in one continuous seam (Illustration 3).

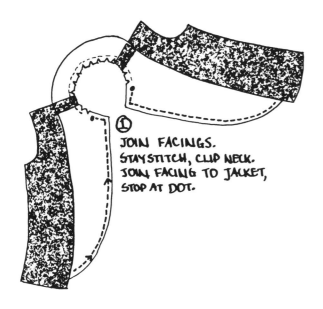

③ JOIN UNDER COLLAR TO JACKET.

① JOIN FACINGS. STAYSTITCH, CLIP NECK. JOIN FACING TO JACKET, STOP AT DOT.

Jacket Lapels Made Easy

To close the ends of the lapels, now forming a V shape, place the ends' right sides together, matching outer collar and undercollar, then jacket to facing. Match the dots exactly. Sew from the outer edge of the matched facing and jacket to the center of the V and stop. Now sew from the outer edge of the upper and undercollar to the center of the V and stop (Illustration 4).

In this process, you are never sewing through more than two thicknesses at a time. Because the seam is not sewn continuously where the four seams join, a small 1/8-inch unsewn spot will manifest itself at the joint of the four seams. This is needed to allow for trimming of bulk, ease in turning, and continuous movement during later pressings.

Press all seams open and stagger trimming of the seams to 1/4 and 1/8 inch. Make the wider seam allowance the one closer to the outside of the garment.

Turn the collar and facings right side out and place the open seam allowances together at the neckline. To anchor these two seams together, hand-baste the seam allowances together in an invisible fashion, preferably with a stab stitch (Illustration 5).

Put lapel and front facings on the tailor's ham, mold, and steam-press. Pound the lapel flat with a tailor's clapper. To eliminate stretching, let the lapel dry completely before lifting it off the tailor's ham.

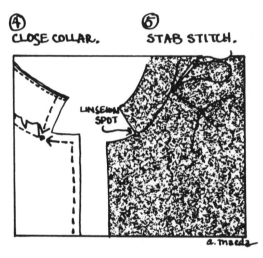

④ CLOSE COLLAR.

⑤ STAB STITCH.

UNSEWN SPOT

a. maeda

■ Read through all pattern instructions before beginning so you will have an idea of what steps are involved and be able to substitute improved methods of construction that you have learned.

Felt Undercollar Technique

A felt undercollar in a man's or woman's jacket is far preferable to an undercollar made in the jacket fabric. The lightweight felt used in tailoring (which can be found in the interfacing section of fabric stores) works much better with collars and lapels because it eliminates considerable bulk.

By cutting the felt undercollar and hair canvas interfacing on the bias, the collar is given a nice, sharp roll at the neckline, perfect for today's styling.

Pattern markings are very important on the collar and lapel. Make sure yours are visible when cutting out pattern pieces.

Sew the front facing to the jacket front, stopping at the large dot (the place where the jacket joins the lapel). If you are using a back facing, join the back and front facings at the shoulder.

Now join the upper collar to the facings, right sides together, matching the large dots and sewing only between the large dots. Press seams open and trim to $\frac{1}{4}$ inch. To eliminate bulk, miter the outside edge of the upper collar and press in $\frac{5}{8}$ inch on all outside edges.

If the undercollar pattern includes seam allowances, these should be removed from outside undercollar pattern edges, cutting off an additional $\frac{1}{8}$ inch. Do not trim seam allowance from neck edge. Join the two bias pieces of the hair canvas undercollar at the center back by centering them over a piece of bias tape and zigzagging.

The undercollar of felt may be cut in one piece, using the joined hair canvas as a pattern. After cutting out the felt undercollar, trim an additional $\frac{1}{8}$ inch off all edges of the hair canvas. Sew hair canvas and felt together by machine sewing through the roll-line.

Clip neck edge of the jacket along the curves. Overlap neck edge of the undercollar $\frac{5}{8}$ inch over the neck edge of the outside of the jacket. Handwhip raw edges of felt into place between the dots. Because tailor's felt does not ravel, it is not necessary to turn edges before stitching to garment.

To finish the collar, place the undercollar and upper collar with wrong sides together. Handwhip the outside edge of the felt to the outside of the collar. Felt undercollar will be a little smaller.

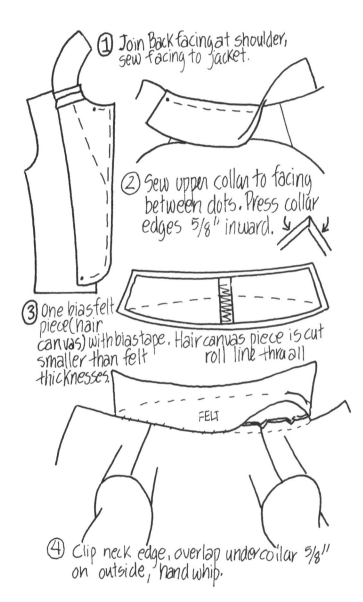

① Join back facing at shoulder, sew facing to jacket.

② Sew upper collar to facing between dots. Press collar edges $\frac{5}{8}$" inward.

③ One bias felt piece (hair canvas) with bias tape. Hair canvas piece is cut smaller than felt thicknesses. roll line thru all

FELT

④ Clip neck edge, overlap undercollar $\frac{5}{8}$" on outside, hand whip.

Roll Line Memory

If you are able to build roll line memory into a jacket or coat as it is constructed, your finished product will always hang as well on you and on the hanger as it did the day you finished it. This technique takes fifteen minutes.

Whether you are making a shawl collar or a tailored collar, this technique can be applied to assist the lapel and the jacket to work as one unit at the roll line. Before the lining is applied, hand tack a narrow strip (¼ inch wide) of fusible web along the roll line. As the jacket is pressed, this web of glue will melt, fusing the upper and under lapel together at the roll line. If a non-fusible interfacing was used in the lapel, an additional strip is needed between the top collar and the non-fusible interfacing to make the two layers act as one at the roll line.

If the pattern does not indicate a roll line, try on the jacket. Determine your own roll line by adjusting the collar or lapels to your liking. Place a row of pins on each side of the jacket indicating the desired roll line. Lift up the collar or lapel. Hand tack a strip of fusible web along the pin line. Press and the two layers will fuse lightly and act as one.

This technique could be your solution to the unlined jacket syndrome of the slide-out facing problem.

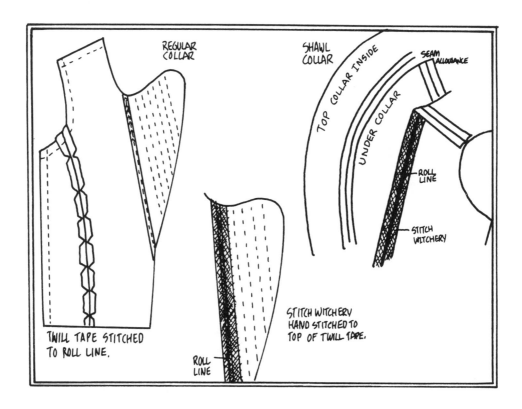

Poor Sleeve Design

Sleeves in ready-to-wear often have a quite different look from sleeves in home-sewn garments. Although you may have perfected the technique of inserting a sleeve without puckers, you may still detect a slight ripply effect at the cap itself.

Poor sleeve design is usually the cause, not poor fit. Learn to recognize the sleeve with this problem. The sleeve cap is tall and thin. Not every sleeve is cut this way. With a few pattern changes made on the sleeve before it is cut out, a smoother cap will result.

Trim $\frac{1}{4}$ inch off the top of the sleeve cap. Add $\frac{1}{4}$ inch to each side of the sleeve cap. Move the shoulder placement on the sleeve cap $\frac{1}{4}$ inch to the front of the sleeve. By allowing a little more ease across the cap of the arm, the sleeve is allowed to fall with greater ease, thus eliminating puckers.

In a knit garment, the sleeve seam allowance should be trimmed to $\frac{1}{4}$ inch after the sleeve is sewn on. In a woven garment, trim only the area between the notches under the arm. The seam allowance gives a lift to the sleeve cap, which is quite flattering, especially to a person with heavy arms. Cut small triangles out of the sleeve cap seam allowance to eliminate excessive bulk.

In better dresses and coats, it is often preferable to pad the sleeve cap a little with a strip of polyester fleece or several layers of lambswool. Cut a strip of polyester fleece $\frac{1}{2}$ inch wide and the length of the cap or the distance from the front notch to the back notch over the cap of the inserted sleeve.

Place the strip of polyester fleece between the sleeve and the sleeve seam allowance. Sew the strip of fleece to the seam allowance with a hand backstitch using thread that has been run through beeswax for strength. Do not flatten the fleece with your stitch.

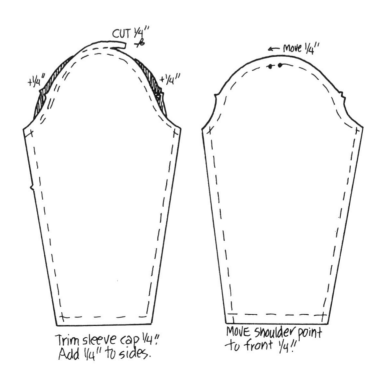

CUT ¼"

+¼" +¼"

Trim sleeve cap ¼"
Add ¼" to sides.

← Move ¼"

MOVE shoulder point
to front ¼"

Sleeve Ease Surprise

If you are one of those people who is willing to take out a sleeve in an attempt to eliminate "ease" puckering, you may be surprised to know that sleeve ease is positioned differently in tailored ready-to-wear. Instead of easing from front notch to back notch over the sleeve cap (as pattern indicates) ease is positioned from back underarm seam over cap past shoulder placement dot stopping 2 inches toward the sleeve front (Illustration 1).

Repositioning sleeve ease in the cap accomplishes two things: First, ease is positioned across entire back where needed for reaching; second, a smooth sleeve without ease is visible from the jacket or coat front, an area prone to scrutiny. Smooth puckerless sleeves read quality tailoring.

This requires repositioning either the sleeve shoulder dot or the underarm seam. Comparing an expensive European ready-to-wear jacket to several patterns, I discovered that the ready-to-wear sleeve was rotated slightly, positioning the shoulder dot ¼

inch toward the back and the underarm side seam indicator ¼ inch toward the front. Experiment on your next jacket and see if this works for you. So much depends on the pitch of the arm.

Sometimes a sleeve will not hang properly because the cap is too shallow to accommodate a larger shoulder pad. To give yourself flexibility, use a one inch seam allowance on sleeve cap when cutting out the sleeve. Pin in the sleeve and slip in desired shoulder pad. On the sleeve cap, cutting a wider seam allowance gives flexibility in fitting a sleeve. Some of the wider seam allowance in the cap can be stolen to accommodate desired pad or fuller arm.

Very often the shape of the back upper arm near the shoulder is different than the shape of the sleeve cap. If there seems to be excess fabric in the back of the sleeve, trim sleeve cap in back ¼ to ½ inch from shoulder dot to back notch to eliminate excess fullness.

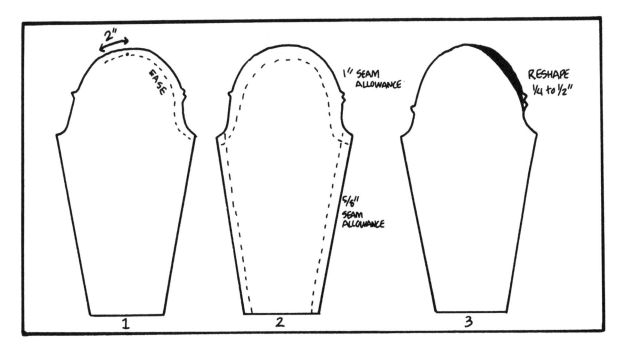

Sleeves for the Large Arm

Increasing the size of the sleeve usually requires an increase in the bodice at the underarm to make the armhole large enough for the larger sleeve. This creates another fitting problem by making the bodice and armhole too large. Other alternatives are preferable.

Examine the arms carefully from the side. Are they full from armhole to elbow, from the armhole to wrist, or are they full all the way from the shoulder to the wrist?

The shape of the arm determines where the additional fabric is needed. If the whole arm is full, split the sleeve vertically from the shoulder dot to the wrist and add the desired amount.

How much is the desired amount? Measure the arm at its fullest part. To this measurement add 1½ to 2 inches of ease. Measure the pattern at the same place between the seamlines. The difference between the flat-pattern measurement and you, plus ease, equals the amount you need to add.

If the addition is not needed at the lower part of the sleeve, simply taper the sleeve at side seams. If the fullness is not needed in the cap but only in the muscle area, make additions at the side seam, tapering when necessary.

After both of these additions, easing the new sleeve into the armhole can be a problem. If some addition is also needed in the bodice, the amount eased in will not be so great. If not, run an easeline along the whole upper part of the sleeve, not just between the notches. Pull in as much ease as possible. Press with steam over a tailor's ham to shrink in more fullness.

These two techniques can eliminate about 1 inch additional ease. If more is needed, choose a sleeve style with gathers or pleats in the cap.

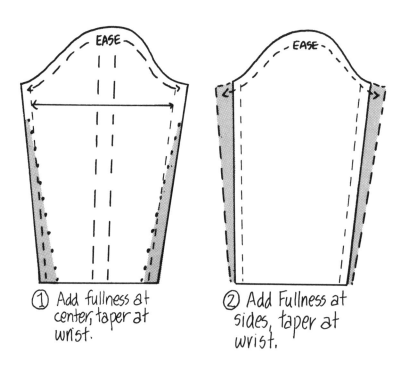

① Add fullness at center, taper at wrist.

② Add Fullness at sides, taper at wrist.

Silk Sleeves

What is the difference between a $400 lined silk jacket and a $90 lined silk jacket both with set in sleeves? On the more expensive jacket, certain steps were taken to prevent the armhole from stretching as the sleeve was set in. Stretching at the armhole is the culprit for wiggly seams and shoulders which ride to the back. Try this trick from one who specializes in tailored silk garments and your problems will be over.

Using the front and back bodice pattern pieces as a guide, cut two front and back templates (one set for each sleeve) from medium-weight paper to mimic the armhole of the pattern pieces. Use tracing paper to transfer the armhole seamline from pattern to paper. Remove pattern from paper. Reduce paper to 2 inches, mimicking the outline of the armhole.

Overlay paper templates on the wrong side of front and back bodice pieces at armholes. Staystitch armholes at $\frac{1}{2}$ inch through the fashion fabric and the paper template. The presence of the paper while stitch-ing prevents the silk from stretching. With paper in place, sew shoulder and underarm seams of bodice through fabric and paper.

Thread tracings on the sleeve itself (to mark seam placement) ensure accuracy on a silk sleeve, where small inaccuracies become more obvious. Ease sleeve cap at $\frac{1}{2}$ inch. No paper is included during sleeve easing. Sew underarm sleeve seam.

Set in sleeve into the armhole, placing pins sleeve-side up. Sew armhole seam through sleeve, bodice and paper templates. After seam is complete, pull paper templates away from the fabric.

Paper templates eliminate stretching while stitch-ing. To prevent armhole stretch while wearing, run a line of hand stitches $\frac{1}{2}$ inch from cut edge or $\frac{1}{8}$ inch from machine sewn seam, within seam allowance. Use heavy-duty thread or buttonhole twist as you backstitch around the armhole. The armhole seam can now be finished in an appropriate manner.

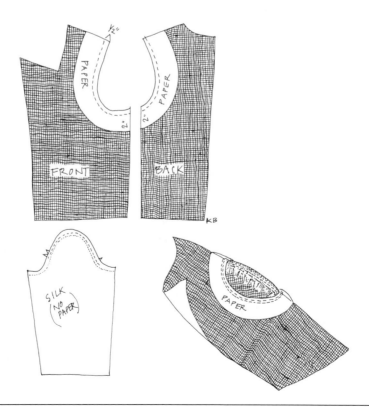

Sleeve Ease with Ease

Setting in a sleeve need not be a problem if you take a tip from ready-to-wear dress factories: Always set the sleeve in flat. What this means is that the sleeve is inserted before the underarm seam is sewn, right after the shoulder seam is completed.

The industry itself uses a method to ease called "crimping." Crimping on a sleeve cap is accomplished by sewing the sleeve cap into the armhole with the sleeve side against the machine and the armhole side against the presserfoot. By pushing the underside (sleeve cap) into the machine, the feed dog actually assists in easing the sleeve cap, which is larger, into the armhole. If you hold the top layer (the garment) up slightly with your left hand, you are able to push the sleeve cap in toward the feed dog with your right hand. While this technique takes a little practice, after a sleeve or two you will feel confident that the feed dog will do its job of easing even though you can't see the process as you sew.

If you are uncomfortable not being able to "see" the ease while you are sewing, try the technique called "staystitch plus."

To ease the cap of the sleeve, simply place your finger in back of the presserfoot as you sew. Push with medium pressure on the back of the presserfoot. Your finger, acting like a fence, keeps the fabric from coming out the back of the presserfoot as it would like to. This drag under the presserfoot is what causes the fabric to gather up lightly, creating just the right amount of ease at the sleeve cap. Do not be afraid to put your finger behind the presserfoot. Feel the pressure of your finger against the presserfoot. If you cannot feel it, you are not doing the process correctly.

Stitch length and pressure for staystitch plus is determined by the weight of the fabric. A light fabric calls for a medium-length stitch with light pressure. A heavy fabric calls for more pressure with a long stitch length. If the fabric is very heavy, you may have to do two rows of staystitching plus next to each other. Staystitch plus is done at $1/2$ inch.

After the ease process is completed, try the sleeve in the armhole to see how it fits. If you have eased too much, simply snap a thread. If more ease is needed, pull a thread or do another row of staystitch plus. Before sewing in the sleeve, steam-press the sleeve cap over the tailor's ham. This pressing helps set the ease and shrink in the sleeve cap a bit. The pressing before the sleeve is inserted is important to remove the gathered, puckered appearance. Sew the sleeve in with the sleeve side on top, flattening out

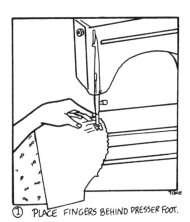

① PLACE FINGERS BEHIND PRESSER FOOT.

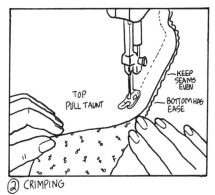

TOP PULL TAUNT — KEEP SEAMS EVEN — BOTTOM HAS EASE

② CRIMPING

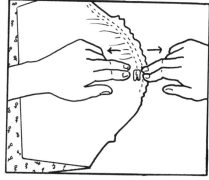

③ FLATTEN SLEEVE CAP AS YOU SEW.

Sleeve Ease with Ease

the sleeve cap as you sew. Press. After the armhole seam has been completed, sew the underarm seam in the bodice and the underarm seam in the sleeve in one continuous seam.

Coat and jacket sleeves are more comfortable set "in the round" after the underarm seam is sewn.

Try this tip from European ready-to-wear. Since most of the ease on a sleeve is needed in the sleeve back, do not ease between notches. Instead start easeline in front two inches before dot marked for shoulder placement. Continue ease in back all the way to underarm seam.

■ If the fabric is very difficult to ease, such as wool gabardine, try running an easeline all around the sleeve, from underarm to underarm.

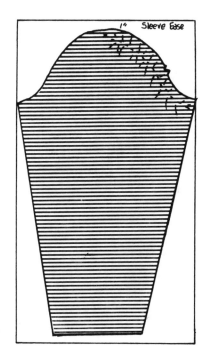

Setting Sleeves in Difficult Fabric

One thing is common in easing a sleeve cap in leather, Skinner's Ultrasuede®, or wool gabardine—the difficulty of achieving a smooth, puckerless sleeve. A few years ago, the following technique was demonstrated to me by a men's tailor, and I have been using it ever since.

Cut a 2-inch-wide bias strip of hair canvas (Seams Great® is a good substitute) the length of the area to be eased, from one notch to another over the sleeve cap.

For best results, the sleeve cap must be eased from the top of the cap to the notch. Place the bias strip against the wrong side of the sleeve cap.

Stretch the bias strip, starting at the top of the sleeve and following the shape of the sleeve cap. Sew the bias strip to the cap at ½ inch, stretching the strip as you sew. Work about 1 inch ahead of where you are sewing. Do not stretch the sleeve cap.

After you have sewn the bias strip in its stretched state, it will return to its unstretched condition, bringing ease to the sleeve cap with it.

You will be amazed how much ease can be brought in with this method. The eased area will be smooth and puckerless.

Repeat this procedure for the other half of the cap, working from the top of the sleeve to the notch. One continuous line of sewing will not yield the same results as working in two steps from the cap to the notch.

After the ease has been completed, insert the sleeve into the armhole. Leave the bias strip in the sleeve for extra lift at the sleeve cap.

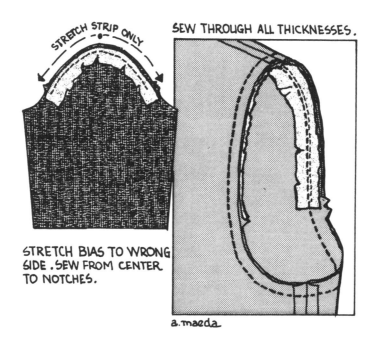

STRETCH STRIP ONLY

SEW THROUGH ALL THICKNESSES.

STRETCH BIAS TO WRONG SIDE. SEW FROM CENTER TO NOTCHES.

a. maeda

Demonstrated on *Power Sewing* Video #5: *Construction Difficulties.*

Puffed Sleeve Support

Sleeve support can be obtained by several methods. This technique is one I learned from Bobbie Carr, whose knowledge on fashioning sleeves could fill several textbooks.

If the desired sleeve effect is overall puffiness, your best method is to underline the entire sleeve with nylon organza. Nylon organza is preferable to silk organza. The stiffness of silk organza changes and softens with wear. Nylon organza is washable and never changes its original body, so it is a good choice for interfacing where body is needed and a press-on interfacing is undesirable.

If puffiness is desired only in the cap of a full sleeve, a sleeve head in double nylon organza is desirable. To make a pattern for a sleeve head, simply fold down the pattern tissue at dots on the cap of the sleeve. This folded tissue portion becomes the pattern for the sleeve head.

Folding the nylon organza on the bias, place the straight side of sleeve head pattern along the fold, thus cutting the nylon organza double. To attach the sleeve head, simply lay the folded organza sleeve head on the wrong side of the sleeve. Hand-baste layers together.

Run the gathering stitch through all thicknesses of the sleeve. Set the sleeve into the garment. To get the maximum benefit from the sleeve head, gently tug the sleeve head and the sleeve apart at the stitching line. This allows the sleeve and sleeve head to act independently, giving the maximum effect.

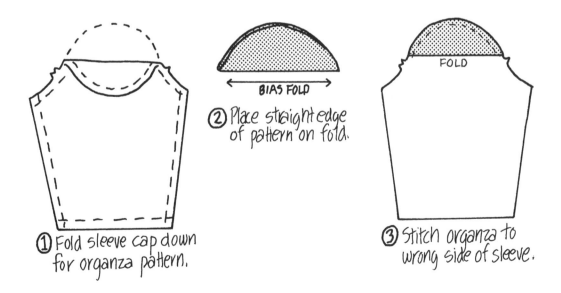

① Fold sleeve cap down for organza pattern.

BIAS FOLD
② Place straight edge of pattern on fold.

FOLD
③ Stitch organza to wrong side of sleeve.

Shoulderpad Shaping

The challenge of a better-fitting shoulderpad continues. Here is a method for covering any shoulderpad with fashion fabric using a combination of machine and hand stitching to mold shape. Choose a pad with as much built-in shaping as possible.

Cut a 14 inch square of lightweight fashion or lining fabric. Fold fabric square into quarters along bias grainlines. Along the center of one foldline, sew a fish dart 8 inches long and $5/8$ inch wide, tapering to zero at ends. With wrong sides out, place the center of the dart at the center of the pad, perpendicular to the pad edge which will be placed along the armhole. Slide the pad close to the bias fold without the dart. Trace outside curves of the pad on the wrong side of the 14-inch square pad cover. Slip out the pad.

With right sides together, sew pad cover closed, sewing pad cover $1/4$ inch larger than tracing line indicates. Leave end of the pad open so that cover can be turned right side out and pad inserted.

Trim excess cover fabric which extends beyond the sewing line. Turn right side out. Insert shoulderpad. Slipstitch end of pad closed. Shape pad on sleeve roll or fold in half parallel to sewn dart. Steam press and shape.

Shape pad and cover with hand stitching, using a stab stitch at $1/2$ inch intervals. Strengthen thread used by running through beeswax. Use a long stitch on top of the pad and a short stitch on concave underside of the pad, which will be placed against body.

Place the pad in the garment, lining up the dart on the convex side of the pad against the shoulder seam of the garment. If the garment has a set in sleeve, the edge of the pad extends $1/2$ inch into the sleeve from the armhole seam. If the sleeve style is dolman or raglan, pad placement is determined by comfortable placement on the shoulder.

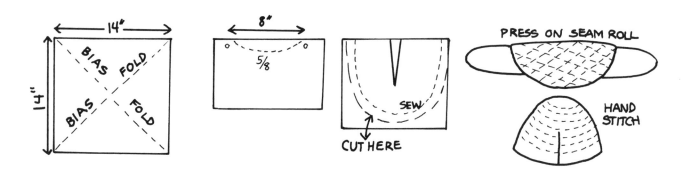

Demonstrated on *Power Sewing* Video #6: *Easy Linings.*

Eliminating Shoulderpads

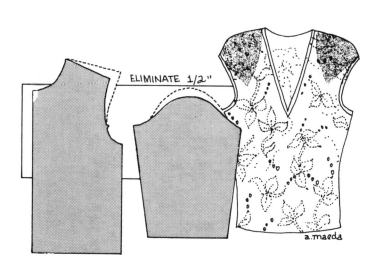

ELIMINATE 1/2"

a.maeda

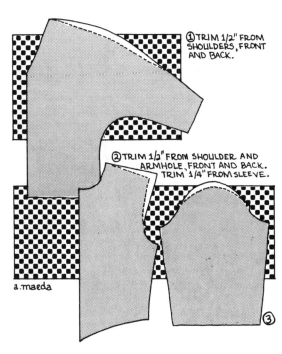

① TRIM 1/2" FROM SHOULDERS, FRONT AND BACK.

② TRIM 1/2" FROM SHOULDER AND ARMHOLE, FRONT AND BACK. TRIM 1/4" FROM SLEEVE.

a.maeda

③

Despite the hard sell on shoulderpads by the ready-to-wear industry, not every individual agrees. Many women exclaim, "I hate them!" If you are not a fan of shoulderpads, you need to know how to alter the pattern to eliminate the built-in allowance for the pad. Simply eliminating the pad itself won't work because eliminating the height caused by the pad creates wrinkles along the shoulder line.

Read on the back of the pattern envelope under "suggested notions" to determine what size pad was intended. For most garments a $\frac{1}{2}$ inch pad is suggested. What this indicates is that $\frac{1}{2}$ inch of height and $\frac{1}{2}$ inch of width extension was added to the sloper (basic pattern) to accommodate the $\frac{1}{2}$ inch pad. Along the shoulder seam, cut off $\frac{1}{2}$ inch tapering to zero by the neckline. At the arms-eye, cut off $\frac{1}{2}$ inch at the shoulder, tapering to zero at the notches. Complete alterations on both front and back.

Height has also been added to the sleeve to accommodate the pad so cut out $\frac{1}{2}$ inch from the top of the sleeve cap.

These alterations can also be made on ready-to-wear garments. Rather than eliminating the pad altogether, a smaller pad might be more to your liking.

One complaint about shoulderpads is that they don't stay in their proper position. Consider purchasing one of the lace undershirts with shoulderpads attached. Buy the undershirt a size smaller than you normally wear to keep the shirt from shifting and the pads well placed.

In all fairness to the fashion industry, shoulderpads do give balance to the bottom half of the body, thereby creating a slimmer silhouette. Shoulderpads can also give a garment a better hang, especially if you have sloping shoulders.

Cover and Placement of Shoulderpads

The easiest way to lose ten pounds without dieting is to wear shoulderpads with everything you own. If you have shied away from shoulderpads because you thought they were too stiff or you didn't know how to wear them, it is time for an education. To begin with, the selection of shoulderpads has increased considerably. Four or five types of pad are readily available, ranging in both size and shape. The pads are soft and conform easily to the shape of your body. Initially you might want to buy a pair in every shape and experiment to find which pad you are most comfortable with.

A covered shoulderpad gives a finished look to the inside of the garment and protects both the pad from soil and you against the scratchiness of the pad itself. Choose a soft fabric such as lightweight knit, cotton batiste, or lining fabric to cover shoulderpads.

Because so many shapes are available, here are pattern dimensions for the largest pad, used by many designers.

Cut a circle 11 inches in diameter. Draw a line through the center as a grainline. For a snug fit over a large pad, a dart is usually necessary. At $2\frac{1}{2}$ inches to the left of the grainline, draw in a dart 4 inches long and 5 inches wide (Illustration 1). Sew in the dart. Wrap the pad with the fold along the high part of the pad and the dart along the top (Illustration 2). Now that the lining is forming a half-circle around the pad, pin the raw edges together. Sew the lining close to the outside edge of the pad with an overlock or zigzag stitch. Trim off excess fabric. For smaller pads, the dart may be eliminated by using a smaller circle for a lining pattern.

To determine the correct placement for the shoulderpad, try on the garment. Slide the pad in with the thin side close to the neck and the fattest part of the pad at the shoulder. Slide the pad out toward the shoulder until the edges of the pad are the most invisible and the silhouette the most flattering. To anchor, sew the pad along the seam, catching the middle of the pad (in line with the dart) and the shoulder seam. For ease in transferring the pad from garment to garment, attach a strip of Velcro® on the underside of the pad and a strip on the garment at the shoulder seam.

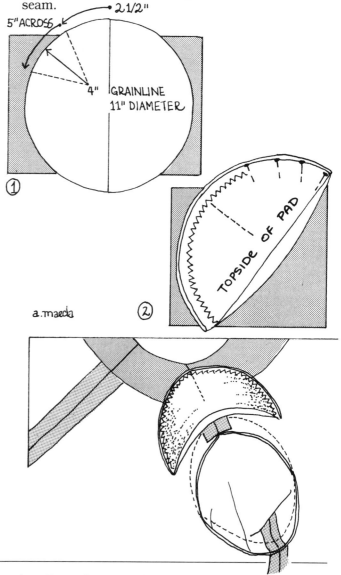

5" ACROSS · 2 1/2"

4" GRAINLINE 11" DIAMETER

①

a. maeda ②

TOPSIDE OF PAD

Demonstrated on *Power Sewing* Videos #5: *Construction Difficulties* and #12: *Handwoven and Quilted Garments.*

Easiest Sleeve Vent

Here is an easy way to make a professional-looking sleeve placket—it's especially handy for difficult-to-work-with fabrics.

Begin by making a mark on the sleeve piece at the place you want the placket (Illustration 1). If a sleeve placket isn't marked on the pattern, you can approximate its location by dividing the sleeve into thirds. The placket opening will lie approximately one-third the distance from the back of the sleeve.

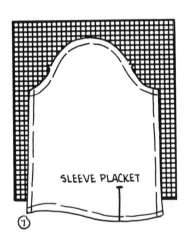

To make a traditional tailored welt, slash the fabric as described above but make a cut 3 inches high with two $\frac{1}{8}$-inch cuts on either side at the top. Cut a separate strip of fabric on the bias $1\frac{1}{2}$ inches wide and 8 inches long. Interface this strip with press-on interfacing, also cut on the bias.

Place the right side of the strip against the wrong side of the sleeve at the opening, raw edges together. Sew the strip to the opening with a $\frac{1}{4}$-inch seam allowance in one continuous line of stitching, letting the bias strip curve around the top of the slash. The $\frac{1}{8}$-inch cuts allow the strip to be sewn on in a straight line (Illustration 2). Turning under the raw edge on the strip, wrap it around the two seamed raw edges so that no raw edges show. Pin the top and stitch into place (Illustration 3).

Overlap the top welt (on the top side of the sleeve when worn) onto the bottom welt (Illustration 4). This forms a small pleat above the welt. Topstitch a little triangle at the junction of the top and bottom welts to anchor the pleat into place. Press and pound with a tailor's clapper.

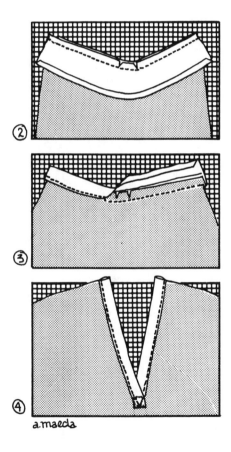

a. maeda

■ Sleeve fullness on expensive shirts are pleated, not gathered into a two-button cuff, and open with a tailored placket.

Cuff Perfection

For sleeve cuffs as good as or better than those on expensive ready-to-wear garments, cut the outer cuff, the undercuff, and cuff interfacing on the bias. This enables the cuff to circle the wrist smoothly. If a bias cuff would look awkward due to the fabric design, cut outer cuff on the straight grain and cut undercuff and interfacing on the bias.

For the interfacing, use a lightweight press-on interfacing. On silk, use organza hand-basted to the undercuff as interfacing.

After cutting out interfacing for the undercuff, cut $\frac{1}{2}$-inch strips of interfacing to press on the seam allowance on the wrong side of the outer cuff (Illustration 1). Press it along the edge that will be sewn to the sleeve.

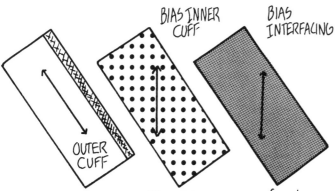

BIAS INNER CUFF
BIAS INTERFACING
OUTER CUFF

① Interface inner cuff and long seam of outer cuff (wrong side.)

Trim $\frac{1}{8}$ inch from all edges of the undercuff to make it smaller. This will eliminate wrinkles in the finished cuff.

Placing right sides together, sew undercuff and outer cuff together on three sides, sewing only halfway up cuff ends, leaving the interfaced outer cuff edge free (Illustration 2). Use small stitches and remember to handwalk the machine for two stitches at corners for a sharper finished corner. Trim sewn edges to $\frac{1}{8}$ inch.

Place right side of undercuff against wrong side of gathered sleeve, raw edges together and extending $\frac{5}{8}$

inch beyond the vent opening. Stitch and trim seam allowance to $\frac{1}{4}$ inch.

With right sides of outer and undercuff together, stitch remaining short sides of cuff $\frac{1}{16}$ inch beyond edge of vent (Illustration 3). This will keep cuff flush with vent edge when turned.

Turn under the interfaced edge of the outer cuff and topstitch in place. The interfacing prevents outer cuff from stretching while being topstitched.

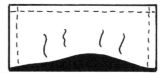

② Trim under cuff smaller and sew top half of both pieces.

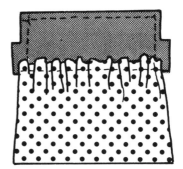

③ Trim cuff. Attach under cuff to sleeve, close ends turn to right side.

Fake Cuffs

Three-quarter-length sleeves are not only comfortable but flattering. This length has yet another advantage: sleeve vents can be eliminated.

Since most patterns feature long sleeves, a simple pattern adjustment will be needed. Shorten the sleeve pattern 4 to 5 inches in the lower half of the sleeve (Illustration 1).

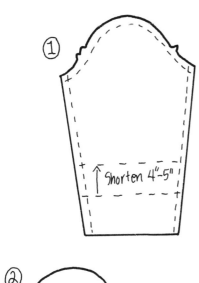

To determine the length to cut the cuff so it will fit comfortably, measure your forearm and add 2 inches. Cut a strip of fabric this length. As for width, cuffs for these shorter sleeves are cut narrower than for full-length sleeves. Most comfortable finished widths are between $1\frac{1}{2}$ and 2 inches. Cut cuffs $4\frac{1}{4}$ to $5\frac{1}{4}$ inches wide.

Fold one cuff length in half lengthwise. Pin ends together the width of seam allowance. Slip it on your arm. Would you like it looser or tighter? Remember that the gathers at the sleeve will take up about $\frac{1}{2}$ inch, making the cuff feel a little tighter. Cut sleeve cuffs and interfacing on the bias for the nicest look.

Gather the bottom of the sleeve. Placing the right side of the cuff and the right side of the sleeve together, sew a $\frac{5}{8}$-inch seam. Trim seams to $\frac{1}{4}$ inch. Sew underarm seam and cuff seam in one long operation. Turn half of cuff and seam allowance to the underside and handstitch into place, turning under seam allowance (Illustration 2).

If you want buttons on the cuff but don't want to go to the trouble of a vent, try this. Complete the same process as described above, but use a cuff length of your forearm plus 4 inches. Completed, the cuff is wide enough to fold over and button. Pinch together about an inch and sew a buttonhole in the cuff. This cuff can button over, giving the appearance of a vent (Illustration 3).

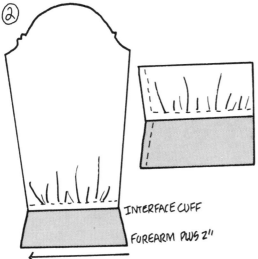

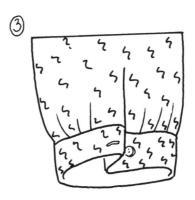

Jacket Sleeve Vent

A jacket sleeve vent can be intimidating at first glance, especially because correct sleeve length must be determined before constructing the vent.

I recommend cutting the sleeve in a scrap fabric and inserting it in the blazer. Fold up the sleeve at the hemline as indicated.

Determine at this point whether the sleeve is the correct length. Check the ease at the elbow to see if it falls at the right place. This will give you an indication of whether to shorten the sleeve above or below the elbow.

You should finish the sleeve vent before you insert the sleeve; a smaller piece is much easier to work on.

Begin by joining the underarm and top sleeve pieces together, matching the notches and leaving the portion below dots A and B open (Illustration 1).

Next, match dots B and D, right sides together (Illustration 2). Sew this portion. Press open seam. Trim to ¼ inch.

Turn right side out and pound with a tailor's clapper. This finishes the vent on the upper sleeve.

The undervent could be finished in the same manner, matching dots A and C, but I find a seam here is too bulky (Illustration 3).

Instead, simply match dots A and C with wrong sides together. Use a wide zigzag of small stitches on edges. Trim close to stitching. Overlap top vent and catchstitch into place (Illustration 4).

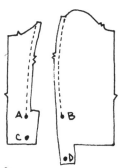

① JOIN UNDERARM AND TOP SLEEVE

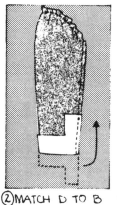

② MATCH D TO B

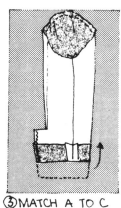

③ MATCH A TO C

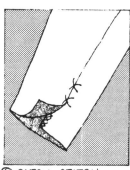

④ CATCH STITCH

Sport Zippers

Sport zippers—zippers with giant teeth—make a fashion statement with their high visibility. Sport zipper application is easier than you imagine. To insert a zipper in a seam such as on a jacket front, interface the seam allowances and use centered zipper application.

If zipper is not in a seam, such as one being used as an opening for a pocket, it's best to stabilize the fabric with interfacing before zipper application. This is necessary to support the weight of the zipper and prevent the fabric from stretching as zipper is applied. Interface behind desired placement.

Carefully measure the zipper from the bottom of the zipper stop to the top of the last teeth. On an interfacing-stabilized piece of fabric designated as the facing, draw a rectangle on the wrong side of the facing, ½ inch wide and the exact length of the zipper. The facing piece should be 4 inches wider than the rectangle in length and width. With right sides together, place the facing against the garment, positioning the drawn rectangle on the exact spot you want the sport zipper.

Using small reinforcing stitches, stitch the rectangle through the garment and facing. Handwalk two stitches at each corner. Cut opening in rectangle, similar to that used in bound buttonholes, clipping close to the stitching at each corner. Through the opening, turn facing to the wrong side of the garment. Press rectangular opening so that facing is not visible.

Position zipper under rectangular opening. Topstitch zipper in place, using a zipper foot, sewing close to the facing edge.

On very expensive garments, topstitching is not visible on the garment. To attach the sport zipper invisibly, cover the outside edge of the zipper with fabric glue such as "Unique Stitch." Position the zipper under the rectangular opening, and let sit until glue dries. Lift up the garment fabric until the seam allowance which joined the facing and the garment is visible. Sew the seam allowance to the zipper ⅛ inch away from the original facing seam. Start and stop 1 inch from the zipper tab. Unzip the zipper and complete the seam, attaching zipper to seam allowance.

Cover completed zipper with presscloth. Press well with zipper open and closed.

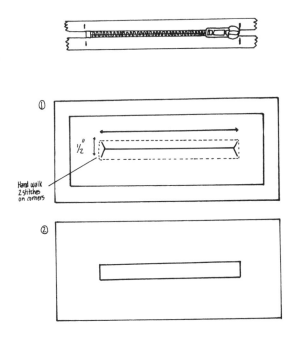

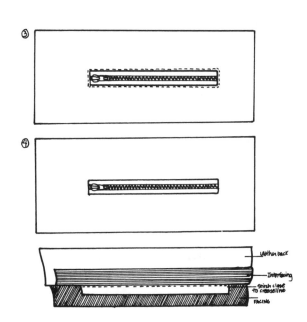

Zipper Refinements

For those who have mastered zipper techniques, here are a few pointers to make your results even more professional.

Zipper weight is very important. A lightweight fabric demands a lightweight zipper. A zipper also needs flexibility. A stiff plastic zipper has a mind of its own and will not conform to the shape of the garment. If strength is needed, for example in a fly front for tight-fitting pants, a metal zipper would be a better choice.

Always interface the zipper placket or seam allowance where zipper will be set. Use ½-inch strips of lightweight press-on interfacing behind seam allowance for the length of the zipper.

This little bit of added support in the seam allowance eliminates any rippling in the zipper area in lightweight fabric or bias fabric.

In observing expensive European ready-to-wear, I noticed the use of a very narrow lap in the lapped zipper—¼ to ⅜ inch. Experiment to see what width lap still covers the zipper tab. The width of the lap is narrowed by sewing close to the teeth of the zipper.

To eliminate the gap between the top of the zipper and the waistband, buy the zipper 1 to 2 inches longer than you need.

Sew in zipper, letting excess extend above the waistline, and attach waistband before cutting off excess zipper tape. Hand-walk the machine carefully between the teeth of the zipper when sewing waist seam. Cut off excess zipper and finish waistband.

After the zipper has been completed, always press across the zipper, toward the placket fold. An up-and-down ironing technique will produce a ripply effect.

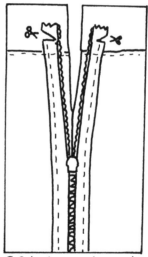

③ Extend zipper beyond waist seam. Trim excess.

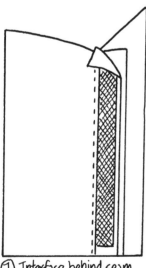

① Interface behind seam allowance.

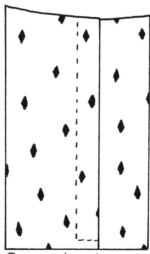

② Narrow lapped zipper.

Centered Zipper

Mastering a lapped zipper or fly zipper can be pretty intimidating to a new sewer. I made my own clothes for ten years without knowing how to do anything but a centered zipper. You can, too.

A zipper is usually in a pretty inconspicuous place. If you want to put in a fast, easy zipper, try this method.

Sew the seam with permanent stitches up to the spot where you want the zipper. Switch the stitch length to "baste" (larger stitches) and continue to the end of the seam.

Cut two thin strips of interfacing $1/2$ inch wide and the length of the zipper. On each side of the seam allowance where the zipper will be, press a strip of fusible interfacing on the wrong side of the seam allowance (Illustration 1).

Interfacing helps stabilize the seam and keep it from rippling as you sew. Place the interfacing close to the basted seam. When you press the basted seam open, you will no longer be able to see the newly applied strips of interfacing. If you don't have any interfacing and the fabric is stable, it is okay to put in the zipper without it.

Place the right side of the zipper down against the pressed-open seam allowance. Pin. Tape across zipper a few times to hold in place (Illustration 2). Remove pins. Turn the right side of the garment so it faces you. Center a piece of tape over seam. Use edge as guide for sewing. (Do not sew on the tape.)

Get the zipper foot out of your machine supply box. It is structured so that the needle can be moved from one side to the other. Begin with the needle on the right side of the foot. Start sewing on the left side of the zipper as the zipper faces you with the top away from you. The needle will be on the side closest to the zipper teeth.

Following your chalk guideline, sew with a permanent stitch over the chalked guide (Illustration 3). Sew down one side; stop; leave the needle in; pivot; sew across the bottom; stop; pivot; sew up the other side.

Remove tape. Remove the machine-basting stitch that held the seam together while you worked (Illustration 4). Press. Your zipper is finished!

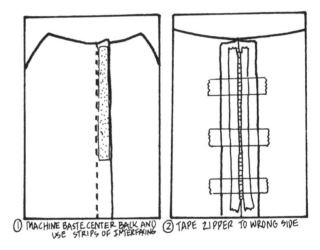

① MACHINE BASTE CENTER BACK AND USE STRIPS OF INTERFACING   ② TAPE ZIPPER TO WRONG SIDE

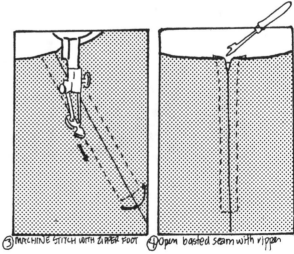

③ MACHINE STITCH WITH ZIPPER FOOT   ④ Open basted seam with ripper

---

Lapped Zipper

The lapped zipper, although slightly more time consuming than the centered zipper, yields a much more professional closing with a truly hidden zipper.

Sewing the garment from the bottom up, switch stitch length to basting stitches at the point indicated for zipper opening. If the fabric is lightweight, press half inch strips of interfacing behind the seam allowances in the indicated zipper area.

Looking at the wrong side of the garment with the basted seam at the top, begin zipper construction on the left side.

Open the zipper and place the zipper face down on extended seam allowance. Line up the zipper teeth with the basted seam. Start stitching 1 inch above the bottom of the zipper stop. This eliminates irregular stitching around the zipper tape. Sew only the seam allowance and the zipper tape in the first step.

Close zipper and turn the zipper so that it lies face up. Place fabric away from zipper. Machine stitch through the fold created by the basted seam and the first line of stitching just completed. Begin stitching at the bottom of the zipper. No stitching should show through to the right side of the garment.

Spread the garment flat and allow the zipper to relax into position. The zipper will lie a little to one side. Stitch across the bottom and up the unsewn side of the zipper using the woven guideline on the zipper as a guide. This is the first time you are sewing through the main part of the garment.

Remove original seam basting. Press lapped zipper toward the fold. Do not press with up and down strokes on a zipper or you will produce wrinkles.

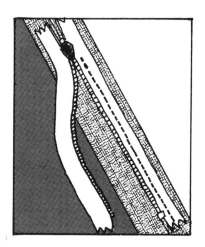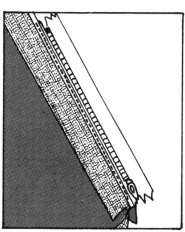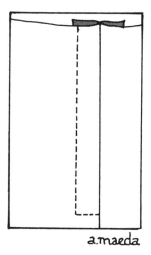

a.maeda

■ Invisible zippers are back with lighter weight and more flexible teeth—a great choice for close fitting garments in lycra blends. Don't forget to purchase the special foot needed to sew invisible zippers.

Fly Front

One of the surest signs of a homemade pair of slacks is a clumsily made fly front. Most instructions are so complicated that we usually give up in midstream and put in the lapped zipper, which really has little resemblance to the fly front.

A fly front can go on any pant or skirt by merely adding an extension of 1⅜ inch beyond the seamline for 8 inches. Sew the two front pieces with small stitches starting one inch beyond the inner leg seam to one inch beyond the bottom of the fly front extension. Switch stitch length to basting and sew the remainder of the seam to the waistline, clip curve at the bottom of the extension.

Go over to the iron and interface the entire fly extension on the wrong side, from the seamline to the raw edge, with fusible knit tricot.

By purchasing a zipper 9 inches or longer, you can eliminate the space between the bottom of the waistband and the top of the teeth. This is an opportunity to use up old zippers. The zipper will not be trimmed off until after the waistband goes on.

Looking at the pants from the wrong side, position the zipper, teeth side down, against the right fly extension. The left edge of the zipper should butt against the basted seamline. The bottom of the zipper is positioned one inch above the bottom of the extension. Sew the right zipper tape to the right fly extension, attaching only the extension and the zipper together. Pulling everything to the left except the right zipper tape, do a second row of stitching on the same side, ⅛ inch from the seam formed by your first row of stitching. This will flatten the fabric against the zipper tape. No stitching will show on the outside of the pants.

Pull the left zipper tape extension toward the left fly extension as far as it will go and still lie flat. The zipper tape will not match the raw edge of the fly extension. Pin the left zipper tape to the left fly extension, sewing close to the teeth and including only the fly extension and the zipper in this line of stitching. Still, no stitching shows on the outside of the pants.

Turn the pants around so that the outside of the pants faces you. Flatten the sewn zipper by pulling it a little to the right side, as it faces you. Mark desired topstitching line 1¼ to 1½ inch away from the center seam with chalk. Use this as a guide for sewing. Through all thicknesses on the right side, sew the zipper placket into place. It is not necessary to catch the zipper tape in this step, as the zipper has been anchored on each side in the previous step. To eliminate rippling, sew from the bottom of the zipper, around the curve to the waistline. With a very narrow zigzag which is very close together, sew a bar tack at the bottom of the fly at the seam. Remove basting and admire your fly front.

The fly facing is optional, but it really makes a nice finish. Cut a piece of fabric 4 inches by 8 inches. Fold in half lengthwise with right sides out, and sew a little curve in at the bottom.

Attach the fly facing to the fly by sewing the two raw edges of the fly facing to the right fly extension. Overlock to give a nice finish.

Press the fly with press and lift motions to avoid ripples. Doesn't it look great?

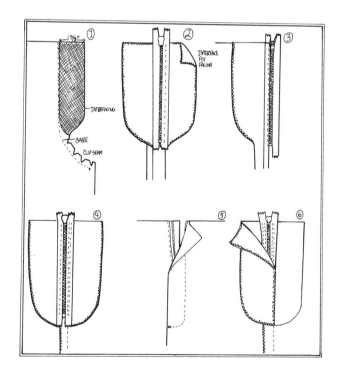

Demonstrated on *Power Sewing* Video #5: *Construction Difficulties.*

Button Loops

If your buttons are large, if your fabric is very loose weave, or if machine buttonholes intimidate you, button loops from self fabric or tubular rayon braid can be your solution. The loops go into the seam which attaches the front facing to the garment. If your pattern features a fold back facing, create separate facing pieces by adding seam allowances on both sides of the foldline indicated on the pattern.

If your fabric is not suitable for making self fabric loops, check out the braid department for tubular rayon braid in a matching or even a contrasting color. The key to professional looking closures of this type is that they lay almost flat against the seam from which they protrude.

Often the decision to do a loop closure is made after the garment is completed, when choosing a button or buttons which are too large for conventional buttonholes. No problem. Simply try on the garment to determine desired placement of buttons. Then mark the desired location of the loop closure. The next step requires a little experimentation. The goal is to find the smallest loop which will accommodate your button. If the seam has not been sewn, position the center of the loop ¼ inch away from the seamline indication, bringing the ends of the loop into the seamline as soon as a loop is formed large enough for the button to pass through. Experiment by moving the ends in towards the center and out away from the center to create a larger and smaller loop. The closure is made larger by lengthening the loop not by making the loop stick out farther into the garment. You may have to baste and rebaste ends into position a few times to try your button. This is par for the course.

If your facing and garment seam has already been completed, create openings with a ripper where ends of tubing can be inserted. Experiment to get the smallest loop possible to pass button through. Resew seam openings stitching twice to anchor the loop well.

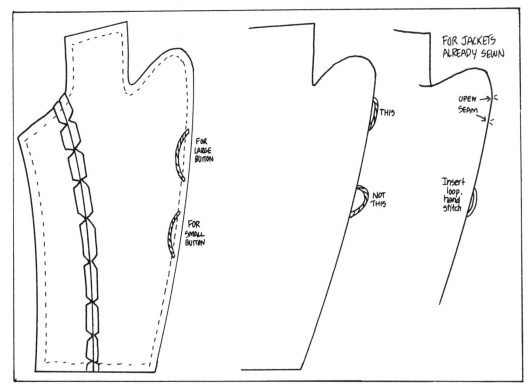

FOR JACKETS ALREADY SEWN

OPEN → SEAM

FOR LARGE BUTTON

FOR SMALL BUTTON

THIS

NOT THIS

Insert loop, hand stitch

Demonstrated on *Power Sewing* Video #12: *Handwoven and Quilted Garments.*

Foolproof Bound Buttonholes

Bound buttonholes go in and out of fashion. Jenny Hake showed me a wonderful method of making them, definitely the easiest I have seen.

Begin by making a trial buttonhole on a scrap of the fabric you will be using for your garment. This gives you a chance to try the technique and will forewarn you of any problems you might have. When you work with your garment, interface the area where you intend to put bound buttonholes to give support.

For each buttonhole, cut a 3-inch square of fabric. If fabric has a loose weave, apply press-on interfacing.

On the garment, make two vertical buttonhole, placement lines to mark ends of buttonholes. Make one horizontal placement line to run along center of each buttonhole. Baste these placement lines through garment and interfacing with contrasting thread (Illustration 1). Tailored buttonholes seem to look better if they are at least 1 inch long.

Pin the 3-inch square diagonally over buttonhole markings with right sides of garment and right side of square together.

With interfaced side of garment facing you, baste center of buttonhole and then baste two lines ¼ inch away from center line and parallel to it (Illustration 2).

On right side of garment, pin bottom triangle up as far as it will go. The basting line you did earlier will hold it in place (Illustration 3).

On interfaced side of garment, sew a line ⅛ inch from center placement line through garment and two thicknesses of outer square piece. Use small stitches and stop exactly within the basted boundaries. Use your previous line of stitching as a guide. Sew right on top of it.

Repeat this process for the top side of the square, pulling the top triangle down toward bottom. On interfaced side, sew ⅛ inch from center placement line (Illustration 4).

Pull out all basting lines. Cut an opening as small as possible in center of buttonhole. From that opening, cut a slash toward each corner, making triangles as long as possible. Slash to within one stitch of corner (Illustration 5). Turn square of fabric through opening.

If a corded look is desired, thread yarn through a large needle and pull through the welts forming the buttonhole (Illustration 6).

Baste the center of the buttonhole closed. Lift up garment and you will find small triangles, which need to be secured at the ends of the welt.

Sew the triangle to the welt, getting close to end of buttonhole with small reinforcing stitches. If fabric is heavy, use zipper foot for this step.

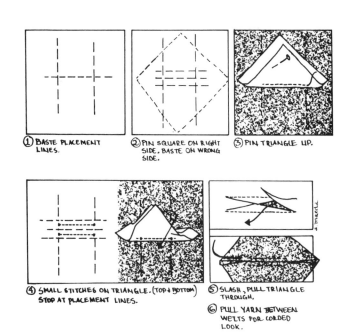

① BASTE PLACEMENT LINES.

② PIN SQUARE ON RIGHT SIDE. BASTE ON WRONG SIDE.

③ PIN TRIANGLE UP.

④ SMALL STITCHES ON TRIANGLE. (TOP & BOTTOM) STOP AT PLACEMENT LINES.

⑤ SLASH, PULL TRIANGLE THROUGH.

⑥ PULL YARN BETWEEN WELTS FOR CORDED LOOK.

Hand Buttonholes

If you find machine-made buttonholes unsatisfactory, and if you enjoy doing handwork, try making a handworked buttonhole. Like machine buttonholes, the handworked ones are made after the garment has been completed. A handworked buttonhole is often made on a jacket in lieu of a bound buttonhole.

Mark placement line for buttonhole on right side of garment. Machine-stitch a rectangle around placement line that is a little more than $\frac{1}{8}$ inch from placement line (Illustration 1). Slash through the buttonhole placement line, being careful not to cut beyond this line in any direction.

The best buttonhole is made with a thick thread called buttonhole twist.

Insert the needle at one end of the buttonhole. Backstitch to make a knot (Illustration 2). Cut off excess thread, then begin using the buttonhole stitch, working from left to right, along the slashed placement line.

The buttonhole stitch is the same one you use when making a knot. Simply pull thread through the loop formed by the first stitch.

Fan out stitches at the ends of the buttonhole (Illustration 3). On each end of the buttonhole, bar-tack for extra strength. To bar-tack, take several stitches across the end of buttonhole (Illustration 4) and go over these stitches in the opposite direction with the same stitch you used to make the rest of the buttonhole (Illustration 5).

Always make a sample buttonhole on scrap fabric first. The shape of the button often determines buttonhole length.

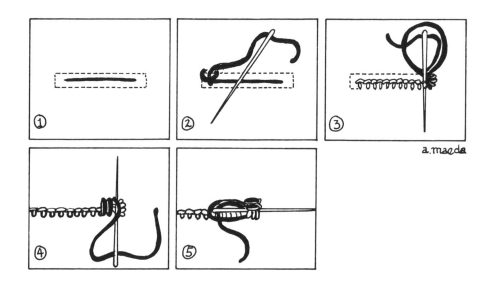

a. maeda

Buttonhole Placement and Sewing on a Button

Sewing on a button sounds easy, but surprisingly few people know how to do it correctly.

Pin the garment together in the position you would like it to be when it is finished. For proper button placement, place a pin through the outer edge of the buttonhole or the buttonhole edge closest to the edge of the garment. Push the pin down to mark the placement (Illustration 1). Unpin the garment, leaving the button placement pin in place.

To strengthen your thread and keep it from knotting while you sew, pull your thread double through beeswax. Beeswax can be purchased in any notions department or candle store. Knot the doubled thread.

Start the knot on the backside of the garment at the pin point. If the garment is heavier than a lightweight cotton, you must allow for a shank when sewing. This keeps the button a small distance away from the garment so that, when buttoned, there is plenty of room for the buttonhole side. If the button is sewn tight against the garment, the buttonhole side will bunch behind the button.

Bring the needle through the button and then back into the fabric, holding the button about ¼ inch away from the garment for the shank. When you've sewn back and forth about twice the number of times you'd normally think necessary, your button is secure.

Wind the thread around the allowed shank many times to give a neat appearance (Illustration 2). Pull your thread to the wrong side and make a knot by pulling it through the loop (Illustration 3).

■ If you own a buttonhole attachment for your machine, take the time to make up a sample buttonhole from each template. Open up the buttonhole and mark the size of the template beside it. Keep the samples with the buttonhole attachment. The next time you do buttonholes you will know from your samples exactly which template fits your button.

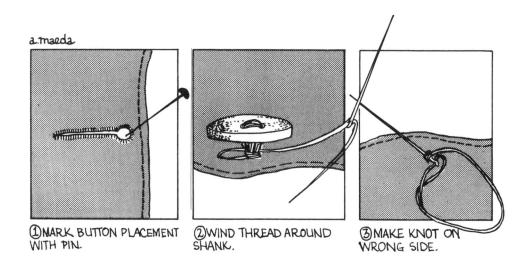

a.maeda

① MARK BUTTON PLACEMENT WITH PIN.　② WIND THREAD AROUND SHANK.　③ MAKE KNOT ON WRONG SIDE.

Waistline Finish Tab

When using a waistband, you are faced with the dilemma of how to finish the skirt or pants at the top of the zipper. The hook and eye solution is never permanent as well as a hassle to find in the back of the garment. Try this method for a quality solution to the problem.

Complete the pants or skirt past the stage of zipper and waist facing application. Facing has not yet been anchored by hand to the inside of the garment at the zipper.

Cut a piece of fashion fabric $2\frac{1}{2}$ inches long by $3\frac{1}{2}$ inches wide. Interface. Fold fabric in half so that you now have a piece of fabric $2\frac{1}{2}$ inches long and about $1\frac{3}{4}$ inches wide. Sew a $\frac{5}{8}$ inch seam on the remaining side, shaping one end into a point or a curve. Don't forget to handwalk two stitches at the end of any point. One end of the tab is left open for turning. Press seam open. Trim and grade seams removing as much bulk as possible. Turn tab right side out. Press and pound flat with a tailor's clapper.

Go to your button box and find a small flat button, no bigger than one half inch, which matches your fabric. Near the finished end of the tab, make a buttonhole which will accommodate your button.

On the lapped side of the zipper, remove enough stitches to allow the raw end of the tab to slide between the zipper and the lapped seam allowance. Slip the tab in far enough so that only the end of the tab with the buttonhole extends beyond the fold of the lap zipper. Pin into place. Resew stitches removed on the lap side of the zipper, permanently sewing the tab into place at the same time.

On the inside of the garment, trim off excess fabric from the end of the tab, overlock raw edge if desired. Sew button on the opposite side of the zipper opening on the outside of the garment. Makes a pretty neat finish, doesn't it?

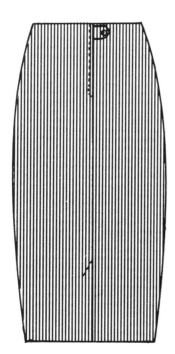

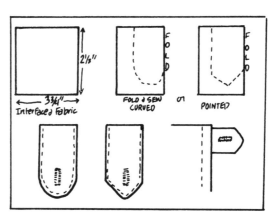

Alterations on Ready-to-Wear

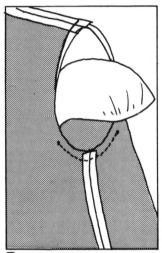

① REMOVE SLEEVE AT SHOULDER, TRIM BODICE.

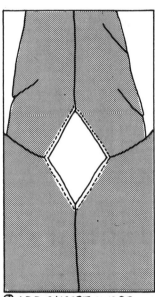

② ADD GUSSET UNDER THE ARM.

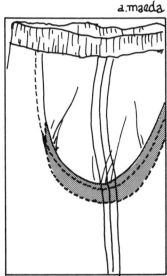

a.maeda

③ SEW CROTCH DEEPER.

Not everyone has the time nor the inclination to sew a garment from start to finish. Given the wide range of body shapes, alterations on ready-to-wear garments are often needed both for comfort and overall appearance.

Alterations for narrow shoulders rarely take more than a few minutes. Using a seam ripper, remove the stitching between the sleeve and the armhole. It is not necessary to remove the entire sleeve. Leave the armhole seam intact for 2 inches on either side of the underarm seam. Trim excess from the armhole on the bodice *only*, not the sleeve. Trim $\frac{1}{4}$ to $\frac{3}{4}$ inch at the shoulder tapering to zero about two-thirds down the front and back armhole (Illustration 1). Pin the unsewn part of the sleeve in place. Re-sew seam.

Sometimes a garment feels too tight underneath the armholes. Usually the problem is caused by not having enough fabric in the sleeve and the bodice. Using fabric which matches the garment fabric closely, cut a small angular gusset 5 inches long and 4 inches wide. The size of the gusset may vary depending on how tight the garment is. Open the underarm seam for 2 inches on either side of the armhole seam. Slip the gusset under the opening and spread the seam to within $\frac{1}{2}$ inch of the raw edges of the gusset. Pin in place. Topstitch gusset into place (Illustration 2).

A crotch seam which is too short is not only unflattering but uncomfortable as well. To lower the crotch in a pair of ready-to-wear pants, sew the crotch $\frac{1}{2}$ inch to 1 inch lower at the intersection of inner leg and crotch seams, tapering to zero about one-third of the distance up the crotch in both directions (Illustration 3). Connect the lowered crotch seam in a smooth transition between lowered seam and existing sewn seam.

Replacing a broken zipper can be a time-consuming affair, but by removing the few teeth at the zipper bottom, zipper function can usually be restored. After the zipper is working again, create a barrier with waxed thread $\frac{1}{4}$ inch in front of the missing teeth. This creates a new stop and will prohibit the zipper from slipping off at the bottom.

Pants Philosophy

Although pants are flattering to a limited number, everyone needs a few pairs in her wardrobe. Style choice is important in pants that are flattering. If you have fullness in the tummy or the hips, a style with deep front pleats will draw attention to the pleat and away from the problem. Pocket placement should be carefully considered if your hips are wide. Slant hip pockets that end at your wide hip act as an arrow pointing to the problem. Loose non-fitted styles conceal figure faults, whereas snug-fitted styles draw attention to them.

Unless you are tall, be careful of a pant leg that is too wide. Wide legs make you look shorter and wider. Correct length is also an issue. Before hemming, try on pants with the shoes you intend to wear with them. Heel height affects pants length. Pants should end at the break in front and be ½ to 1 inch longer in back, long enough to cover part of the shoe in back.

Fabric choice is also important to flattering pants. For very tailored pants, choose a fabric with body so that the pants will hold their shape—wool gabardine, wool flannel, or firm cotton. Be careful of corduroy, which adds weight. For full pants, choose a fabric that drapes well—wool jersey, wool crepe, cotton knits. If you try to use a firm fabric with full pants, the result is extra unwanted pounds.

Finally, how you wear pants is extremely important. Tops tucked into pants are only for the very slim. If you have any tummy fullness or love handles, do not tuck in your shirt. Wear the shirt on the outside of the pants, belted loosely, or wear pants with a camisole and the blouse acting as a loose jacket. If you are unsure whether to tuck in, have a friend take two pictures of you from the rear, tucked in and not tucked in. The photos will tell the true story.

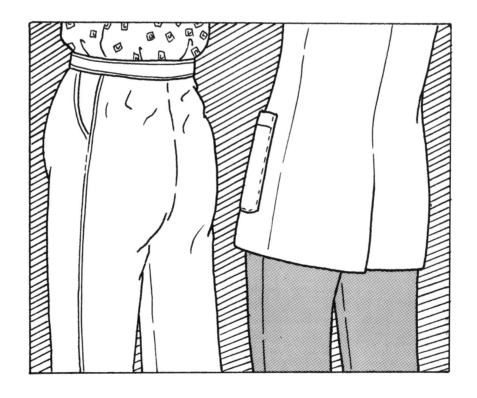

Flat Bottom, Baggy Seat

Perhaps the most difficult figure to fit in pants is the individual with a flat bottom. Not only is the derriere flat, but the individual often locks the knees when standing, making it impossible for the pants to hang in a straight line from the derriere to the floor. The pants actually get caught on the back calf on the way to the floor. While this problem can be minimized, the most sag you can eliminate is 60 percent. 40 percent will remain caught on the back calf.

To begin with, you must understand the difference between a flat bottom and a wide bottom. An individual may have one or both. To accommodate a wide bottom, additions are made at the side seam. To accommodate a flat bottom, the distance between the crotch point and the center back seam must be reduced. A narrower scoop on the back crotch accommodates the flatter derriere.

If you are using a multisized pattern, this can be accomplished quite easily by using a smaller size from the crotch point to the hem on the back inside leg seam. If your pattern is not multisized, feel free to reduce this seam by ½ inch (see Illustration 1). Be conservative—if you take away too much, you will not

have enough room to sit down.

Another fitting problem which seems to go hand in hand with the flat derriere is a low bottom. Unless some accommodation is made for this, the derriere pushes down the crotch seam, resulting in wrinkles right under the crotch in back. Lower the crotch ½ inch (see Illustration 2).

A third fitting problem which often accompanies the flat derriere is a larger waist and fullness in the high hip area right under the waist. If this is the case, back darts can be eliminated completely, replaced with slight ease—using the rest to accommodate the large waist. If the high hip is full but the waist is small in proportion, a curved dart can be used in this area. A curved dart starts and ends at the same place but curves in slightly towards the fold, letting the fabric mold itself over the high hip.

After you try on the pants, it is often necessary to lift the center back slightly (½ inch or so) to get the pants to hang correctly. After you determine the amount you can eliminate at center back, simply cut off this amount at center back, tapering to zero at the side seam every time you cut out pants.

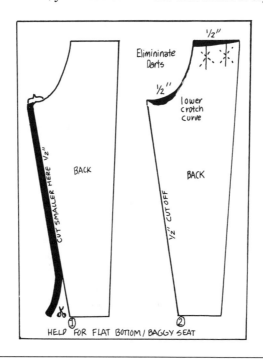

Pants and the Pot Belly

Do front pleats pull open on every pair of tailored pants you put on even if the waist and hip fit? Instead of pleats falling gracefully from the waist, are pleats anxious for the opportunity to pop open under the topstitching? Do side seams pull toward the front as they near the waist? Believe it or not, it is possible to make pants which hang like those worn by skinny runway models even if you have a pot belly and haven't worn a size 10 since eighth grade. The secret lies in cutting the front pant one, two, or more sizes larger than the back pant. Let's see how this works.

Wearing a pair of tights or opaque hose, stand sideways facing the mirror. Along your side, pin a piece of seam tape from the center of the leg at the knee to the waist, placing the tape where an ideal side seam would be in a straight line from knee to waist. Repeat procedure on other side.

Viewing your body from the side, it becomes apparent that the front half of the body is much larger in the tummy area ($2\frac{1}{2}$ inches down from the waist) than the back. Make a mark with chalk $2\frac{1}{2}$ inches down from the waist along the seam tape on each side of the body. Measure seam to seam across the front half of the body and back half of the body separately. Measuring tape will be positioned slightly closer to the waistline at center front and center back than the distance from the waistline at side seams, to allow the tape to go in a straight line from side seam to side seam. To these measurements, add 1 inch ease to front body and $\frac{1}{2}$ inch ease to back body.

Front measurement plus 1 inch ease in the tummy area is the amount needed in the pant to eliminate stress over the pleat area, allowing the pleats to fall freely, hanging closed. Back measurement plus $\frac{1}{2}$ inch ease in the tummy area (sometimes called the high hip) is the amount needed to fit smoothly over the love handles in back without horizontal stress lines.

The next step is to prepare the pattern for measurement. On the front, pin out pleats from the waist to the front crotch; on the back pin out darts. If you have a flat bottom, elimination of back darts gives more room in the high hip area and waist, while deemphasizing the flat bottom. If you don't intend to use a back dart, don't pin it out. What now remains is the pant without design elements as it would be on the body. On the pattern, make a mark $2\frac{1}{2}$ inches from the waist along the side seam, on front and back pant pieces. Draw a horizontal line from this $2\frac{1}{2}$ inch point on the side seam to center front and center back, keeping horizontal lines parallel to grainline. Horizontal line from side seam to center front or center back will be positioned slightly closer to the waistline at center front and center back in order for a straight measurement on the pattern to simulate the same measurement, as taken on the body.

Measure front and back pant pattern pieces separately, along the horizontal lines from center front or center back to side seams. Multiply each measurement times two, since your pants will have two fronts and two backs in construction. Now, going back to your actual measurements in this area plus 1 inch ease on front and $\frac{1}{2}$ inch ease on back, compare your front measurement to the front measurement with the pleats folded out. The difference is the alteration or the amount you must add to the front piece for the look you want.

Divide the front alteration in half and add this amount to the side seam of the pattern. Make this alteration from the waist tapering to zero by the full hip at the side seam. If your tummy measurement is larger than your hip measurement, pants are more flattering if they hang from the tummy and do not curve in at the hip. This method deemphasizes the large tummy/small hip comparison. If this is you, make addition from waistline to the bottom of the pants at the side front.

Now compare the pattern measurement of the back multiplied times two to the body measurement of the back plus $\frac{1}{2}$ inch ease. The difference between these two measurements is the alteration which will have to be made for the back to fit properly. Divide the back alteration in half and add or subtract from waist to full hip.

Do not be surprised if your calculations lead you to add to the front and take away from the back. This alteration is common for flat-backed individuals with a tummy.

No additions are ever made on the side front, which is actually part of the pocket. Never "steal" from the

Pants and the Pot Belly

side front by moving the front placement line to accommodate the larger tummy. Bulging pockets will result.

For the pants to hang properly, alteration has been made in the waist as well as the tummy area. Before putting on the waistband, it may be necessary to deepen the front pleats slightly ¼ inch on either side—resulting in a slanted sewing line for front pleats. Do not sew pleats ¼ inch deeper over its entire length, only the upper pleat area near the waistline seam. Back darts may be deepened or reduced to accommodate waist size. Waistline of pants should measure 1 inch bigger than band before joining. Run an easeline on the pants within the seamline before joining to waistband, easing in 1 inch. Stabilize waistline with staytape before fitting. Flatten ease by steam pressing lightly.

For those of you who are allergic to anything to do with measurements, numbers, or calculations, try this alternate method. When cutting out the pants, allow 1½ inch seam allowances on the side seams and the waistline seam. Mark pattern side seam and waistline position with tracing paper. Construct pants including pleats, darts, pockets and zipper except for the side seams and waistband. Run a machine-basted easeline in contrasting thread on front and back traced waist seamline. Press slightly with steam to remove obvious ease puckers. Machine baste staytape or ¼ inch strip of selvage along traced waist seamline. Machine baste side seams in contrasting thread, using 1½ inch allowed seam allowance.

The pants are now ready for fitting. Attempting to fit pants without stabilizing the waistline seam with staytape results in a hit-or-miss pants fit. Position the pants on your waist. If the pants seem too short in the crotch, reposition the staytape higher, using some of the 1½ inch seam allowance at the waist. If the pants seem too tight, rebaste entire side seams using some of the 1½ inch side seam allowance.

Once a satisfactory fit is achieved, turn the pants wrong-side out. Compare the actual seamlines used for the good fit to seamline on pattern. Transfer new seamlines to the pattern. The next time you make these pants, trial and error fitting will not be necessary. Providing you haven't gained 10 pounds before you make them again, the pants should fit perfectly.

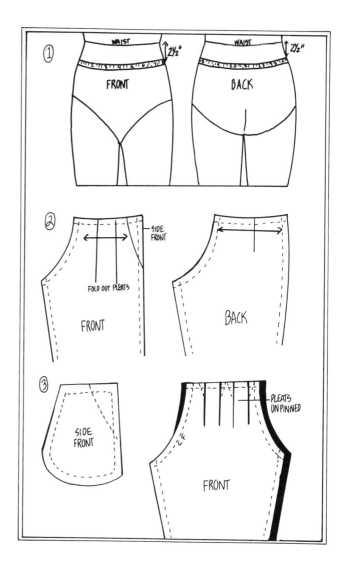

Demonstrated on *Power Sewing* Video #4: *Foolproof Pant Fitting.*

Pant Lining

If you sit in an office or if you travel often, you might want to start lining your pants. Pant linings take very little time in construction, but will save you lots of time between wearings by cutting down on wrinkles.

Pant lining is cut from the same pattern as the pants themselves, except shorter. Cut lining to the finished length of the pant. This is accomplished by merely folding up the pant hem as you cut out the lining.

Ambiance, a rayon lining by Bemberg, is by far my favorite lining for pants. Prewashed, it can be used for pants which are hand-washable or dry-cleaned.

Sew front and/or back darts in lining. Front pleats in lining are sewn half their width. Extra fullness is then eased at the waist.

At one time I used to sew pant lining seams $1/8$ inch deeper, using the principle that something which fits inside must be smaller. This method resulted in linings which pulled out the hand stitching at the zipper.

The problem lies in the fact that lining fabric has no give, while the pant fabric itself is able to give a bit as necessary to mold to the body. Further experiments have proven that pant linings accomplish the same task and are more comfortable if the seams are sewn $1/8$ inch less, using $1/2$ inch seam allowances to compensate for the lack of elasticity in the lining fabric.

Construct pant lining as you would pants. Press open seams. Trim and overlock crotch seam at $1/4$ inch. Press back seam allowance at zipper opening. Slip lining into pant before the waistband is applied. Lining is eased to fit the pant at the waist.

Using thread strengthened with beeswax, hand sew lining to zipper seam allowances. Hem pants and pant lining separately. Attach lining at hem with a hang tack on inner and outer leg seam allowance. Failure to do this will result in lining which peeks out of pant hem when you cross your legs.

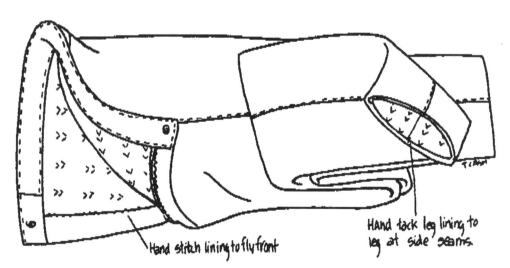

Hand stitch lining to fly front

Hand tack leg lining to leg at side seams.

■ Do your pant linings peek out at the hem when you're sitting down? The finished hem of pant linings should never be longer than the beginning of the hem allowance of the fashion fabric pant. Couture designer Tove Clausen attaches lining to pant hem with a loose tack at seams.

Demonstrated on *Power Sewing* Video #6: *Easy Linings.*

Handwoven fabric works well in simple cardigan style from a *Vogue* pattern (see page 90 for handwoven tips). To stabilize fabric for eyelets, 1 1/2 inch circles of fusible knit interfacing are fused to the wrong side of fabric at eyelet positioning. Over interfacing, 2 inch circles of Ultrasuede are glued to cover interfacing to give something extra for the eyelet to hold onto. Set islet. Braided Ultrasuede strips form drawstring.

Handwoven fabric (see page 90 for tips) when made into a bolero from a Vogue pattern takes on a whimsical touch when trimmed with Ultrasuede (see page 211) and embellished with fruit and vegetable charms found in a Guatemalan shop.

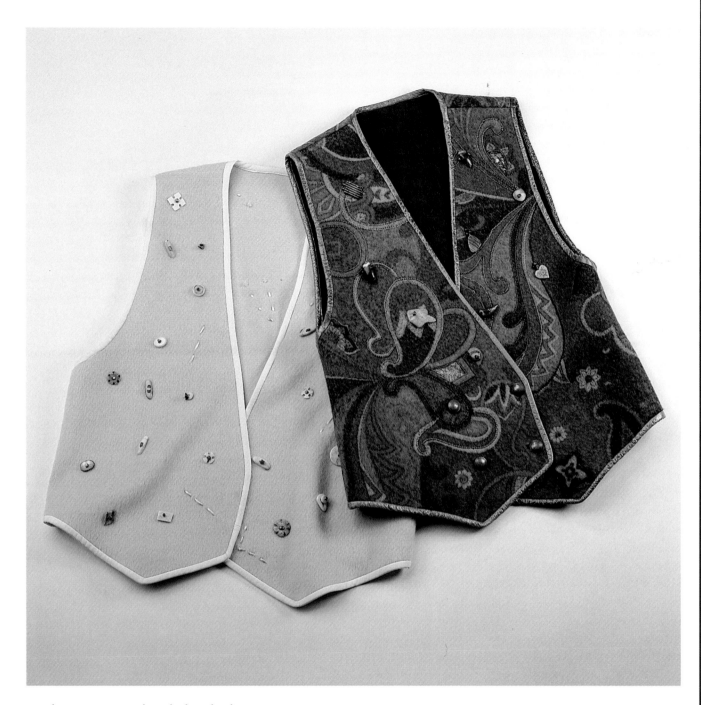

*Both vests are unlined, finished
along edges with ultraleather and
embellished with buttons and charms.
Both vests are made from a Burda man's
vest pattern. **Off white vest** is made
from a heavy camel hair fabric (see page
87 for seam treatment). **Brown paisley
vest** is made from a cashmere wool blend
using reverse applique.*

Cut on sleeve styling using a McCall's pattern eliminates matching difficulties when cutting coat from a Pendleton blanket. Coat is unlined and interfaced only in upper collar with Suit Shape. Leather trim (see page 211 for technique) is used around jacket and sleeves, eliminating facings and hems. Leather undercollar and antique oversized button draw attention to the face.

No More Smiles and Frowns on Pants

It may amuse you to think of pants smiling and frowning, but look closely at an ill-fitting pair of pants—they do just that. This can be caused by a problem in the crotch length or in the crotch depth or both.

If you are certain that your pants have enough crotch length, the fitting problem is probably one of crotch depth. Smiles on pants show in the front if the pants are too tight across the thigh. Frowns on pants in the back are caused by not having enough seat room.

To alter the pattern for full thighs, add ¼ to ½ inch to the front at the inner leg beginning at the crotch. Taper the addition to zero about 7 inches down the inner leg. If your fullness extends to the knee, do not taper to zero until 1 inch beyond the knee. This will add room for the thigh and prevent the pants from riding up while sitting or walking.

Frowns in the back of pants are caused by not having enough crotch depth or not enough sitting room.

Every woman has a different shaped derriere, so the pattern's existing crotch curve won't necessarily fit everyone. In crotch depth alterations a small addition goes a long way, so don't add too much to begin with.

For more crotch depth in back, add ¼ to ½ inch to the back piece at the inner leg beginning at the crotch. Taper the addition to zero about 7 inches down the inner leg.

Besides this crotch depth alteration, you may find it necessary to deepen the crotch curve. This gives additional sitting room and keeps the pants from riding down in the back when you sit down.

Begin deepening the crotch seam in back at the crotch and lower the crotch curve about ½ inch for about 1½ inches. Taper back to the original sewing line.

This alteration may take a bit of experimentation, but the comfort in the finished pair of pants is well worth the effort.

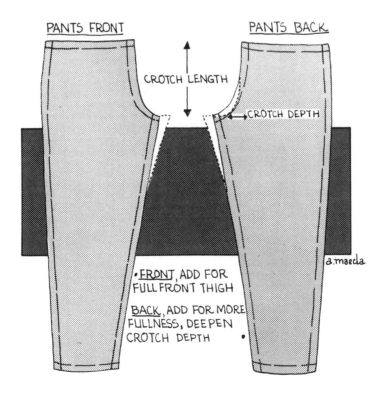

PANTS FRONT   PANTS BACK

CROTCH LENGTH

CROTCH DEPTH

• FRONT, ADD FOR FULL FRONT THIGH

BACK, ADD FOR MORE FULLNESS, DEEPEN CROTCH DEPTH

a.maeda

Small Thighs

Will we ever conquer the fitting problems of pants? Here's another problem—and its solution.

On an individual with small thighs, pants will hang in vertical wrinkles from the end of the fly front zipper. Taking in the seam at the inside of the leg does not completely take care of the problem, and taking in the crotch seam actually worsens it.

The alteration that seems to be the most effective is lifting up the center back of the pants. Pulling the pants up in front makes the problem worse, but lifting the center back $\frac{1}{2}$ to 1 inch eliminates the wrinkles.

Stand in front of a mirror and have someone pull up the pants at the center back. Watch carefully what happens to the inner leg seam and the fitting problem.

The best time to determine the exact amount to be trimmed from the waistline seam in the center back is before the waistband has been sewn on. Pin the waistband into place and keep lowering the band in the center back until the problem disappears. Taper the amount trimmed off at center back to zero by the side seams.

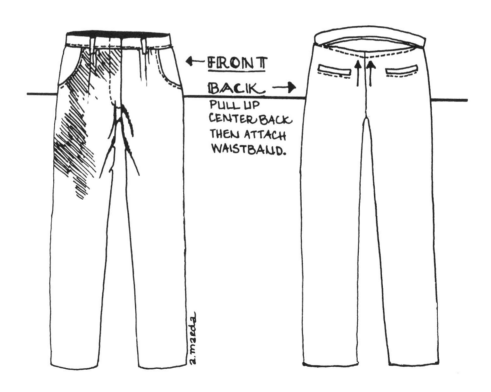

← FRONT

BACK →

PULL UP CENTER BACK THEN ATTACH WAISTBAND.

a. maeda

Altering Ready-to-Wear Pants

What is the best you can do for a pair of pants that doesn't fit?

The most common complaint is a crotch that is too short. Considerable comfort can be achieved by simply dropping the crotch curve $1/2$ to 1 inch (Illustration 1). Make this alteration only at the bottom of the curve. Resew the seam, zigzag, and cut out the excess fabric.

To correct pants with a crotch that is too long, take off the waistband, cut the excess off the top of the pants, and put the waistband on again. This may shorten the zipper a bit, but this shouldn't cause a problem.

If the pants wrinkle under the waistband in the back, the problem is caused by a sloped waistline. Determine the amount of wrinkling, $1/2$ to 1 inch. Remove the waistband from the back. Cut off the excess fabric from the top of the pants, tapering to zero by the side seam. Sew the waistband back on. If you have a bit of a potbelly, you may be able to achieve a more flattering front if the waistline seam

allowance has not been cut off. Remove the waistband at the center front and drop the center front of the pants $1/4$ inch, tapering to zero by the side seam. Resew the waistband in its new position.

To taper wide-leg pants, taper both the inner and outer legs, starting 2 inches down from the crotch (Illustration 2).

To eliminate or at least minimize a baggy seat, pinch and pin out the amount you wish to eliminate under the seat. Measure this amount; it's usually between $1/2$ and 1 inch.

Take out the stitching in the crotch seam for about 3 inches where all seams meet at the crotch point. Remove the stitching in the inner leg for 7 inches.

Working with the back leg only, trim off the amount you pinched out, tapering back to the original width 7 inches down the leg (Illustration 3).

Resew seams and you will find that the bagginess has been minimized. If you have a flat bottom, you can also take some fullness out of the crotch curve in the back only

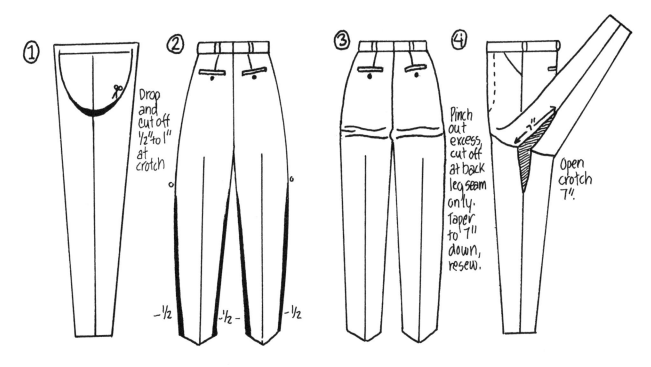

Remedy for Baggy Knees

Why do knees bag out in some pants and not in others?

For starters, the fabric may not be suitable for pants. A loose, unstable weave will lose its shape. Stretch a piece of sample fabric before you purchase it. If the fabric does not return to its original shape rapidly, it's a poor choice. Move on to another.

No matter how stable the fabric, the knees will bag out in pants if the pants are hanging off-grain. Pay particular attention to grainline when cutting.

Poor posture or swayback can also cause the pants to hang off-grain. Try lifting the pants in the center back $\frac{1}{2}$ inch. Look in the mirror. Does the seam hang straight now?

If that simple adjustment changes the hang of the pants on you, cut off $\frac{1}{2}$ inch at center back, tapering to zero at the side seams on all of your pants before putting on the waistband.

It might be a good idea to correct this on your ready-made pants too.

Lining the knees of pants can also be a great help, especially if you sit all day, putting prolonged stress in the knee area.

Simply sew in a 6-inch-wide piece of pocketing or lining fabric cut to match the shape of the front leg in the knee area.

Baste this piece at the inner leg and side seam to the front pant leg. Sew in the side seam and inner leg seam when you join the front and the back legs.

It is perfectly acceptable to let the top and bottom of the stabilizing piece hang free; you may tack it into place if you can do so invisibly.

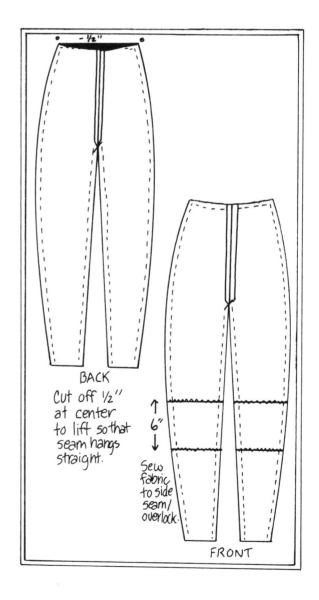

BACK
Cut off $\frac{1}{2}$'' at center to lift so that seam hangs straight.

6''
Sew fabric to side seam/overlock.

FRONT

Demonstrated on *Power Sewing* Video #4: *Foolproof Pant Fitting.*

Copying Your Favorite Pants

Copying a style from a designer is called "knocking off" in the fashion industry. Many of us would like to copy a pair of pants we already own because they fit well. Here's how:

Choose a pair of pants that are not completely stretched out of shape. A woven pair can be copied more accurately than a knit pair, but either will be successful. The technique is called "making a rubbing."

You'll need enough lightweight muslin or pattern tracing cloth—a see-through cloth with 1-inch grid, for one front and one back leg—about 1⅜ yards should be enough. Pattern tracing cloth works particularly well; since you can see through the material, making a rubbing much easier.

Find the grainline (see illustration) on the front leg of the pants by matching the inner and outer leg seams from the hemline to the knee. These seams will not match from the knee up. The fold formed in the front of the leg by matching these seams from the knee down is the front grainline. Run a line of hand-basting in contrasting thread along the grainline from the hem to the waist. Then do the same for the back grainline.

Cut the pattern tracing cloth in half lengthwise. Draw a line the entire length of the pattern tracing cloth halfway from the edge that will be matched up to the pants grainline. Be sure to leave enough room on both sides of the line to stretch to at least 1 inch past the seamlines.

Lay the line drawn on the pattern tracing cloth directly over the basting stitches, marking the front grainline on the pants leg (see illustration). Smooth the pattern tracing cloth over the leg and pin it onto the outer seamline. Keeping the pattern tracing cloth very smooth, pin it also from the crotch seam to the hem. Now do the back leg.

Place a tailor's ham under the top part of the pants and mold the pattern tracing cloth over the pants. Pin the crotchline first and then the side seam. Any excess fabric in between will be used in the dart and for ease. Pin dart in the pattern tracing cloth at the waistline. Now run pins along the waistline seam. Make sure all pins are directly on the seamlines and placed fairly close together. Mark with a pen the placement of every pin—i.e., trace the seamlines. Mark the dart at the waist. This should be close to the size and placement of the dart on the original pants. Mark the hemline.

Unpin the pattern tracing cloth and connect all marked lines.

Smooth out any jags in the lines. Add 1-inch seam allowances all around and use this as your pants pattern. Make a trial pair to work out any corrections.

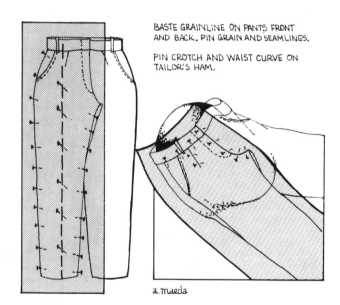

BASTE GRAINLINE ON PANTS FRONT AND BACK. PIN GRAIN AND SEAMLINES.

PIN CROTCH AND WAIST CURVE ON TAILOR'S HAM.

a. maeda

Fast Pants Construction

Making a lined pair of pants can be a simple two-hour task. Cut lining and pants exactly the same size, leaving a 1-inch seam allowance at the side seams for flexibility (Illustration 1).

If you are planning to use a fly front, add a $1\frac{3}{8}$-inch extension at center front for 9 inches. Use press-on interfacing behind extension and fly will not wrinkle later.

Start by putting in the fly. Then sew in the darts or pleats. Taking each leg separately, sew the inner leg and outer leg seams.

Turn one leg right side out. Insert this one into the other leg (Illustration 2). This makes sewing the crotch seam easier. Use small reinforcing stitches between the notches. Trim seam to $\frac{1}{4}$ inch.

Pin on waistband and try on the pants for fit (Illustration 3). Unpin the waistband. Sew the side seams permanently.

Construct lining the same way you did the pants, leaving an opening for the fly and sewing the side seams $\frac{1}{8}$ inch deeper. This allows for the fact that the lining will be on the inside.

With wrong sides together, slip the lining inside the pants. Attach the lining to the pants at the crotch, fly, and waist. Sew waistband on.

Determine the finished length of the pants by comparing them with a finished pair at the side seam or by trying them on. In order to get the pants long enough to cover the shoe in back without breaking in front, the pants must be $\frac{1}{2}$ to 1 inch longer in back.

For pants to hang properly, the lining and pants should be hemmed separately. Cut 1 inch off the bottom of the pants lining. Run an easeline around the lower pants edges to eliminate excess fullness. Finish raw edges with a zigzag or overlock stitch. Use a tailor's hem, but knot the thread every four stitches to keep the hem from pulling out easily.

Attach the pants and the lining to each other at the inner and outer leg at the bottom with a loose catchstitch as you would for a loose lining in a coat.

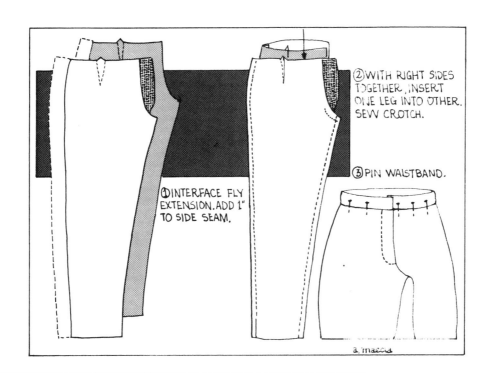

① INTERFACE FLY EXTENSION. ADD 1" TO SIDE SEAM.

② WITH RIGHT SIDES TOGETHER, INSERT ONE LEG INTO OTHER. SEW CROTCH.

③ PIN WAISTBAND.

Planning Your Leather Pants Projects

Leather continues to be a fashion headliner—especially leather pants. If ready-made pants don't fit you or you can't afford the quality leather pants you'd like, perhaps you are toying with the idea of making your own.

Even experienced sewers are intimidated by leather, for two reasons: Leather is not purchased by the yard, but in odd-shaped skins rarely large enough to accommodate the whole pattern piece, and the expense of the skins (at least $100 for pants) makes experimentation out of the question.

Do you dare tackle such a project? Perhaps I can eliminate some of the risks so you'll get results that will make you want to make another pair immediately.

Get the pattern right before you begin. Altering seams in leather often leaves permanent holes. Make up a pair of pants in corduroy, which will approximate the bulk of leather. This will give you an idea of the finished garment. Any altering or tapering of the leg should be noted on the pattern.

Since most skins are not large enough to accommodate the length of the whole leg, piecing will be necessary. A seam at the knee makes the pants hold their shape better.

Measure the distance from the finished hem to the knee at the side seam. This will probably be 13 to 15 inches. Measuring up from the bottom of the pants, mark a point at the inner and outer leg of the pants the same number of inches from the bottom. Draw a line between these points. This line may not be exactly perpendicular to the grainline. The discrepancy is caused by differing shapes on the inner and outer leg. Follow the above instructions and your seamlines will match up in construction. Make an X on either side of the line to remind yourself to add seam allowances when you cut out.

Write "back" and "front" below the line so you know which piece to join to which after it is cut out. Cut the pattern apart at this line.

Put all pieces concerning the pants in an envelope and take it all to the leather store. You can actually lay the pieces out to find out how much you need.

A pair of pants usually calls for about 30 square feet. If you have too much, you can always make a belt or purse. Better to spend $20 more than to end up with Bermudas.

Choice of leather: Do not choose leather that is too heavy unless you have access to an industrial sewing machine. Most home machines handle lamb suedes, chamois, and cabretta quite well. To go heavier, you are asking for problems.

If you are in doubt, purchase a few scraps of the weight you have in mind and try to sew through at least three thicknesses. Any problem will quickly manifest itself.

LEATHER

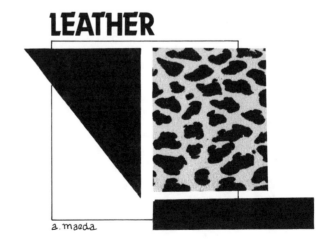

a. maeda

Leather Pants Construction

Since pinning the pattern to the skins puts holes in the leather and tears the pattern tissue, use of pattern weights is preferable. I like to use Weight Mates®. Cans or rocks can also be used. Place the skins carefully to avoid flaws or discolorations in the leather. Cut with sharp scissors. Mark all pattern pieces on the wrong side with chalk or colored wax. Do not use a tracing wheel as this will put holes in the leather.

Sometimes it is possible to pin suede skins, much as you would fabric, but leather is usually too tough and will bend the pins. I have had great success holding the seams in place with small clothespins, clips, or even Scotch tape (Illustration 1).

Join the lower leg to the upper leg for your first seam and then construction is identical to that of your pretested pants. For easy sewing, an even feed foot is a must. You can sew leather without it, but the even feed foot keeps the top piece in alignment with the underside effortlessly. A Teflon® foot is also effective for controlling creeping.

Machine leather needles are a must—size 14 or 16. If you do not use a leather needle, the thread will break continually. Cotton or polyester thread will work equally well. A medium-length stitch will give you the most even stitching.

After you have sewn the seam, press the leather or suede seam open on the wrong side with a dry iron at the wool setting. After the seam has been pressed open, run a bead of Soloman's SOBO glue behind the seam allowances (Illustration 2). Finger-press the seam flat. Topstitch the seam allowances flat from the right side.

Use interfacing on leather and suede in the same manner you would for any garment. In the case of pants, interface behind the zipper placket. Use stay-tape to reinforce pockets and keep them from bulging (Illustration 3). A waistband in leather or suede has a tendency to stretch, but the use of Armo's Easy Shaper® or Stacy's Waist Shaper® solves the problem. Not only is the waistband a nice firm one that will not roll, but bulk is eliminated.

Hems are usually glued into place. Any hand sewing will need to be done with a glover's needle, which is a special hand sewing needle for leather.

Don't be intimidated by leather or suede. My first garments looked great. Yours will, too.

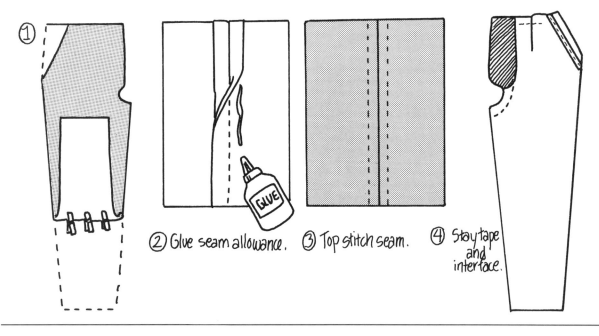

① ② Glue seam allowance. ③ Top stitch seam. ④ Stay tape and interface.

High Waist Extension

High waisted pants and skirts can give one the illusion of longer legs, help balance a long-waisted figure or simply be style of choice. To fit properly, each high-waisted pattern must be fit to the body; therefore allow one inch seam allowances on side seams when cutting out.

Before fitting, pin pants to twill tape along the actual waistline as indicated on the pattern. Because you are using a high-waisted style, the position of the twill tape will not be at the top of the pants but at the actual waistline. Pin-fit pants at the side seam to mimic your body at the hip, waistline, and midriff. If your high hip or tummy measurement is larger than your actual hip measurement, the pants may be more flattering if they actually hang from the tummy, not from the hip.

After side seam adjustments have been made on the pants, make identical adjustments on the facing. Stabilize the facing with a medium-weight interfacing. Trim seam allowances on facing to 1/4 inch. Clean finish the bottom edge of the facing with an overlock or Hong Kong finish.

With right sides together, seam top edge of pants and facing together. Grade and trim seam to 1/4 inch. Reduce bulk by understitching seam, attaching seam allowance to facing, 1/8 inch away from original seam.

Boning is necessary to retain the shape of the high waist and prevent the extension from wrinkling and rolling over when you sit. Rigilene, see-through polyester boning, is the boning product most comfortable to wear. Purchase boning in 1/4 inch width if possible; 1/2 inch width will also work. Boning is positioned at center front and side seams on the wrong side of the facing.

Cut boning lengths the width of the facing from the waistline seam to 1/2 inch shorter than bottom of the facing. On the facing, position the boning between the seam allowance and the facing, sliding one end of the boning under the seam allowance at the top of the pants. Since the ends of boning are sharp, sear ends of boning with a match; then cover ends of boning with ribbon or a fabric patch. The first time you wear a garment with boning, you will be glad you padded the ends.

Overcast baste or scotch tape the boning into position on the wrong side of the facing. Machine sew boning into position by stitching in the well of the seam through the facing and the boning strip. Strips of boning are sewn at side seams and center front.

Anchor facing to garment at center front and side seams with a 1/4 inch swing tack, a crocheted 1/4 inch thread extension.

Hand-baste facing and high waist seam together with silk thread. Press and pound flat.

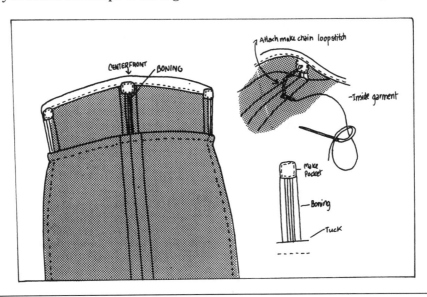

Waistbands That Fit

Is the fit of your waistbands on skirts and pants still a gamble? Are some too tight and some too loose? The excuse of weight fluctuation has some validity, but not much. The real problem is that every waistband is a trial and error proposition. It need not be.

Measure your waist with a tape measure—honestly, for once. Don't look at the numbers until the tape feels comfortable. To this measurement, add 1 inch. This inch will be needed for ease and bulk taken up by darts and seams. (If you make the band without ease, it will be too tight.)

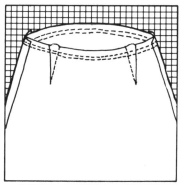

EASELINE ACROSS WAIST.

If you have a waistband that fits well, measure this band from zipper teeth to zipper teeth or button to buttonhole.

Cut a waistband and two lengths of interfacing 4½ inches wide and the length of your waist measurement plus 1-inch ease plus 3½ inches for any overlap. Notch the waistband 1¾ inches from either end. Your skirt or pants must now fit between the notches (Illustration 1, page 171).

The waistline of the skirt or pants will always measure at least an inch bigger than the notched waistband to allow for ease over the tummy. If you have a little pot belly, you might let out the side seams so that the waistline is 1½ to 2 inches bigger than the waistband.

Do not confuse this stomach ease with the actual waistband ease of 1 inch previously mentioned. The eases are two separate entities. If you measured your skirt without band from zipper teeth to zipper teeth, it should measure 2 inches bigger than your waist measurement, 1 inch for bulk of waistband and 1 inch to ride gracefully over the stomach.

If either of these eases is eliminated, the skirt will ride up and form little folds under the waistband. Sound familiar? Now how do you get the larger skirt or pants eased so that they fit between the notches you marked on your waistband?

Run an easeline ½ inch from the cut edge all around the waistline. Fit skirt or pants onto the waistband between the notches. If the garment is big, run another easeline near the first. Try again for fit. If the garment is too small, pull out a little of the ease.

If the waistline of the skirt or pants is still too big to fit between the notches, you might take in the side seams a little or fatten up a few darts.

If the waistline of the skirt or pants seems too small or doesn't need an easeline to match the band between the notches, do the reverse. Reduce the side seams a little or slim down a few darts. Remember, the garment should be 1 inch larger than the waistband between the notches.

After the garment fits between the notches, steam press the easeline to achieve a flat appearance with invisible ease.

After you have completed the skirt and are pleased with the fit of the band, keep the extra length of interfacing with the cut notches as a permanent waistband pattern.

Since the front half of the body is ½ inch larger than the back, do not divide the band in equal quarters for application. Use ½ inch more of the band for the skirt or pants front than for the back.

When the skirt fits the band, pin the waistband to the skirt with the right side of band against the wrong side of the skirt, matching the zipper teeth with the notches. Sew a ⅝-inch seam (Illustration 2).

Finish the ends of the band by turning in ⅝ inch on each lengthwise edge and sewing vertically with right sides together. Sew two threads past garment on band to give the band room to turn. Make underlap one inch longer to allow for a button or hook and eye (Illustration 3).

Waistbands That Fit

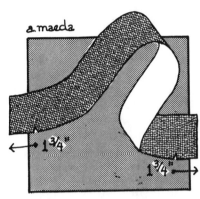

a.maeda

1¾"   1¾"

① LENGTH-YOUR WAIST MEASUREMENT PLUS 4 1/2." WIDTH-DESIRED WIDTH PLUS 5/8", DOUBLED.

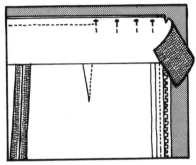

② MATCH NOTCH TO ZIPPER, SEW 5/8" SEAM TO JOIN WAISTBAND.

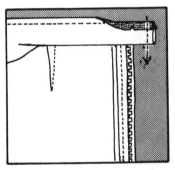

③ TURN SEAM EDGES DOWN AND SEW 5/8" AT END.

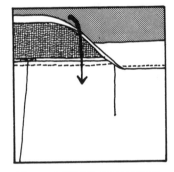

④ TURN OTHER RAW EDGE 5/8", FOLD WAISTBAND OVER AND TOPSTITCH (RIGHT SIDE).

Trim seam allowances to ¼ inch. Turn waist-band right side out, turn under ⅝ inch on front edge and topstitch into place (Illustration 4). If your fabric is very heavy, cut waistband 3⅞ inches wide with one long side along the selvage. Apply the right side of the band against the right side of the garment. Do not turn under ⅝ inch seam allowance along selvage. Handstitch selvage to underside at waistline seam. This method eliminates bulk.

■ When cutting out the pattern, cut off the thick black cutting line entirely. Most people cut on the outside of the black line, which accounts for the common complaint that the pattern measurements are off.

Contoured Waistband

Most waistbands are sewn to the pants or skirt at the waistline and extend an inch or two above it.

Many women, however, look better in skirts and pants that have a contoured waistband, one that is sewn to the pants or skirt at the high hipline and that ends where the waistline starts. This waistband is especially flattering on short-waisted women because it gives a longer line from shoulder to waist.

To make the pattern for a contoured waistband, use the front and back skirt or pants pattern pieces. Using a yardstick, extend the grainline to the top of the pattern, including the seam allowance.

Measure $1\frac{1}{2}$ inches down from the waist seamline (not the cutting line) and draw a line across the pattern. This is called the style line. It will have a slight curve, like the seamline.

Mark an X on either side of the style line to remind yourself to add a $\frac{5}{8}$-inch seam allowance on both sides of the style line (Illustration 1).

Cut the pattern along the style line. Bring dart lines on waistband together and pin or tape them.

This will give the piece a sharper curve.

Forget about the remaining dart in the pants or skirt pattern; simply take in $\frac{1}{8}$ inch from the top of the side seams (Illustration 2). You will ease the skirt to the contoured band.

To ensure that the contoured band fits smoothly, cut it on the bias. Don't forget to interface the band pieces. Remember to cut the waistband's interfacing on the bias, too.

Now that you have your front and back waistband pattern pieces, you are ready to cut them out of your fabric. You will need four fronts and four backs, since this waistband is faced for a smooth finish.

Be sure you have added a $\frac{5}{8}$-inch seam allowance to both the lower edge of the waistband and top of front and back skirt (or pants) pattern pieces (Illustration 2).

If your pants or skirt has a front zipper closing, extend the left front waistband pieces $1\frac{1}{2}$ inches for a lapped closing.

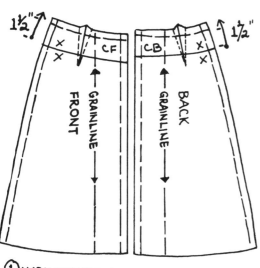

① MARK STYLELINE $1\frac{1}{2}$" FROM WAIST SEAM. INDICATE CENTER SEAM, AT WAIST.

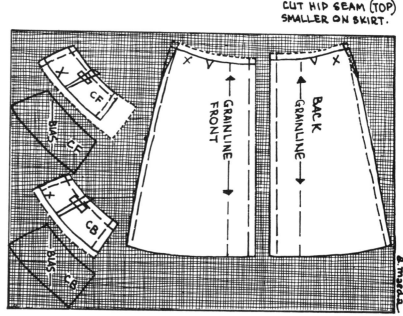

② CLOSE DARTS ON WAISTBAND. CUT HIP SEAM (TOP) SMALLER ON SKIRT.

172

Pockets

Add a Pocket in a Side Seam

It's an easy matter to add a pocket to any skirt or dress by slipping a small, teardrop-shaped one into the side seam.

Begin by cutting out four teardrop shapes approximately 6 inches wide and 8 inches long. If garment fabric is heavy, cut pocket pieces out of lining-weight fabric.

These pockets are usually most comfortable for use 4 to 6 inches down from the waist, but you can raise or lower them to suit yourself. Place one pocket piece against skirt front, with wide part of the teardrop down, right sides together and the straight edge of the pocket against side seam allowance (Illustration 1). Stitch together with a ¼-inch seam. Repeat with pocket back and skirt back. Press seams open. Understitch seam allowances to pocket if fabric is heavy (Illustration 2).

Place front and back skirt pieces with right sides together. Sew side seam of garment, sewing up 1½ inches from bottom of pocket, continuing along pocket seam and sewing down 1½ inches from top of pocket (Illustration 3). This will help keep pocket inside garment.

Press skirt seam open and press pocket to front of garment. Clip back seam allowance at top and bottom of pocket to permit pocket to lie flat.

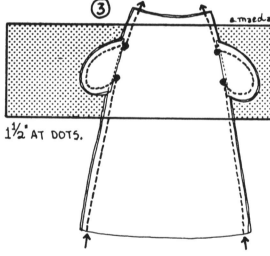

③

a.maeda

1½" AT DOTS.

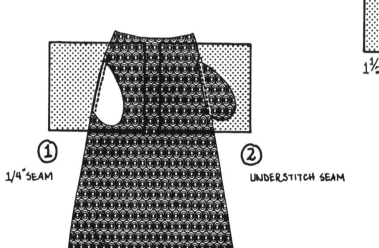

①
1/4" SEAM

②
UNDERSTITCH SEAM

■ Directional stitching is important because it keeps the fabric from stretching as you sew. If you always sew a skirt from the bottom of the garment toward the top, you will find that you will not have to cut off that extra ½ inch or so at the bottom.

Patch Pockets

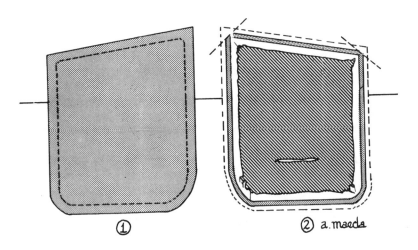

① ② a. maeda

Patch pockets show up everywhere: on shirts, loose jackets, pants. Why not learn a technique to simplify the process? The difficulty with the patch pocket technique as described in the pattern instructions comes in trying to make two pockets that look identical. After the top hem of the pocket has been sewn down, the instructions call for you to press in a $5/8$-inch seam allowance on the remaining raw edges. This may sound easy enough, but pressing an exact $5/8$-inch seam allowance on a rounded corner quickly poses difficulties. Try this technique for a fast foolproof solution to the problem.

Cut two pocket shapes for every one pocket. If the garment fabric is mid-weight or heavier, use a lighter weight fabric for the underpocket. Cut the top piece on the grainline indicated on the pattern piece. Cut the underpocket piece on the bias. Trim $1/16$ inch off of all edges on the underpocket. Placing right sides together, pin upper and underpocket together, stretching the bias underpocket a bit so that all raw edges match up. Sew the pocket all the way around $5/8$ inch from the raw edge using small machine stitches. Don't forget to hand-walk the machine two stitches diagonally at the corner so that the points will have a place to turn (Illustration 1). Press seam open by pressing one seam allowance back against the pocket. Trim seam allowances at corners diagonally within one stitch of the hand-walked stitches. Trim remaining seam to $1/4$ inch.

Make a small 2-inch slash on the bias under pocket (Illustration 2). This slash will enable you to turn the pocket right side out. Use a point turner on corners rather than risking a hole poked through with scissors. With the outer pocket facing you, press and pound pocket with a tailor's clapper. To close up the slash on the underpocket, slip in a small strip of press-on interfacing behind the slash against the wrong side of the pocket. Press. If you do not want to use press-on interfacing, simply close the slash with a loose hand stitch.

■ Hold patch pockets in place with stick-style glue as you topstitch into position.

Invisibly Stitched Patch Pocket

A lined patch pocket is often used on coats and better dresses since no stitching shows on the outside of the pocket. One might think that the pocket had been attached with an invisible hand stitch, but that alone would not be strong enough if the pocket were actually going to be used.

To make a lined patch pocket, first cut two pockets exactly the same size, one from the fabric and one from the lining. Cut 1 inch off the top portion of the lining pocket only. Placing the right sides of the pockets together, run a 1/4-inch seam along the top edge. Press this seam open and then press the pockets with wrong sides together.

A fold will form along the top edge of the pocket, keeping the lining hidden. Make a snip at the foldline on each side of the top edge. Starting at the snip and sewing in the direction of the lining, staystitch from snip to snip around the lining at 5/8 inch. Continue the stitching at the snip onto the fabric pocket but sew at 1/2 inch.

To attach the pocket to the garment, place the right side of the lining pocket against the right side of the garment. Starting at the snip or fold at the top of the pocket, sew reinforcing stitches (18-20 per inch) from snip to snip through the pocket lining and the garment.

Press the seam allowance in toward the pocket. Bring the fabric pocket down over the lining pocket, folding in the 1/2-inch seam allowance shown by the original staystitching line. The fabric pocket will completely cover the lining. Attach the fabric pocket with an invisible hand stitch. No stitching will show, but the pocket is very strong because its lining is attached to the garment with reinforcing stitches.

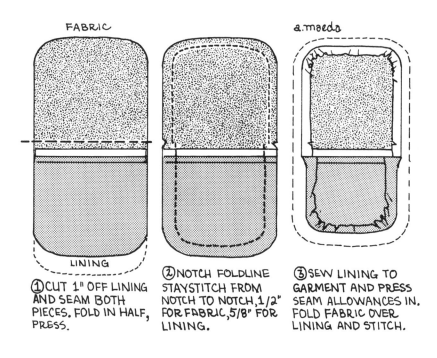

FABRIC

a. maeda

LINING

① CUT 1" OFF LINING AND SEAM BOTH PIECES. FOLD IN HALF, PRESS.

② NOTCH FOLDLINE STAYSTITCH FROM NOTCH TO NOTCH, 1/2" FOR FABRIC, 5/8" FOR LINING.

③ SEW LINING TO GARMENT AND PRESS SEAM ALLOWANCES IN. FOLD FABRIC OVER LINING AND STITCH.

Hip Pockets That Lie Flat

After taking special care to construct perfect pockets in a skirt or pants, it is disappointing to have them gap open. The solution is this construction technique.

Cut a piece of stay tape or narrow selvage the length of the seam that attaches the pocket facing to the skirt or pants front. Place the pocket facing and garment right sides together. Pin stay tape into place. Sew over stay tape as you sew seam at ⅝ inch (Illustration 1). Trim seam to ¼ inch. Pull trimmed seam toward pocket facing and understitch seam ⅛ inch from sewn seam on the pocket facing (Illustration 2). Fold pocket facing into finished position. Steam press and pound with a tailor's clapper.

Pin side front back pocket piece into place by matching notches at outer pocket edge. Sew with a ⅝-inch seam. Pin finished pocket into place at waist; baste.

Now for the trick for eliminating pocket gap: Before sewing pocket into place at the side seam, place garment with pocket inserted over a tailor's ham. The tailor's ham will simulate how the pocket will fit over the body. Smooth your hand over the pocket surface allowing excess fabric to roll out at the side seam. You may find that the seam allowances in this area vary ⅛ inch to ¼ inch depending on the fabric (Illustration 3).

This difference is what causes the pocket gap on the body. Pin the pocket into place at the side seam before moving it off the tailor's ham. Baste into place. Proceed with garment construction.

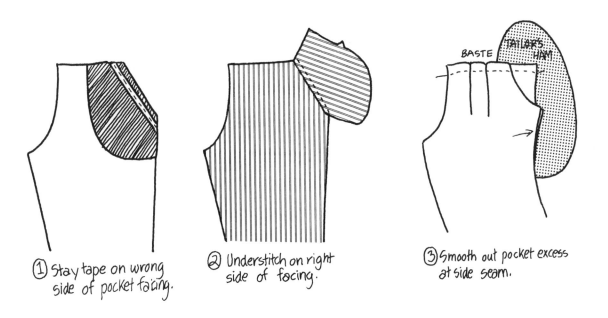

① Stay tape on wrong side of pocket facing.

② Understitch on right side of facing.

③ Smooth out pocket excess at side seam.

Demonstrated on *Power Sewing* Video #4: *Foolproof Pant Fitting.*

Drawstring Pockets

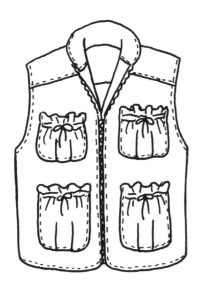

A great deal of sportswear has been inspired by army fatigues. These garments are not only distinguished by fabric, but by pocket style. My favorite is placed very low on the hip wrapping around the side seam attached to a loose vest or jacket or pants.

For each pocket, cut a piece of fabric 12 inches wide by 14 inches long. Fold down a 2-inch hem along one 14-inch length. Press (Illustration 1). With the right side of the pocket facing you, measure the center of a 14-inch long piece and make a marking for two $\frac{1}{2}$-inch buttonholes 1 inch apart, $\frac{1}{2}$ inch from the top fold. Use a small piece of interfacing behind these buttonhole markings. Through one fabric thickness and the interfacing, keeping pocket hem free, sew two buttonholes (Illustration 2). They should be 1 inch apart in the center of the pocket and $\frac{1}{2}$ inch below foldline at top of pocket. Cut open buttonholes.

Fold the previously pressed 2-inch hem toward the wrong side of the pocket. Turn under a $\frac{1}{2}$ inch raw edge and pin finished hem into place. Machine-or hand-sew. Parallel with this line of stitching and, directly above and below buttonholes, sew two parallel lines of stitching that will form channels for a drawstring with the pocket and the pocket hem.

Cut two pieces of drawstring 12 inches long. Starting at the side of the pocket, insert one drawstring at each end through the channels. Bring each drawstring out at corresponding buttonholes (Illustration 3). Anchor opposite ends of drawstring at the pocket sides with a machine stitch.

Fold under $\frac{5}{8}$-inch seam allowances at the sides and bottom of pocket. Hand-baste and press into place. Fold in a 2-inch inverted pleat at the bottom of pocket. Baste into place. Place pocket over side seam and make sides of pocket parallel to the side seam. Sew sides and bottom of pocket into place. Pull up drawstring and tie into place. Trim off drawstring to desired length.

The size and fullness of this pocket can be altered to suit your taste. The pocket does not need to be cut in a perfect rectangle. The top edge of the pocket could be cut much wider to allow for more fullness when the drawstring is pulled.

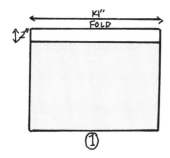
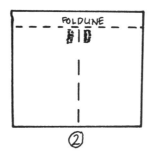
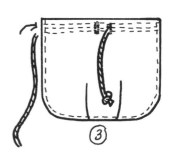

Free Floating Pockets

If I had to choose one word that distinguishes sports-wear, the word is pockets. Pockets are bigger in size and more visible than ever. Although the pattern companies do feature some great skirts, the absence of the newer-looking pockets is definitely noticeable. On a recent trip to New York, I saw two particularly good pockets that were free-floating. These can be attached to either skirts or pants.

The first pocket is totally self-contained and but-toned onto the skirt with three buttons at the waist-band. For each pocket, cut a piece of fabric 19 x 12 inches. On each short end, fold under 1½ inches and press. Fold under ¼-inch raw edge and pin into place. Topstitch these hems at the tops of the pocket into place. Placing right sides together, sew seams in sides of pocket.

Press seam open. Trim. Turn pocket right side out. Press and pound with a tailor's clapper. Sew three buttonholes in evenly spaced intervals through all thicknesses at top of pocket (Illustration 1). Sew three buttons on the waistband with the middle button positioned at the side seam. Space buttons a little bit closer (about ½ inch) than buttonholes. This spac-ing allows for some play so that pockets do not pull at the hip. Button pocket onto skirt. This same pocket idea in a smaller size would be great on a shirt or jacket as breast pockets.

The second interesting pocket is also free-floating, except for an attachment at the side seam. Cut a piece of fabric 22 x 14 inches. Turn down a 2-inch hem along the one length of 22 inches. Press in place. Turn under a ½-inch raw edge to form a finished edge for hem and top-stitch into place. Fold the 22 inches in half with right sides together. Sew seam in bottom of the pocket (Illustration 2). Press. Trim. Turn pocket right side out.

Press and pound with a tailor's clapper. Starting 2 inches from the waist, insert the raw edges on the side of the pocket into the side seam. Pin into place. Sew side seam. The front edge near the fold and top of the pocket is then secured in one of two ways—with a buttonhole and button as described above or with a tie—one end attached to the top of the pocket, the other end secured at the waistband. The two ties then tie together.

You might make up these pockets in scrap fabric and try them on your pants and skirts. Sizes can be varied to suit personal taste.

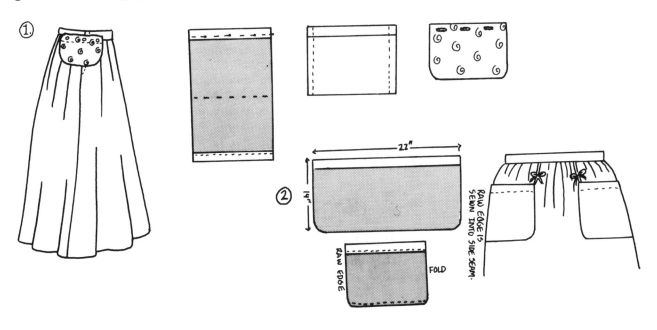

Buttonhole Welt Pocket

Making a welt pocket will remind you of making a giant bound buttonhole. The technique is similar. The traditional welt pocket has one large welt. The buttonhole pocket is similar with two small welts instead. For a pocket 5 inches long with two $\frac{1}{4}$-inch welts, follow these instructions.

Cut two crosswise strips of fabric exactly $1\frac{1}{8}$ inches wide and $6\frac{1}{2}$ inches long (Illustration 1). Mark location of pocket using tailor's tacks. Mark ends accurately; placement line is 5 inches long.

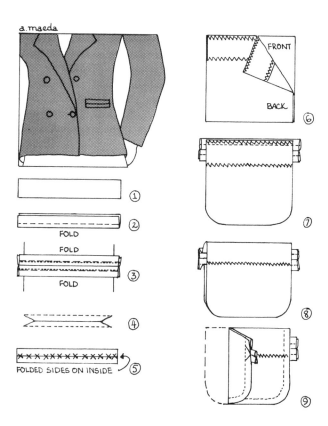

Cut out a piece of fusible interfacing 6 inches long and $1\frac{1}{2}$ inches wide. Fuse on wrong side of fabric behind pocket placement line. If you are interfacing with hair canvas, do not make pocket through hair canvas.

Press crosswise strips in both directions and then fold in half lengthwise and press again with plenty of steam. Stretch strips in both directions while pressing to prevent further stretching from wear. Machine-baste strips $\frac{1}{4}$ inch from fold (Illustration 2). Be accurate. This becomes your sewing guide.

On the right side of the garment, place the raw lengthwise edges of strips against the pocket placement line. The folded edge of strip is away from marking line. Pin. Using previously sewn basting line as a guide, sew strips into place, ending exactly at end pocket placement marks. Sew with small reinforcing stitches. Check to make sure stitch ends line up precisely (Illustration 3).

On the wrong side of garment, cut a slit at placement line, going into triangles in corners. Clip within one stitch of corner (Illustration 4). Do not clip welt. Turn welts to inside. Hand-baste folded lengthwise edges of welt together (Illustration 5).

Cut two strips of lining fabric 6 inches by $6\frac{1}{2}$ inches and one strip of garment fabric 2 inches by $6\frac{1}{2}$ inches. Place strip at top of one pocket piece, lining up three raw edges. Zigzag into place (Illustration 6). This is the back of the pocket. Sew the right side of the back of pocket, the side with fashion fabric attached, to top welt (Illustration 7). Sew front pocket to bottom welt. Fold pocket back up to form pleat that covers welt (Illustration 8).

Attach cut triangles and welt ends to pocketing fabric. Close bottom of pocket (Illustration 9).

Press with steam and pound with a tailor's clapper. Allow to dry. Remove basting.

Welt Pocket
With Flap

■ One of the features of expensive coats is a deeper pocket. Whenever possible, deepen pockets 1 to 2 inches. Substitute pocketing fabric or preshrunk flannelette in pocket interiors. Pockets are much stronger and cosier to put your hands into.

Welt Pocket With Flap

A welt pocket with flap is featured on many of the better ready-to-wear blazers today and can be quite an accent if the garment is a solid color.

Cut four flap pieces 6¼ inches long and 3¼ inches wide. Interface flaps. Seam three edges with a ⅝-inch seam (Illustration I). Press seam open. Trim off corners. Turn right side out. Press and pound with the tailor's clapper.

Machine-baste a 2-inch by 6-inch strip of interfacing behind pocket placement lines, following the placement lines for flap pocket. Use contrasting thread. End-marking lines should be 5¼ inches apart, ¼ inch wider than the flap itself.

Cut a strip 1¼ inches wide and 12 inches long for each pocket. This will form the welt. Fold strip in half lengthwise and sew a line of regular length machine stitching ¼ inch from the folded edge. Trim off one half of the lengthwise strip so that the newly cut edge is the same distance away from the stitching as the fold (Illustration 2). Cut strip into 6-inch strips.

Place the two strips so that the newly cut edges butt each other on the placement lines. One half inch of excess strip will extend beyond the end placement lines. Sew over the original line of stitching on the two strips, stopping the stitching at the end placement lines. Use small reinforcing stitches.

Lay the flap over the top strip, placing the right side of the jacket and flap against each other. The raw edge of the flap is lying along the placement line (Illustration 3). Pin in place. Turn the garment to the wrong side and sew over the original top line of stitching.

Remove placement basting and slash an X-shaped opening as you would for a bound buttonhole (Illustration 4). Turn all raw edges inside, leaving the flap hanging in its final position on the outside. Hand-baste the pocket closed. Stitch the ends of the triangles onto the ends of the welts.

Cut a piece of fabric 6¼ inches by 11 inches. Cut in half. These two pieces will be used to complete the pocket. Placing the short edges of the lining against the raw edges of the welts with right sides together,

sew the lining to the welts, one piece to the top welt and one to the bottom welt, with a small seam allowance (Illustration 5). Close the sides and bottom of the pocket. Don't worry if pocket lengths do not match. Trim off excess after sewing.

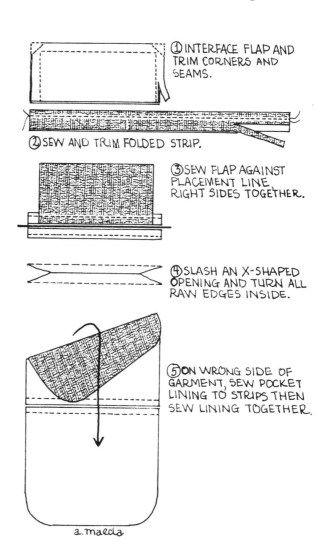

① INTERFACE FLAP AND TRIM CORNERS AND SEAMS.

② SEW AND TRIM FOLDED STRIP.

③ SEW FLAP AGAINST PLACEMENT LINE, RIGHT SIDES TOGETHER.

④ SLASH AN X-SHAPED OPENING AND TURN ALL RAW EDGES INSIDE.

⑤ ON WRONG SIDE OF GARMENT, SEW POCKET LINING TO STRIPS THEN SEW LINING TOGETHER.

a. maeda

TRICKS OF THE TRADE

■ To eliminate stretching when sewing on pre-pleated fabric, push pleats gently into the needle.

■ Do your garments hang shorter in seamed areas? In drapey fabrics, use a small zigzag (narrow width, .5mm) and a regular stitch length. The slight zigzag will allow the seam to relax as it is pressed, eliminating the thread draw-up you get with a straight stitch.

■ "Gather potential clothes in the front of your closet or on a separate rack. Think of assembling outfits from `head to toe,' including accessories. Before you sew or purchase another garment, develop a plan to give you the clothes you need. Start with a group of garments in one color family: pants, skirt, jacket, blouse, dress. Matching shades in the same general color family add up to a look that can be pulled apart to make other looks. Limit colors to a maximum of two; each should stand on its own or mix with the other."

—Andrea Geisreiter and Joan Jensen,
Travel Handbook

Design Detail Inspiration

One way to eliminate the homemade look in your sportswear is to apply some of the detailing found in the expensive ready-to-wear lines.

Pattern companies provide us with good shapes, but they are often found lacking when it comes down to details. Here are some clever details that will give your sportswear a distinctive touch.

If you find the pants legs too full and continued tapering does not solve the problem, consider pinch pleats at the bottom of the pants at the side seam. Think about using two or three inverted pleats of an inch or so that come together on the side seam.

Topstitch the pleats into place for 2 inches. This detail was used by Soprani on men's trousers (Illustration 1).

The waistline on pants is always a focal point. How about trying something new on the waistband? Taper off the top corners of the ends of the waistband. This detail was shown on high-waisted pants by Baldassari (Illustration 2).

How about extending the length of the waistband and fastening with an interesting buckle (Illustration 3)?

Instead of normal belt loops, try the triangle-shaped

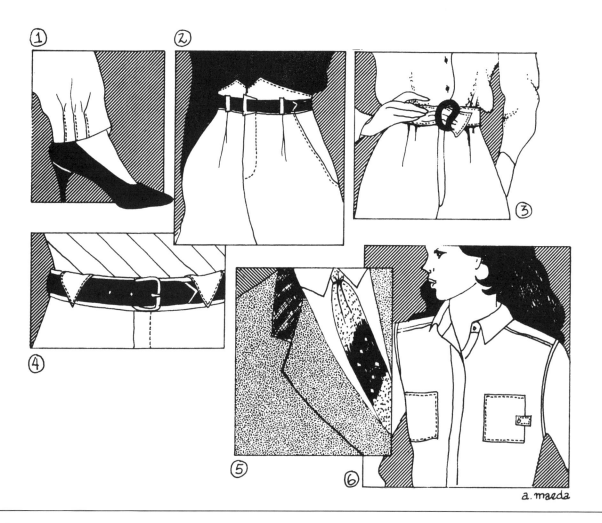

a. maeda

Design Detail Inspiration

belt loops used by Gianni Versace (Illustration 4). For the tailored jacket, soften the look with an upper collar in leather or suede. This detailing is used on jackets by Touché (Illustration 5).

From the same designer, how about leather button tabs on a tweed jacket? Combine these with rectangular suede or leather elbow patches used by Uoms.

One of the details that distinguishes the woman's tailored blouse from a man's shirt is the breast pockets. Far more attention is given to these pockets than a mere patch pocket. Try this trick—turn the pocket sideways and use a tab with a buttonhole for a closing (Illustration 6).

Recently I saw two details on a shirt well worth passing on: The shirt featured a wonderful free-floating pocket as well as an added panel attached at the yoke in back.

To make the back detail, cut two strips 11 inches wide and the length of the back from yoke to hem plus $2\frac{1}{2}$ inches. Placing right sides together, sew three sides leaving one small end open. Trim, turn, and press well.

Center this panel at center back. Insert raw edges of panel between the bodice back and yoke seam.

After hemming the back of the shirt with a $\frac{1}{2}$-inch hem, top-stitch the bottom of the panel into lace, matching lower edges.

Since the added panel has been cut a little longer, the panel will sit away from the jacket a little, giving a nice detail. You may vary the length depending on fabric and personal taste.

This pocket is a great one if you like welt pockets. This welt construction also allows for mistakes, since it's done on a separate piece that will be added to the bodice.

Cut two fabric pieces $7\frac{1}{2}$ inches wide by $8\frac{1}{2}$ inches long. Insert a $4\frac{1}{2}$ inch welt, in one piece, 2 inches from the top, centered. Pound and press with a tailor's clapper.

Place the two cut pieces' right sides together. Sew all around the rectangle. Trim seam allowances.

Turn pocket right side out through welt. Press and pound with a clapper.

Try on shirt. Move pocket around until it looks good on you. Topstitch onto shirt $\frac{1}{8}$ inch from the very top of the finished pocket and let pocket hang free or topstitch entire piece onto the blouse.

Whenever you shop, always keep a little notebook handy to jot down a note or sketch a detail that can be incorporated into a later garment.

■ Always carry a 6-inch ruler with you when you shop. Use it to measure details from ready-to-wear—cuffs, collars, belts—that can be incorporated into your sewn garments.

■ Carry a little notebook when you shop to jot down sewing ideas and measurements. This way you can keep abreast of fashion changes.

Cover That Mistake

The very design details that can make a garment a pleasure to own can also ruin the entire garment if they are less than perfect. Wearing the garment is not pleasurable because all you see is your "mistake."

There can be a good side to errors, though. Some of my most creative touches have resulted from covering up a mistake.

Suppose you made a mess of a welt pocket on a jacket. Leave it as is and make a flap ¼ inch longer than the welt pocket. Topstitch the flap over the top of the welt pocket. The pocket is still usable, but the flap covers the unsightly problem.

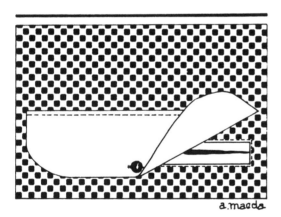

a.maeda

What if your buttonholes are of assorted sizes and perhaps less than perfectly placed? Sew a small button—identical to the one used to close the garment—on the buttonhole itself. Use the side away from the edge of the garment.

Your attention will be drawn away from the buttonhole to the beautiful button. When the garment is buttoned, the two-button effect is interesting.

Suppose you cut a hole in the garment while you were trimming something. Don't panic and throw it away. Take a small piece of press-on interfacing and place it behind the cut. Press. The bonding will bring the two edges together. For a more secure bond, zigzag over the slash if the area is not too visible.

A slash can also be fixed at a reweaver's shop.

Suppose you incorrectly placed the sleeve placket right sides together and turned the placket to the inside. Disaster? No. Simply take your stitches out carefully with a ripper. Close the slash with a piece of press-on interfacing on the wrong side. Proceed again.

What if you pressed the interfacing on the wrong side of the collar? Can you pull it off? No. Throw out the collar and interfacing and cut new ones.

Anytime you make a mistake, take a break. Come back refreshed, maybe even a day later, and you will get a new perspective about how to fix it.

■ Very often the seams in polyester garments simply refuse to lie flat. Put 1 tablespoon of white vinegar into a cup of cold water and pour it into a spray bottle. Spray a little of this solution onto the seam allowances.

■ If you can't see a mistake from 3 feet, forget it. No one is looking that closely for mistakes. If they are, perhaps you should question the friendship, not your sewing.

Maintain the Shape with Stay Tape

So much frustration and disappointment in sewing could be eliminated with the knowledge of where and when to use stay tape. Patterns seldom mention stay tape application and sewers are puzzled as to why the pattern pieces do not fit together as indicated.

What is stay tape? It is a cotton twill tape $1/4$ inch to $3/8$ inch wide used as a stabilizer in areas that have a tendency to stretch—such as a V neckline or shoulder seam in a loose weave or knit fabric.

My recommendations for stay tape are: Use on all necklines and armholes in unstable or stretchy fabrics, as well as shoulder seams, waistline, and crotch seams. Stay tape helps the garment keep its shape during construction and maintain its shape while it's being worn. Determine the length of stay tape by measuring the pattern piece. Do not use the cut fabric piece as your guide, as stretching may have already occurred.

For example, in putting a strip of stay tape in a shoulder seam, I discovered that the shoulder of the handwoven fabric had stretched 1 inch during the time I had removed the paper pattern and pinned the front and back together. If I had not used tape,

the shoulder seam would be longer than the style intended, giving a saggy, baggy look at the armhole.

Most likely it will be necessary to ease the fabric to fit the stay tape. This can usually be done during the sewing process by pulling on the tape and gently pushing the fabric under the presser foot as you sew. Stay tape is applied at the shoulder, crotch and waistline seam at the same time the seam is sewn.

To stabilize the neck and armholes, stay tape cut to size by the pattern is applied to the neck and armholes $1/2$ inch away from the cut edge, within the seam allowance—*before* collar or sleeve is applied—through one fabric thickness. Once you have stabilized the shape of these pieces, you can give your full attention to sleeve ease and application as well as perfectly shaped collars.

In the lightweight fabrics such as silk, I often use the selvage edge of the silk itself, a $1/4$-inch strip, in lieu of twill tape. The selvage is lighter in weight but still provides the stability necessary. A strip of selvage in lightweight cotton is often a good substitute on any fabric.

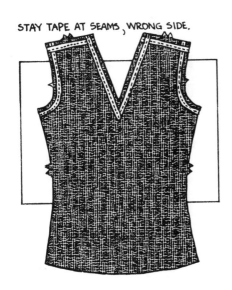

STAY TAPE AT SEAMS, WRONG SIDE.

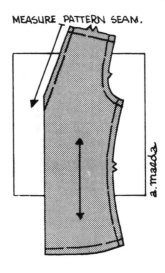

MEASURE PATTERN SEAM.

a. maeda

Corner Secrets

Knowledge of how to handle corners in sewing is crucial to a professional looking garment. Without it, you will have pointed collars with fat rounded ends, V necks that pucker and refuse to lie flat, pockets of undefined shape, etc.

The technique is really very simple: Whenever you are approaching an angle that is a right angle or smaller, you must switch your stitch length to small reinforcing stitches and hand-walk the machine diagonally before continuing on the other side of the angle (Illustration 1). These two small diagonal stitches give your fabric "room to turn" without causing bulk.

Small reinforcing stitches allow you to trim or slash very close to the stitching line without fear of weakening the seam. On a collar, slash diagonally within one stitch of the corner (Illustration 2). In corners such as on a V-neck or on pockets, slash inward toward the seam within one stitch of the seamline. Trim bulk out of the seams.

When turning the garment right side out, do not use scissors to assist in getting sharp points. The scissors themselves will often punch through the seamline or the fabric and create a hole. Use a point turner made specifically for this purpose. Press seams open.

Suppose you can't find your point turner and have poked a hole with your scissors. Don't panic. Simply deepen the entire seam by $\frac{1}{8}$ inch, sewing the entire seam again at $\frac{3}{4}$ inch.

After the garment has been turned right side out, hand-baste the corner or the whole seam, if you wish, with silk thread. The basting will hold the seam in place while you press and pound with a tailor's clapper. Silk thread is finer with more elasticity than other threads, thus eliminating lasting basting impressions.

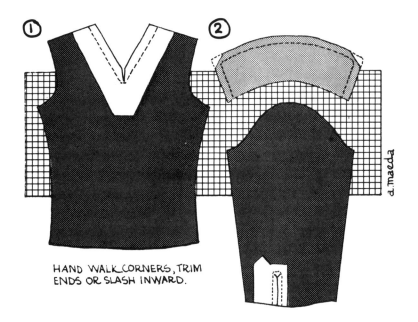

HAND WALK CORNERS, TRIM
ENDS OR SLASH INWARD.

Strapless Secrets

When summer approaches, many of us eye strapless bathing suits and dresses, trying to figure out how we can make one that will stay up.

The secret of strapless garments lies in boning. For 400 years prior to 1860, whalebones were used to give shape to corsets and hoops. Whaleboning was replaced by steel "bones," which are still used today in corset and costume construction. Corset stays may be purchased from corset companies and cut with tin snips. The ends are sealed with a thick tipping solution. Steel boning is rarely comfortable and restricts movement.

For lighter support in bathing suits, strapless dresses and camisoles, polyester boning (available in notions departments) is preferable—and it's washable. Dritz™ Featherweight boning is available by the yard.

Boning is one of the last steps in garment construction. After the facings have been attached, cut boning the correct length, ¼ inch shorter to allow for play. Pad the ends of the poly boning. Sear with a match.

After the boning has been cut to size, pad the ends by wrapping well with adhesive tape. Your comfort depends on this. Although the poly boning is encased in a tape, I prefer encasing the boning strip again in twill tape or grosgrain ribbon. The reason for this is twofold: First, the encasement will further protect you from rough edges; second, the inside of the garment will have a more finished appearance.

Sew lengthwise sides of the tape or ribbon, leaving ends free. Turn under ½ inch on each end of the encasement to the back side. Hand-stitch ends into place. One-inch seam allowances on the bodice give ample room to attach boning (Illustration 1).

Clip curved seams before pressing. Lay the encased boning strip against the seam allowance. (Ribbon encasement has been eliminated in illustration to make the procedure clearer.) Hand-whip the ends into place. Using buttonhole twist or strong thread, cross-stitch back and forth over the encased boning. This method keeps the boning firmly in place without the stitching showing on the outside (Illustration 2).

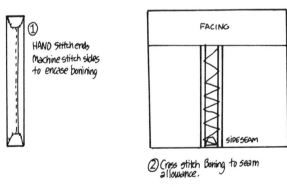

① HAND stitch ends. Machine stitch sides to encase bonining

② Cross stitch Boning to seam allowance.

■ Kenneth King provides in-depth construction of a bustier in *Threads* magazine issue 46

Flattering Peplums

If you have never tried a peplum because you thought you couldn't wear one, you might be missing something. The peplum flatters most figures.

The length of the peplum and fabric choice are crucial. The peplum should never extend to the fullest part of the hip.

Experiment with scrap fabric to determine the most flattering length for you. A peplum may be altered by merely shortening or extending the shape. Keep in mind that the longer the peplum, the lighter weight the fabric must be. Never interface or it will become too stiff.

The peplum may be faced in its own fabric, or a better choice might be a lighter weight fabric. Cut peplum and facing, paying careful attention to grainline for the proper drape.

If any pattern alterations were made on the skirt, remember to make the same adjustments on the peplum pattern. Such adjustments include large waist, fullness at tummy, large hip, or swayback.

To construct the peplum, sew the pieces at the side seams. To join the peplum and the facing, sew the outside edges with small stitches. Clip, grade, and trim seam.

Turn peplum right side out. Roll seam slightly to the underside toward the facing. Hand-baste with silk thread. Using silk thread is important because its inherent stretch will not leave an imprint when it is pressed. Press and pound outside edges with a tailor's clapper.

Machine-baste peplum and facing at waist. Pin peplum onto the jacket with the facing side of the peplum against the right side of the jacket. Carefully match center front, center back, and side-seam markings.

Baste peplum to jacket. Placing the right side of the bodice against the right side of the peplum, sew the waistline seam.

FINAL TOUCH

■ Fiber artist Lois Erickson offers these tips for design inspiration: Cut a window from a piece of paper. Look carefully at the fabric through the window. As you move the window around, "Do the images in the window suggest some techniques to get you started—faced shapes, pleating, tucking, layering, piecing, piping, stitching, applique or beading?

"When planning a garment, place fabric, trim and buttons together. Do they relate? Is there some commonality? Are the buttons too dressy for the fabric?" For more, see Sources.

Piped Pocket

Cultivating an Eye for Workmanship

Recognizing quality is a learned skill whether you sew your own clothes or buy them off the rack. Quality clothing can still be obtained if you know what to look for when you shop. Unfortunately, in today's society one pays dearly for a quality garment with a number of design details.

Before making a purchase, you might ask yourself how much wear a garment actually will receive. Some compromise in quality is acceptable in "occasional" garments, such as a dressy blouse, a light-hearted sweater-vest or a pair of pants in the latest style.

Fad garments need not be constructed as well, because either you will tire of them or they will be out of style before they show wear.

Quality should not be compromised in a jacket that will be worn to work every day, a bathrobe, basic skirts and slacks, or accessories such as boots and purses. These items receive a great deal of wear.

If you purchase a well-made item, you will receive joy from it every time it is worn. The garment will retain its styling and shape throughout the years.

What should you look for when you want quality and a long-lasting garment?

FABRIC, FABRIC, FABRIC. I cannot stress enough the importance of this.

If the fabric is not pleasurable to touch, it will receive little wear. If you have some doubt, rub the fabric along your neck under your chin. Is it scratchy? If so, forget it.

Is the fabric pleasing to you in design, pattern, and color? Looking at the fabric should give you pleasure. If the color is not flattering to you, no amount of styling can save it; put it back.

I have found that natural fibers seem to retain their shape and finish longer than man-made fibers. Man-made fibers may look good on the rack, but in wearing, they seem to snag and pill easily. Man-made fibers do not breathe, and many people complain that they are "hot" to wear.

Before you even try on the garment, look at the seams from the outside. Do they pucker? Pressing will not eliminate this problem. The ripples were created in sewing. Now examine the garment from the inside. A lightweight fabric should have French seams or overlocked seams; French seams are preferable,

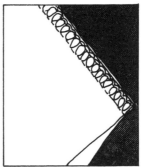

FRENCH SEAM

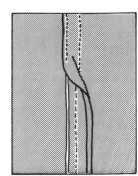

OVERLOCK SEAM   FLAT FELL SEAM

especially if the fabric has a tendency to ravel.

A French seam conceals all raw edges of the fabric, revealing a narrow ¼-inch finished welt on the inside of the garment. The overlock seam covers the raw edges of the fabric with a chain of overlock stitches. It is an excellent treatment for fabrics that tend to ravel.

Sportswear such as pants holds up better with flat-fell seams. The flat-fell is a plain seam that has double strength because it is sewn twice. After the seam is sewn once, one seam allowance is trimmed away. The second seam allowance wraps the trimmed one and is topstitched.

Overlocked seams are perfectly acceptable in skirts and dresses. In an unlined jacket, Hong Kong seams

Cultivating an Eye for Workmanship

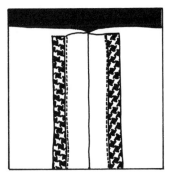

HONG KONG SEAM

give the nicest finish: Each seam allowance is wrapped and sewn with narrow bias tape.

Look at the facings. Are they skimpy? Do they lie flat, or are they fighting with the garment? Examine the interfacing used in the garment. If press-on interfacing was used, can any traces be observed from the outside? Is the interfacing compatible? Does it give support without imposing, or do the collar and cuffs look too stiff?

Check out the zipper. Does the weight of the zipper seem compatible with the fabric? Quality garments usually feature a narrow single-welt zipper often put in by hand for less visibility.

Study the design details. Do welt pockets lie flat? Any design detail should be well executed or eliminated—you will be able to tell the difference. Your eye will be drawn to the problem since the area in question will not lie flat. Are any raw edges visible at the buttonholes? Perfect buttonholes seal in all stray threads.

If the garment is topstitched, look carefully at the workmanship. Are the rows of topstitching even? Are any broken threads or skipped stitches visible?

If trim is used on the garment, check to see if it is compatible with the garment fabric. Does it lie fit or pucker as it goes around a curve? Do the buttons add or detract from the appearance of the garment?

Buttons can be changed, and this change often upgrades the entire look.

Try on the garment. Is the style flattering? Does it make you look fat? If so, you will never wear it. How does it make you feel to look at yourself? If the answer isn't "fantastic," hang the garment back on the rack. You can do better.

Is the hem even? If not, how do you feel about redoing the hem? Look at the sleeves carefully. Do they hang straight without wrinkles when the arm is relaxed? Is the sleeve comfortable or does it feel tight? If the garment is leather, is the leather supple, conforming to the shape of the body?

Purchase of certain accessories is very important. A pair of boots is not a purchase, it is an investment. These boots should be a basic color that blends with most items in your wardrobe, whether that be burgundy, gray, or some shade of brown. Black boots are often heavy-looking and draw attention away from you and onto your feet.

When it comes to purses, quality is especially important. Your purse is with you every day. Inexpensive accessories can cheapen the whole outfit.

After developing the skill of shopping for quality, you are still susceptible to one major pitfall. A sale item is not really a bargain for you unless it is something you already needed. Otherwise it has to be categorized as an impulsive buy.

For example, an impulsive buy might be a bright fuchsia silk blouse reduced from $160 to $90. Unfortunately, you have nothing to go with this blouse. Usually you realize this after you leave the store. You not only need a new skirt or pants to go with the blouse but new shoes, too.

This bargain has ended up costing you considerably more than $90. Use some restraint. Leave these bargains for less sophisticated shoppers.

Standards for the Well Tailored

If you are considering investing time and money in a suit, you would do well to examine an English-tailored man's jacket and note the following:

■ Natural shoulders—padded but not overly; lapels 3¾ inches wide; slightly shaped body

■ Dull horn button opening at waist in a direct line with welt pockets

■ Four buttons at sleeves with hand-made button-holes

■ Fully lined coat.

A man's suit from a Savile Row tailor would cost well over $1000, require four fittings and be expected to last 12 years.

The success of a home-sewn tailored jacket depends on correct fit, correct workmanship, expert pressing and the right choice of fabric.

Most trans-seasonal men's suits are made in 12-ounce fabric. This is the weight of the fabric by the yard. If fabric selection is a sore point for you, check a good men's shop first. Handle the fabrics used in the jacket. Note the weight, weave, and finish. Choose something similar to this for your jacket and you will have success.

Do you want to get really sharp flat lapels similar to those found in a man's jacket? When easing the facing to the jacket in the lapel area, the placement of the ease is very important. If you ease the facing to the jacket from the roll line up, wrinkling will occur at the outer edge of the lapel. Ease the facing to the jacket for 5 inches above the top button; sew the remainder of the seam flat; then ease the last 2 inches again.

The ease near the roll-line enables the lapel to turn out easily. The ease at the very corner of the lapel enables the corner to lie flat. Sewing the remainder of the seam flat yields perfect results.

The amount of ease in a lapel ranges from ⅛ to ¼ inch, depending on the fabric. Hand-baste the seam, press, and check to see if the seam is wrinkling. If it wrinkles you have put in too much ease.

Most home sewers pin everything. Why not hand-baste instead—it's almost as fast.

Flat-fell, French & Strap Seams

While most serious sewers now own a serger (overlock) sometimes an alternative seam finish is preferred if the finished product will resemble something found in better ready-to-wear. For example, flat-fell seams can be turned far easier if ¾ inch seam allowances are used. Decide on seam finish before cutting out the garment, allowing larger seams for special seam treatment.

Flat-fell seams can be done on the wrong side or the right side of the garment depending upon whether the seam is started on the right or wrong side of the fabric. Make a sample of each to decide which side you prefer. For a flat-fell seam on the wrong side of the garment, place the right sides of the fabric together. Sew a ¾ inch seam. Press open. Trim the side of the seam allowance to ¼ inch. Press the long uncut seam allowance over toward the newly cut side. Trim under ⅜ inch on the long uncut seam allowance. Cover the cut side, pinning the folded edge into place. Sew close to folded edge. You may prefer the same technique starting by placing the wrong sides together. This places the flat-fell on the outside. Try a small sample of both techniques and decide which one you prefer.

An enlarged version of the French seam on the outside can be used for shoulder emphasis, eliminating the need for shoulder pads. The result is added design interest as well as a drawn-out line of the garment's construction. Allow 1 inch seam allowances.

Many patterns would look good with this technique, eliminating the seam finish problem. For a French seam that shows on the outside, place the right sides of the fabric together and sew seam at ⅜ inch.

Press seams with wrong sides together aiming for the seam top to be right along the edge. With wrong sides of the fabric together, encasing the raw edges of the seam, sew at ⅝ inch. If the fabric is heavy, hand-baste and press before sewing. Press and pound seam flat with a tailor's clapper.

The French seam on the outside may only be suitable for some seams—the ones you want to draw attention to. For others, such as side seams, you may want to do a traditional French seam with the seam on the inside, or a flat-felled seam.

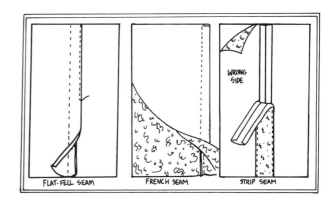

FLAT-FELL SEAM   FRENCH SEAM   STRIP SEAM   WRONG SIDE

For the armhole of a shirt or seams on a silk blouse, a traditional French seam is used. Begin the seam with wrong sides of the fabric together. Sew seam at ⅜ inch. Trim seam to ⅛ inch. Pinch right sides together, enclosing ⅛ inch seam allowance. Press into position. Sew enclosed raw edges. With right sides of fabric together, encasing raw edges of seam, sew at ¼ inch.

Another seam trick that acts both as a fashion accent and a seam finish is the strap seam. Place wrong sides of fabric together and sew seams at ⅝ inch. Press seams open. This places the seam allowance on the outside of the garment.

Cut a bias strip of fabric 3 inches wide and long enough to completely cover the seam. Press ⅝ inch on each side of the bias strip. Place bias strip over the pressed seam allowance on the outside of the garment. Topstitch into place.

The width of the bias strip may be reduced if the sewn seam allowance is trimmed. This can be a great way to accent seams with a companion fabric or suede trim.

Overlock Finish

If you haven't already bought an overlock machine for seam finishing and sewing knits, you can almost justify the purchase by whipping up some overlocked sportswear and selling it to your friends.

When overlocked seams on the outside of the garment appeared in 1982, I was less than enthusiastic. Many ready-to-wear pieces had rippled seams and stretched necklines. Such is not the case for the majority of clothing today. Overlock experimentation has yielded a look that can hold its own in the sportswear market.

The newer overlocks have a stitch length and width adjustment. For the most finished results, reduce the stitch length and width.

Choose a fabric that is not prone to ravelling. Instead of overlocking a single thickness, use one of two methods. For collars and pockets, use a double thickness with interfacing sandwiched in between. Overlock the outside edge. The double thickness gives more body and eliminates the ripple effect (Illustration 1).

If a single-fabric thickness is desired, fold under the seam allowance to the wrong side of the fabric. Press. Overlock along the folded edge. Trim away excess seam allowance from the wrong side (Illustration 2).

For seams, use a $5/8$-inch seam allowance with wrong sides together. Overlock seam at regular seam placement, allowing the knife to cut off the excess. The overlocked seam on the outside may then be left free or topstiched to one side.

For camisoles in knit without gaping armholes, try this trick: Turn under a $5/8$-inch seam to the wrong side at the armhole and press. Slip in a narrow piece of stay tape near the fold from the shoulder to the underarm. Pin in place. Overlock along the fold, overlocking the stay tape in the fold (Illustration 3). Trim off the excess seam allowance. The stay tape will keep the front armhole from stretching. If you have a large bust, you may want to run an easeline in the front armhole at $1/2$ inch before the seam allowance press process.

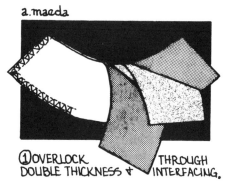

a. maeda

① OVERLOCK DOUBLE THICKNESS & THROUGH INTERFACING.

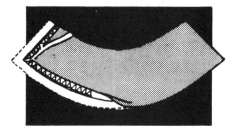

② OVERLOCK FOLDED EDGE, TRIM OFF EXCESS.

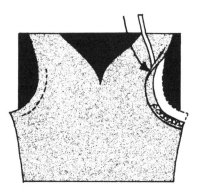

③ ADD TWILL TAPE UNDER FOLD, OVERLOCK FOLDED EDGE. RUN AN EASELINE AT FRONT ARMHOLE

Hong Kong Finish

So often it's the little details that no one but the wearer sees that bring the most pleasure.

How about an unlined jacket with seams and hems finished with the Hong Kong finish? The Hong Kong finish is a technique of wrapping the raw edges of the fabric with a contrasting but related fabric. This makes an excellent finish for armholes and hems as well as seams if you feel truly industrious.

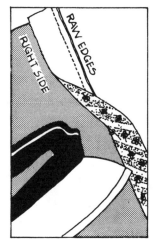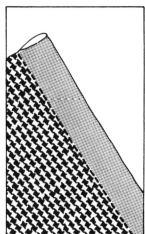

a. maeda

facings, front facings, inside of neckbands, cuffs and pockets. When I mention contrasting but related fabric, I mean the use of a small stripe in the same tones as the outside garment fabric or perhaps a small print that picks up the colors of the garment. The fabric must have a relationship or the subtlety is lost.

Try to pick up $\frac{3}{4}$ of a yard of companion fabric at the same time as the major fabric purchase. You will find many small creative ways to use it.

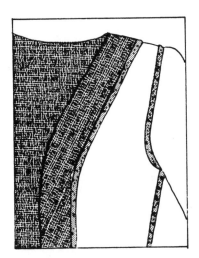

Choose a fabric that relates to the garment fabric but provides some interest. I like to use very small prints or stripes.

Cut bias or well off grain strips $1\frac{1}{2}$ inches wide and long enough to cover the raw edge in mind. Place the right side of the bias strip against the right side of the garment, raw edges together. Sew at $\frac{1}{4}$ inch. Trim seam to $\frac{1}{8}$ inch. Press strip toward raw edge.

Now wrap bias strip around raw edges to the wrong side of the fabric. Pin in place. Sew wrapped edge into place by sewing in the well of the seam from the right side.

Another spot for detail work is the bias strip used to finish the sleeve vent. This is rarely visible. However, a nice statement is made when the vent is finished in a contrasting but related fabric.

Other spots for subtle touches: neck and armhole

Hand Stitches

Although the new sewing machines do almost everything, sometimes nothing is as satisfactory as a hand stitch. But what hand stitch?

The fell stitch is a hand stitch used to hold two edges securely. The most common use of this stitch is to attach twill tape to hair-canvas interfacing on a lapel or a felt undercollar to a collar.

The fell stitch takes one small stitch on the twill tape pushing the needle straight back through the hair canvas.

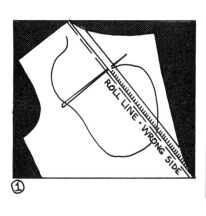
①

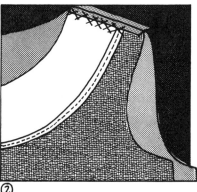
②

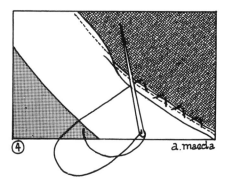
③

from the outside as well as the underside. After pressing up the hem allowance, fold back ¼ inch along the top hem edge and begin stitching. Take one thread on the garment and one thread on the hem ¼ inch down from the top (Illustration 4).

Knot the thread every five stitches, being careful not to pull the thread too tight at any time during the hemming process.

Take one long ¼-inch stitch on the hair-canvas and come back up through the twill tape. This is not a good stitch for hems because it allows no movement (Illustration 1).

The catch stitch is a hand stitch with more flexibility that is used mainly to attach interfacing to the garment at the underarm and the shoulder where the seam allowance has been cut away.

Make one diagonal stitch across the interfacing, catch one thread from the garment and cross diagonally across the interfacing in the opposite direction (Illustration 2).

The slip stitch is sort of a variation on the running stitch used to attach trim, pockets, lining and wide bias in place. Slide the needle along the fold for ¼ inch, picking up a thread in the outside garment fabric (Illustration 3).

The blind stitch—or traditional hem stitch—is a hand stitch used on a woven fabric that is invisible

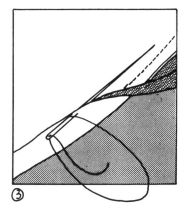
④   a. maeda

The secrets to a good hem stitch are:
■ Use the smallest needle your thread will pass through.
■ Use silk thread if possible.
■ Never beeswax the hem thread (it becomes too stiff).
■ Never pull the thread too tight.

Determining Correct Length

How many times have you finished a garment, turned up the hem and then worn it? Did you happen to glance in the mirror on your way out? Very few individuals can merely turn up a hem and have it hang evenly. Sometimes the whole effect of an outfit is ruined by a skirt or jacket that is too long or too short.

How can the right skirt length be determined? Contrary to what the fashion magazines would like us to believe, fashion does not determine flattering skirt length. This is an individual thing determined by your height, weight, and shape of legs. Everyone has a flattering range. As shorter skirts come into fashion, your skirts can go up, but only to the upper limit of your skirt range.

To find your best skirt range, work with a friend whose taste you trust. Pick out a skirt in your wardrobe that you particularly like. Stand in front of the mirror with the zipper undone and slide the skirt up and down for different lengths. Ask yourself and your friend: What length makes your legs look the best? What length makes you look taller? What length adds or subtracts weight? Have your friend mark these lengths right on your leg with a felt-tip pen. It will wash off.

Now you have a range of lengths that are flattering to you. Stand up straight and have your friend measure the distances from the floor. Keep a record, and, as hems go up and down, your hems will go up and down within this range.

If the back of your skirt habitually hangs lower than the front, try this: At the waistline, cut off ½ inch to ¾ inch at center back, tapering to zero at each side seam. This will lift the back of the skirt after you put on the waistband (Illustration 1).

Does the front of your skirt hike up a bit and seem to want to stick out? At the waistline, add ¼ inch at the center front, tapering to zero at each side seam. This alteration gives the skirt a little more fabric to go over the tummy (Illustration 2).

The most accurate way to get a skirt hemmed equidistant from the floor is to use a skirt marker. Press the skirt well and perhaps let it hang overnight before marking the hem.

During the marking process, wear the shoes you will be wearing. Heel height changes one's posture, thereby shifting the skirt.

Another method, inexpensive but not as easy, is to mark the finished length of the skirt on a doorjamb. Put a nail on either side of the doorjamb, the exact distance up from the floor where you want your finished length (Illustration 3).

Tie a piece of string between the nails. Rub chalk on the string. Stand next to the string and let the chalk touch the skirt at several places.

For a flattering jacket length, try several jackets on in a store. Ask yourself: Which jacket makes me look taller, fatter, in proportion? Many women try to hide large hips with a long jacket that only draws attention to them.

When you have found a good length, measure from the center back of the neck to the hemline. Your range will be about 2 inches. Keep a record of these lengths.

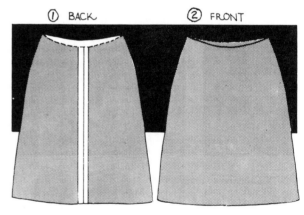

① BACK ② FRONT

③ SKIRT MARKING

a. maeda

Invisible Hems in Difficult Fabrics

One of the telltale signs of a homemade garment is a bulky hem that is plainly visible from the right side of the garment. A number of factors are responsible for the hem's visibility. If you are conscientious about several points, however, the hem's visibility will vanish.

The width of the hem is very important. A full skirt should never have a hem wider than $1\frac{1}{2}$ inches. Too much bulk is created. On the other hand, a slim skirt needs the weight of a $2\frac{1}{2}$-inch hem to create a smooth, straight silhouette.

With some fabrics, an invisible hem is difficult to achieve because of the amount of give in the fabric. Examples of this would be silk velvet, wool jersey and just about anything cut on the bias: When you attach the hem to a thread from the main garment, the thread pulls away and creates a mark on the right side. Here is a solution for this problem. It involves inserting a strip of bias-cut silk organza between the main garment and the hem.

Cut a bias strip of silk organza 1 inch wider than the hem. The silk organza should be preshrunk to soften it a bit. Attach one edge of the strip at the fold of the hem with a catch stitch.

Attach the top of the hem to the bias with a running stitch. Hem carefully, taking one stitch on the garment and one on the hem, never at the same time. The bias organza gives a little support and cushioning. The hem becomes invisible from the right side.

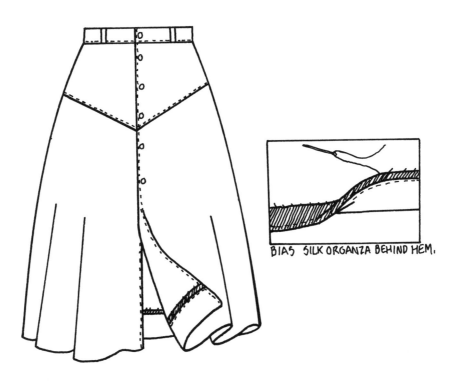

BIAS SILK ORGANZA BEHIND HEM.

Rolled Hems, Hand and Machine

A rolled hem is the best finish for full silk skirts and silk scarves. This kind of hem can be made by hand or by machine, using a special attachment. The hand-rolled hem is nicer and almost invisible, but not everyone has the time for so much handwork.

A machine-rolled hem is fine for skirts but not as good for scarves because it is very difficult to get a neat end with the machine hemmer. The rolled hemmer is an attachment that screws onto the machine where the regular presser foot does. To make a machine-rolled hem, insert fabric under the hemmer, bring fabric up into the roll, and continue pulling fabric a little to the left as you stitch (Illustration 1).

When hemming a scarf by machine, it is easier to begin and end hem with a hand stitch. The rest can be done on the machine.

To make a hand-rolled hem, you will have an easier time rolling under the raw edge if you first make a line of machine stitching ¼ inch from raw edge of fabric. Cut off fabric edge close to stitching (Illustration 2). Roll under machine-stitched edge and pin into place. Sew the rolled hem with a blind stitch by sliding the needle along the roll and taking a thread from the hem and one from the garment every ¼ inch (Illustration 3).

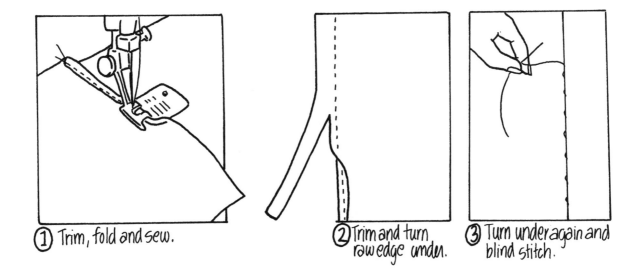

① Trim, fold and sew.　② Trim and turn raw edge under.　③ Turn under again and blind stitch.

Hem Skirts

If you have someone to mark a hem for you, the best method for marking a hem which hangs perfectly on the body is with a hem marker, found in the notions department (see Illustration 1, page 203). If not, locate a skirt in your closet that is a good length for you. Skirt length is determined by comparing the side seams of the old and new skirts from the waistline seam (at the bottom of the waistband) to the hem.

Measure the skirt you plan to shorten in the same manner, from the waistline to the hem at the side seam. This process can be done easily by laying the skirts side by side. Place a pin horizontal to the hem, marking desired finished length. Before cutting off the excess at the hem, a hem allowance for turning under must be determined. For straight skirts, a $2\frac{1}{2}$ inch hem is preferable to give the hem enough weight for a proper hang. For a full skirt, a narrow, 1 inch hem is the best choice. A deeper hem is bulky and prohibits the fullness from hanging close around the legs. For semi-full skirts, such as A-line or gored, a $1\frac{1}{2}$ inch hem is preferable.

With these suggested hem widths in mind, make a chalk-mark the width of a hem allowance below the pin marking desired finished length. Measure this distance from the bottom edge of the skirt all around the skirt. Mark with chalk. Cut off excess skirt length (see Illustration 2, page 203).

Hem tape is rarely used to finish the raw edge of hems. Ready-to-wear skirts sport an overlocked finish. If your machine is capable of an overlock or zigzag, create a finish on the bottom edge of the skirt. If not, a pinked edge, with straight stitch $\frac{1}{4}$ inch away, is attractive and prevents raveling. Now measure up the depth of the hem all around the skirt. Mark with chalk. This will act as a guide for turning the hem up.

If the skirt has some fullness, you will notice that the hem seems fuller than the skirt itself. Some fullness needs to be removed to enable the hem to lie flat. Folding out little pleats in the hem allowance creates ridges when the hem is pressed from the right side. To remove excess fullness along the hem edge, run an easeline $\frac{3}{8}$ inch from the skirt edge by pushing at the back of the presser foot. If more ease is needed, take a pin and pull up slightly on the bobbin thread.

Fold up hem allowance and pin into position. Press lightly. Full skirts are usually finished by machine with a double row of topstitching. Double topstitching can be created by sewing around the hem, on the underside of the skirt, twice by machine—one row $\frac{3}{4}$ inch from the hem fold and one row $\frac{1}{2}$ inch from the hem fold. Use the width of the presser foot as a guide for the second row (Illustration 3). The second method for double topstitching must be done from the right side of the skirt using a double nee

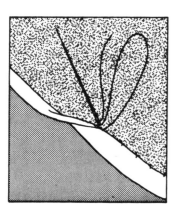

ROLLED HEM.

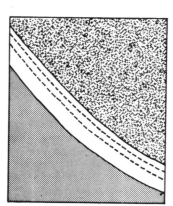

DOUBLE MACHINE STITCH.

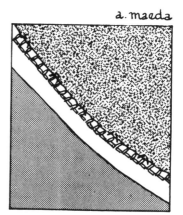

OVERLOCK AND HANDSTITCH.

a. maeda

Hem Skirts

dle. Any machine capable of zigzag can accommodate a double needle (Illustration 4). Refer to double needle in sewing machine instruction manual.

Hems for straight skirts are more visible and therefore put in by hand. When pressing up hem allowance, slip an envelope between hem and skirt. This technique prevents hem imprint from showing through on the outside of the skirt (Illustration 5).

The secret to invisible hand hems is to use a fine needle and a light touch—don't pull the thread too tight. A looser hand stitch will still hold the hem in place. After the hem has been pressed into position, place pins holding up hem 1 inch from raw edge of the hem. As you hand stitch, fold ¼ inch of the hem toward you. Hand stitches will be hidden, formed ¼ inch below the top of the hem. Hem stitches are made ¼ inch apart. Take one thread on the garment, skip ¼ inch and take 1 stitch on the back of the hem allowance, then skip ¼ inch and take one stitch on the garment, and on and on (Illustration 6). For invisible hems, never pick up one stitch from the garment and the hem at the same time.

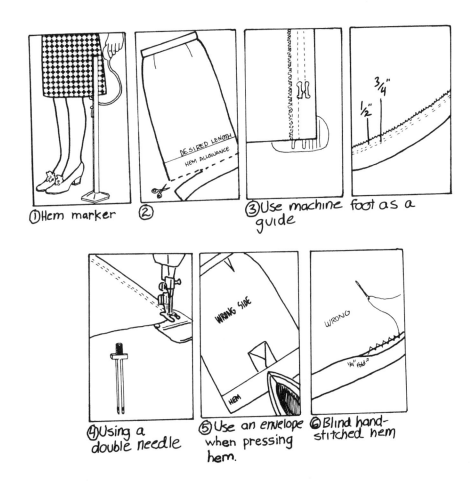

① Hem marker
②
③ Use machine foot as a guide
④ Using a double needle
⑤ Use an envelope when pressing hem.
⑥ Blind hand-stitched hem

Curved Hems

Many overblouse styles call for a thinly rolled hem that curves gently around the corners to slits on the sides.

The difficulty with this kind of hem is making it smooth and flat around the curves. For a roll that doesn't ripple, it is necessary to make the outside edge smaller. This can be done by running an easeline—a row of machine stitching—around the curve $\frac{1}{4}$ inch from the raw edge. Continue the easeline stitching on the straight edge as well.

Pull the thread of the easeline around the curved edge so that the edge turns under $\frac{1}{2}$ inch (Illustration 1). Press up rest of hem $\frac{1}{2}$ inch from edge, too.

You are now ready to turn under the raw edge. Fold raw edge in $\frac{1}{4}$ inch to meet the pressed crease, pin into place, and press lightly over pins. Stitch rolled hem to blouse by hand or machine (Illustration 2). Press and pound with tailor's clapper.

If the fabric has some ease, try using a narrow $\frac{1}{8}$-inch strip of two-way basting tape (Illustration 3). In many cases the easeline may be eliminated. The two-way tape helps hold the edge under.

At the end of the seam, where slit and curved edge meet, bar-tack over the seam to keep slit from tearing. To bar-tack, simply use a small zigzag and very small stitches for $\frac{1}{4}$ inch (Illustration 4).

■ On a blouse or tailored shirt which will be worn tucked in, a better fit is achieved by a rounded shirt-tail hem.

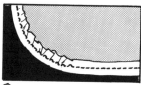

① SEW 1/4" EASELINE, PULL THREADS AT CURVES. PRESS HEM 1/2" FROM HEM.

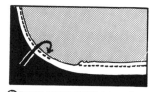

② TUCK RAW EDGE UNDER AT EASELINE AND STITCH.

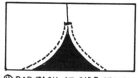

④ BAR TACK AT SIDE SEAM.

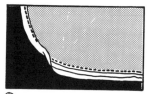

③ SEW NARROW BIAS TAPE.

Hemming with a Miter

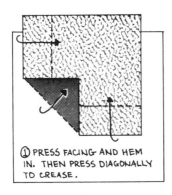

① PRESS FACING AND HEM IN. THEN PRESS DIAGONALLY TO CREASE.

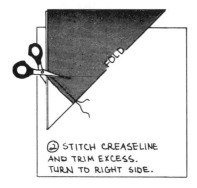

② STITCH CREASELINE AND TRIM EXCESS. TURN TO RIGHT SIDE.

It is a good idea to do this procedure with a basting stitch first, turning it to the right side to be certain that you are doing it correctly before you do any machine stitching or cutting.

Hand-hem the bottom of the coat and the side of the vent with small invisible stitches.

To prevent the seam imprint of miter from showing on the outside of the garment, slip a piece of cardboard or a metal ruler into the corner before pounding to cushion the seam.

Mitering ribbon or braid is also a simple process. Lay braid along front of garment and fold braid up at the bottom of the hem, right sides of braid together. Fold the braid again, this time so that the corner of the braid forms a right angle (Illustration 3). Press well. This foldline is your guide for sewing.

Keeping the right sides of braid together, sew with small stitches along the newly pressed fold (Illustration 4). Trim seam to ⅛ inch. Fold right side out and press.

Attach braid to garment by hand or machine.

Mitering corners gives them the flat professional touch they demand—and it's not as difficult to do as it looks. Mitering is necessary on kimonos and in the treatment of a vent in a coat. The work must be done very methodically for good results. The best way to handle the bulk at the turnback of the vent and the turn-up of the hem is to miter the corner. The size of the vent and hem must be equal.

Press up the hem and press back the vent turnback. Open these out and press up the diagonal edge, matching the crease marks (Illustration 1). This diagonal line will be your sewing line.

With right sides together, sew along this diagonal creaseline with small reinforcing stitches and trim to ⅛ inch. Turn right side out and press (Illustration 2).

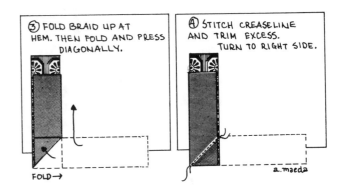

③ FOLD BRAID UP AT HEM. THEN FOLD AND PRESS DIAGONALLY.

FOLD →

④ STITCH CREASELINE AND TRIM EXCESS. TURN TO RIGHT SIDE.

a.maeda

Demonstrated on *Power Sewing* Video #5: *Construction Difficulties.*

Hem-Facing Combo

Often the home sewer is faced with the problem of how to treat the facing and hem when they join at the bottom of a square-cornered jacket, a button-down-the-side skirt, or a shirtwaist type dress. How can the hem and facing be treated to eliminate bulk and achieve maximum flatness?

After the facing has been applied, press seams open, grading seams, trimming the seam allowance of the facing at $\frac{1}{8}$ inch and the seam allowance of the garment at $\frac{1}{4}$ inch (Illustration 1). Press up hem the desired width but preferably no wider than 2 inches. Match the facing seam allowance of the hem to the facing seam allowance of the garment exactly, pinning through the well of the seam. The next step

can be done by machine if you are skillful or by hand if you have trouble sewing in the well of the seam.

With the right side of the garment facing you, sew in the well of the seam, making a firm bond of the hem and garment seam allowances. Sew only the depth of the hem (Illustration 2).

Trim the hem in the facing to 1 inch to eliminate bulk. Turn the facing to the inside of the garment. Complete hem in the garment. Attach edge of facing to hem with an overcast stitch (Illustration 3). Do not turn under an edge here to make it look finished; a bump on the outside of the garment will result.

Press with steam and pound final results with a tailor's clapper.

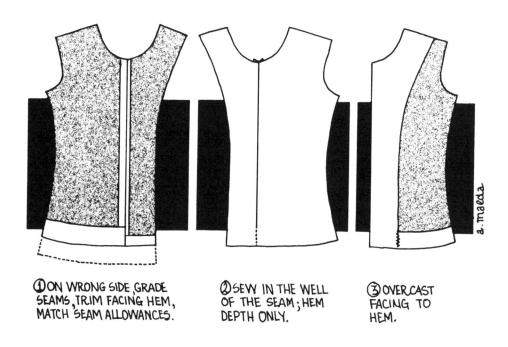

① ON WRONG SIDE, GRADE SEAMS, TRIM FACING HEM, MATCH SEAM ALLOWANCES.

② SEW IN THE WELL OF THE SEAM; HEM DEPTH ONLY.

③ OVERCAST FACING TO HEM.

Jacket Hems

A truly invisible hem in a jacket is possible only if the coat or jacket will be lined. What makes this possible is the insertion of a bias strip of hair canvas that cushions the hem from the outside of the jacket. For a truly professional hem treatment, follow these steps:

Mark the creaseline of the hem with tailor's tacks or a long running stitch. This will enable you to press up the hem and eliminate any dips. Press up the hem. Check to see how much extra fullness is present in the hem after pressing. If there is only a small amount of fullness in the hem, deepen the seam allowances in the hem to take out the fullness. If there is a large amount of fullness in the hem, run an easeline 1/4 inch from the raw edge of the hem. Pull in the fullness with the easeline and press again with steam. Steam will help shrink in the fullness. If the fabric is heavy, you might want to try a combination of both methods.

Trim a small triangle out of the seam allowance at the junction of the seam and the creaseline. This will enable the hemline to have a sharp crease even at the seamline. Trim the seam allowance to 1/4 inch in the hem from the creaseline to the raw edge (Illustration 1).

In the facing, press seam allowances to opposite sides at the creaseline. Press hem seams toward the facing from the creaseline to the raw edge and toward the jacket from the creaseline up (Illustration 2). This will eliminate bulk in the facing hem area.

Cut strips of bias hair canvas 1 inch wider than the hem. Do not overlap bias strips to join, which creates bulk, but simply catch-stitch together.

Place the bias strip against the creaseline of the hem. Baste bias strip loosely in place with silk thread along the creaseline and at the top of the bias strip along the jacket. Catch only a thread on the jacket (Illustration 3). Limit yourself to silk thread for hand-sewing in the jacket hem area; it is finer and has more elasticity than other threads making the stitches less visible.

Fold hem back in place. Press. Pin hem into place 1 inch from the raw edge of the hem. Fold back the raw edge of the hem so that your hand hem stitches will be 1/2 inch from the raw edge of the hem. This will enable you to attach the hem of the jacket and

raw edge of the lining by machine if you desire. Do not rely on the lining to hold up the hem. This will result in a hem that is uneven and sags. Attach the hem to the hair canvas strip which you have already anchored into place. With the raw edge of the hem folded down about 1/2 inch, take one stitch on the hem at the fold and one stitch on the hair canvas. Never take the hem and the hair canvas in the same stitch. This will result in too tight a bond. Take one stitch in the hair canvas, move on about 3/8 inch, and take one stitch in the hem (Illustration 4). Attach lining. Catchstitch the facing to the jacket without turning under the raw edges. This also eliminates bulk at the facing.

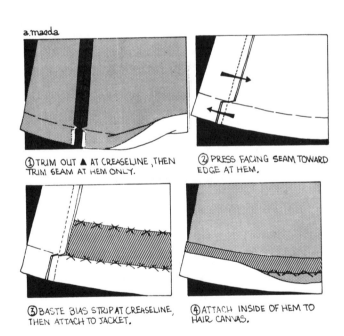

a. maeda

① TRIM OUT ▲ AT CREASELINE, THEN TRIM SEAM AT HEM ONLY.

② PRESS FACING SEAM TOWARD EDGE AT HEM.

③ BASTE BIAS STRIP AT CREASELINE, THEN ATTACH TO JACKET.

④ ATTACH INSIDE OF HEM TO HAIR CANVAS.

Hemming that Bulky Winter Coat

If you have ever hemmed a heavy coat yourself, you probably know how difficult it can be to get good results.

Few, if any, hems should be deeper than 3 inches since anything deeper creates too much bulk at the hemline. Trim all seam allowances that fall within the hem to $\frac{1}{4}$ inch. Run an easeline $\frac{1}{4}$ inch from the raw edge of the hem (Illustration 1).

Pull a thread in the easeline to reduce the fullness in the hem. Press the hem in place on the wrong side with a press and lift motion. This pressing method eliminates a ripply hem. To prevent the hem from making an imprint on the right side, I use a metal hem gauge called Dritz EzyHem®. By inserting the metal between the hem and the coat while pressing, the imprint is avoided (Illustration 2).

For the hem to maintain its nice smooth shape through several dry cleanings, an interfacing should be used in the hem. Cut a strip of bias hair canvas 1 inch wider than the hem itself.

Insert the hair canvas between the coat and the hem, placing the raw edge of the hair canvas against the hem fold. Press along the hem lightly with steam, shaping the bias hair canvas to the hem.

Pin the hair canvas to the hem and anchor the hair canvas to the top of the hem with a machine stitch along the top edge of the hem. The hair canvas is 1 inch wider than the hem so that in later pressings, the hair canvas will cushion the hard edge of the hem.

With a coat, it is necessary to hem twice in order to distribute the weight of the hem. Turn back the hem and hem the coat once halfway down the hem and again $\frac{1}{2}$ inch from the top of the hem (Illustration 3). All hem stitches will go through both hem and hair canvas.

When the facing in your coat or jacket is cut and seamed to the coat front separately, you will get a great deal of extra bulk when the hem is turned up and the seam is turned back on itself.

To eliminate this bulk, turn out the facing and turn up the hem, lining up the seamlines exactly. Now, on the right side of the garment, stitch in the well of the seam for the depth of the hem (Illustration 4). This step will help eliminate the bulk where facing and hem meet.

(The well of the seam is the "groove" you see when you look at a seam from the outside of a finished garment. When you stitch along the well of the seam, you are actually stitching along the threads of your original seam stitches.)

Trim seam allowances to $\frac{1}{4}$ inch, turn facing back to inside of coat and press and pound edge with a tailor's clapper. Stitch facing in place by hand.

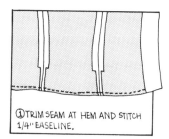
① TRIM SEAM AT HEM AND STITCH 1/4" EASELINE.

② EASE HEM AND PRESS WITH DRITZ EASY HEM.

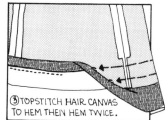
③ TOPSTITCH HAIR CANVAS TO HEM THEN HEM TWICE.

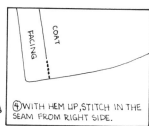
④ WITH HEM UP, STITCH IN THE SEAM FROM RIGHT SIDE.

a. maeda

Demonstrated on *Power Sewing* Video #7: *Hassle-Free Designer Jackets.*

Pants Hems

How many times have you hemmed a pair of men's or women's slacks only to find that they are too short, too long, or somehow just don't look right? And if you only allowed a 1- to 1½-inch hem allowance, a mistake can be disastrous.

Pinning up the hem while the slacks are on the wearer doesn't always work because the hem needs to be longer in back than in front, and without a point of reference, it is difficult to know just how long to make the back of the hem.

Equally disappointing is to compare the new slacks with an old pair, making them the same length at the side seam (Illustration 1). This can create problems because many pants ride lower at the waist than others.

In my experience, the most accurate way to determine the new length is to compare the new slacks with a pair of old slacks that are the correct length. But, rather than comparing them at the side seam, compare them at the inner leg seam (Illustration 2). Most well-fitting slacks are approximately the same length from crotch to hem. Measure your old pants from crotch to hem and use the measurement for your new hem length.

Allow for a 1½- to 2-inch hem, remembering to make the pants ½ to 1 inch longer in the back of the leg (Illustration 3). If you plan to wear the slacks with flat shoes, ½ inch is sufficient. With higher heels, 1 inch of extra length at the back is needed. The longer hem in back allows the slacks to hang much better over the shoe.

Taper the ½ or 1 inch extra length to zero at the side seams. The hem allowance is now curved in the back. To accommodate this, run an easeline ¼ inch from the raw edge in the back. Pull in some of the fullness (Illustration 4). Steam in place. This will allow the hem to lie flat.

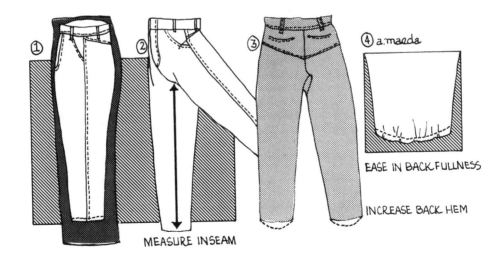

MEASURE INSEAM

④ a. maeda

EASE IN BACK FULLNESS

INCREASE BACK HEM

Bias Application

Sometimes facings create excess bulk in a garment and give the inside an unfinished appearance. If you are making a jacket or vest in a quilted fabric that is attractive on the inside as well as the outside, a bias finish would be preferable around the neck, armholes, or cuffs and down the front.

Wide bias tape could be used, but you have a greater choice of colors and patterns if you cut bias strips out of fabric. They should be 2½ inches wide. Press under ⅝ inch along one lengthwise edge (Illustration 1). If you are experiencing difficulty pressing a ⅝-inch seam allowance, cut bias strip wider than 2¾ inches. Fold strip in half lengthwise and press. Continue sewing two raw edges as one.

Before you sew on the bias strip, decide whether you want to finish the strip by hand on the inside of the garment or whether topstitching on the outside will give you the effect you want.

If you plan to topstitch, place right side of bias strip (the edge without the ⅝-inch fold or two raw edges) against wrong side of garment. Sew a ⅝-inch seam. Trim seam to ¼ inch (Illustration 2). Bring pressed fold just over stitching line and topstitch into place (Illustration 3).

Finishing the bias by hand is a technique I have used on the necklines of several silk dresses and on most children's clothes. To finish the neckline by hand and eliminate topstitching, place right side of bias strip against right side of garment. Stitch, trim, and turn as described earlier, but finish by hand-stitching bias strip into place on inside of garment (Illustration 4).

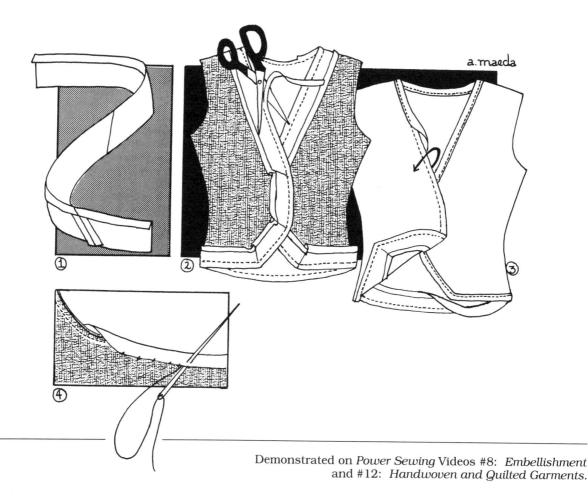

a. maeda

210

Demonstrated on *Power Sewing* Videos #8: *Embellishment* and #12: *Handwoven and Quilted Garments.*

Leather and Suede Trim

Leather or suede trim is one of the simplest ways to upgrade the look of a garment. Synthetic suede is very effective for trim as well as reducing the cost of dry cleaning. In small doses it is difficult to tell the difference between real and synthetic suede. Try these points of interest for suede or leather trim: welts on a welt pocket, undercollar, undercuff, neckband, cording on a slant hip pocket or bias trim around an entire coat.

The term bias trim is misleading when referring to suede and leather, since these skins do not have a grain. Referring to bias trim simply connotes a wrapped finish usually accomplished by wrapping and finishing a raw edge with a bias strip. To use suede or leather as a wrapped finished, simply cut strips $2\frac{1}{2}$ inches wide pieced together with enough length to go around the garment. Many facings can be eliminated by replacing them with this wrapped seam finish.

To eliminate problems when working with leather and suede, always use a leather needle and an even feed or teflon foot. Place the right side of the leather or suede strip against the right side of the garment. Sew a $\frac{5}{8}$-inch seam using care not to stretch the garment fabric or the strip on curves (Illustration 1). Square corners must be mitered. Trim both seam allowances down to $\frac{3}{8}$ inch, grading seams if the garment fabric is heavy. With a dry iron, press the leather or suede strip away from the garment fabric at the seam. This will ensure a standard neat seam wrap. Encase the raw edges of the newly formed seam by wrapping the leather or suede strip around the seam. Pin the wrapped seam into place by placing pins from the right side in the well of the seam. Using a leather needle and the even foot, topstitch the leather strip into place by sewing in the well of the seam from the right side (Illustration 2). On the back side of the garment, trim the leather strip close to the stitching (Illustration 3). Press and pound with a tailor's clapper.

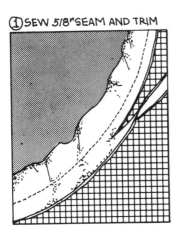

① SEW 5/8" SEAM AND TRIM

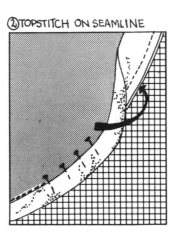

② TOPSTITCH ON SEAMLINE

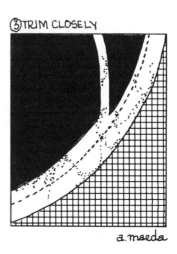

③ TRIM CLOSELY

a. maeda

Corded Seams

Garments with cording in contrasting fabrics periodically appear in the ready-to-wear collections. Using a few tricks, you can make cording that is as smooth and finished-looking as any found in ready-to-wear.

Cording is available in a small variety of colors in the seam tape racks of most stores, but considerably more versatility can be achieved if you make your own. Purchase the cord itself in the notions department. It comes in a variety of widths and has been preshrunk. If you like narrow piping, you can use a soft rayon cord called "rattail" as piping filler.

Cut $2\frac{1}{2}$-inch-wide strips of true bias out of the fashion fabric. True bias in firm fabrics is necessary to avoid a ripply appearance at curves. True bias can be determined by folding the crosswise edge at a right angle (Illustration 1).

If you do not have enough fabric to cut strips on the true bias, a strip cut well off grain (askew) in a soft pliable fabric will usually be sufficient. Strips from a knit fabric cut crossgrain make wonderful piping; $\frac{1}{4}$ yard produces 120 inches of piping strips. Striped fabric cut crossgrain produces an interesting effect when used as piping (see garment photo 14 in *More Power Sewing*.)

Wrap the bias strip around the cord with right sides out. Enclose the cord in the bias strip by sewing close to the cord with a zipper foot (Illustration 2). The zipper foot enables you to sew the bias snugly around the cording, preventing wrinkles. Trim the corded bias strip so that the distance between the line of stitching and the cut edge of the bias is $\frac{5}{8}$ inch.

To attach covered cord to garment, place raw edges of strip along the cut edge of the garment piece. To enable the piping strip to conform to curves or points, clip seam allowance of the piping strip at $\frac{1}{2}$ inch intervals. To avoid shortening garment seam, do not attach piping to garment by machine; attach by hand with a long basting stitch.

You are now ready to join the outer pattern piece, which will enclose the raw edges entirely. Place right sides together, with the side that the cording was previously joined to on top. Sew together. Use the basting line that joined the cording to the first piece as your guideline for joining the second piece. Use of the zipper foot enables you to sew close to the cording.

To avoid shortening piped seam as you join all layers, lengthen stitch slightly. A short stitch length through many layers shortens seams.

To eliminate bulk where two corded seams meet—at the shoulder, for example—pull $\frac{5}{8}$ inch of the cording out of the end of the corded seam and trim off. This will flatten the corded area in the seam allowance.

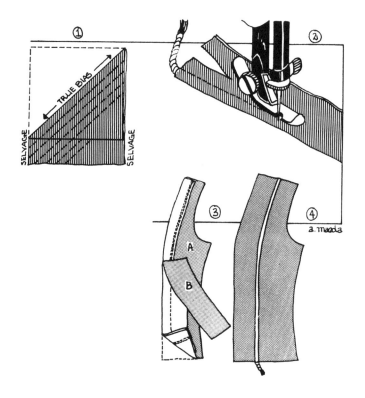

Ruffles

The most important point to know about ruffles is how to choose the right fabric. Any fabric that is stiff or heavy is going to result in disaster. A ruffle demands a soft fabric that drapes well.

In skirts, viyella and challis are good choices. A very soft corduroy can also work, but the ruffle must be cut on the lengthwise grain, so it won't drape as well.

My favorite skirt has a bias cut ruffle 10½ inches wide added to a gathered skirt 24 inches long. The ruffle is double the width of the skirt where they are joined.

For blouses, choose soft rayons, silk crepe de chine and similar lightweight fabrics that are soft and drape well. A circular ruffle is perhaps the most flattering on a blouse because of its cascade effect. Avoid plaids or stripes for this kind of ruffle.

Use narrow hems to finish ruffles—a hand-rolled hem on a blouse, and for the skirt try the rolled hem attachment.

The jabot will always be in style in one form or another because this soft ruffle under the chin is so flattering—even on those without a swan neck.

A jabot can easily be added to any round neck bodice with these simple calculations. Start by making a paper pattern to be pinned to the fabric for cutting.

Using a 12-inch square piece of paper, mark a dot at the center of one edge. This will be your starting point for your radius. Tie a string to a pencil. Measure 9 inches from the pencil and tie a knot in the string. Put a pin through the knot and place this pin at the center dot you made above. Draw a semicircle with a radius of 9 inches by moving the pencil back and forth (Illustration 1).

Shorten the string and draw a semicircle with a 3-inch radius from the same starting point. Cut out shape. Using the same technique, draw another semicircle pattern with outer radius of 7 inches and inner radius of 3 inches. Cut out that pattern (Illustration 2).

Cut out both patterns in fabric. Hem the outside edges by hand or with the narrow stitch on an overlock machine. Gather the neckline edge of both semicircles into ruffles with each gathered edge 2 inches in length. Place the wrong side of the larger ruffle against the right side of the bodice at center front; pin. Adjust gathers evenly. Baste. Press lightly. Place smaller ruffle on top of larger ruffle, right side on top. Adjust gathers. Baste. Press lightly (Illustration 3).

Finish neckline with a facing or bias strip.

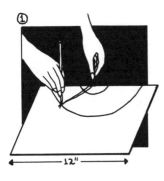

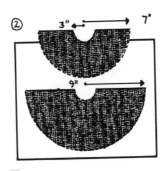

Make two semicircles of different sizes; hem, gather, and place at neckline.

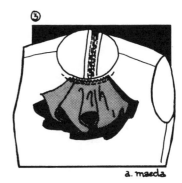

a. maeda

Braid and Cord Application

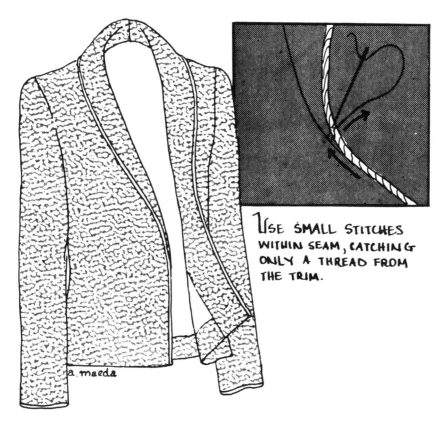

USE SMALL STITCHES WITHIN SEAM, CATCHING ONLY A THREAD FROM THE TRIM.

As we all know, finishing touches are often the details that make a garment unusual.

Narrow twill and satin cordings, as well as various braids, can be very effective, but the use of trim should be subtle so as not to overpower the jacket itself.

Application of trim and cording after the jacket has been completed must be done skillfully to avoid puckers in the jacket or the cording.

Use double thread, which has been pulled through beeswax. Beeswax strengthens the thread and keeps it from knotting.

You will have better luck with braid and trim application if you do not pin it first. Begin the trim in a place that will not receive too much attention. If you are trimming the bottom of a jacket, for instance, the side seam would be a good place to start. Open the seam a few stitches and slide raw end of trim in.

Slide the thread between the seam along the outer garment edge making ¼-inch stitches. In other words, bring out the needle every ¼ inch to catch a thread of the cording or the braid.

The secret of a smooth edge is not to pull your thread too tight. Remember, the garment fabric has some give during pressing, trim usually does not. If you are using trim wider than ½ inch, press the trim with steam into a curved shape before application.

After the cord or trim has been applied, press the trimmed edge well with steam, using a tailor's clapper.

Soutache Braid and Marabou

In lieu of making a new evening jacket this season, you might dress up a jacket you own with soutache braid or marabou feathers.

If the jacket has many sharp turns, it is best to sew on the braid so that it stands upright. Hold it in front of you, over the jacket, in an upright position. Bring the needle up through the material, catching a thread or two along the lower edge of the braid. Insert the needle back through the material as close as possible to the last stitch out of the material. Take a stitch ¼ inch long on the underside of the fabric and repeat the procedure (Illustration 1).

If the jacket is more simple, the braid can be applied flat. Hold it flat over the jacket, taking a stitch through the center of the soutache and the fabric, bringing the thread out on the wrong side of the fabric. Take a ¼-inch stitch on the wrong side of the fabric and very short stitches on the right side through the braid (Illustration 2).

To apply marabou feathers, the marabou must first be sewn to a ¾-inch bias strip of China silk or silk organza. Fold the strip in half with raw edges sitting together. Lay the marabou perfectly flat with the less attractive side up. Lay the bias strip over the stem of the marabou with raw edges next to the stem. Pin in place and sew with ½-inch stitches, using waxed thread for strength (Illustration 3).

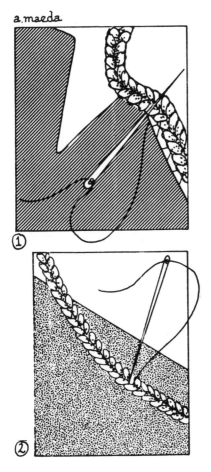

a.maeda

①

②

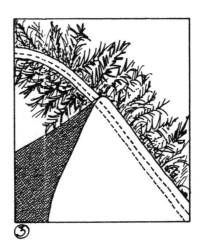

③

Knot Buttons and Frog Fasteners

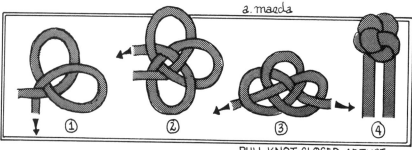

a. maeda

① ② ③ ④

PULL KNOT CLOSED, ADJUST
LOOPS EVENLY.
KNOT BUTTON

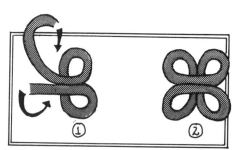

① ②

FROG
LOOP UNDER AND AROUND
HAND TACK ENDS IN PLACE
AND TURN OVER.

■ Pressing every seam as you sew results in a professional looking garment with a flatness seldom associated with home-sewn garments.

Ordinary buttons and buttonholes just don't look right on a quilted or embroidered Oriental jacket. A frog and heavy knot fastener is not difficult to make, and it gives an expensive look to a garment when made in matching fabric-corded tubing.

You might like to experiment with cords of various sizes for different effects. A ¼-inch cord is usually used, but I made fasteners from ⅜-inch cord for a silk jacket and they are very effective. You will need about 10 inches of tubing for each knot and a little more for each frog.

The knot button is merely a series of three loops. Follow the three steps as illustrated. The buttons are

easier to make if the loops are kept fairly loose until the final loop has been made and you are pulling the knot closed. After the knot is completed, cut off the ends about ¼ inch from the knot and sew them to the knot, using thread strengthened with beeswax. Two frogs may be used for each closure, or only one on the "buttonhole" side.

Bead a Dress

If you have been ogling the beaded dresses and jackets at some of the better stores, you may have considered trying some beading yourself. Although it looks difficult, it is easy, relaxing, and very rewarding.

Bead stores carry a large assortment of beads as well as needles fine enough for the work. If you are lucky enough to have some antique beads around, you can begin almost immediately.

Notions departments also carry the fine needles necessary for stitching through the tiny holes of the beads.

The best thread to use is silk thread which is very fine and does not knot easily.

If you are using a strand of antique beads, do not rely on the old thread to hold the beads in line. There is a temptation to use the long strand and catch-stitch a bead every fifth one. Unfortunately, the old thread may break after a dry cleaning or two, so it is best to anchor each bead with new thread.

Sketch out a design on paper and use tracing paper to transfer it to the wrong side of garment. When the design is visible on wrong side, hand-baste, in contrasting color, the elements of the design. This will transfer the design to the right side, where you will be working.

Most fabrics need a little additional support to keep the beaded area from sagging under the weight of the beads. Baste on a piece of silk organza or iron on some very lightweight press-on interfacing. I beaded a zigzag design down one shoulder and sleeve of a black wool crepe dress in jet black beads. I used a lightweight press-on interfacing behind the design on the wrong side of the fabric (Illustration 1).

Bead on the right side of the fabric using double silk thread and a fine needle. Slide bead onto thread, take a short back-stitch through fabric and interfacing and continue on to the next bead (Illustration 2).

The basted thread line following your design is your guide. Remove all basting after beading is completed.

① INTERFACING STRIPS.

② BACKSTITCH WITH FINE NEEDLE AND BEAD.

2. maeda

Chanel-Inspired Styling

While designer Coco Chanel is responsible for a wide variety of innovative styles, to most women the name Chanel conjures up an image of a simple collarless cardigan with knitted braid trim.

If you want to create a Chanel-inspired jacket of your own, many suitable patterns are available. Look for a simple cardigan style with small shoulders and high armholes. If you haven't already purchased your fabric, visit a well stocked trim department to see what's available in knitted or braided flat trims. What you are looking for is an interesting, pliable, flat trim.

You are not looking for fold-over trim to wrap around the Jacket edge. Fold-over trim works well on sweaters, but is unsuitable for Chanel-inspired creations. Knitted or braided trim should be finished on both edges since it will be applied after the jacket is nearly completed. You may even want to purchase a few samples to take with you fabric shopping. When you look for fabric, look for bouclÇs and loosely woven tweeds. These capture the Chanel feeling.

Because the jacket fabric is loosely woven, underlining is necessary to support not only the line of the jacket but pocket detailing as well.

Prewashed silk organza and lightweight silk broadcloth make excellent underlinings. Do not use fusible interfacings for underlining. The original Chanel Jackets of this type were worn somewhat like a sweater soft and comfortable, not overly structured. Fusible, no matter how lightweight, will give the fabric undesired crispness, caused by the glue.

Since no facing was used In the original Chanels of this type, facings are eliminated. Lining comes right to the edge along neck and front. Traditional hems are used on sleeves and jacket body; therefore, lining is attached to the top of the hem. Don't cut lining too skimpy. When cutting lining, allow for 2 inch center back pleat and cut the lining to the finished length of the body and sleeves. When the lining is attached to the top of the hem, small take-up tuck will be formed, allowing movement without tearing the lining.

Chanel-Inspired Styling

Since the body of the jacket is underlined, interfacing is unnecessary for this soft style. If you desire a crisper front edge, a soft sew-in interfacing can be used around neck and down front edges. Attach any desired interfacing to the underlining. If you decide not to use interfacing, sandwich a small strip of fusible web behind all buttonhole placements between the fashion fabric and the underlining. Fusible web will give slight support to buttonholes and strengthen the fabric in this well-used area.

Construct the jacket using a soft lining, such as china silk, silk pongée or silk charmeuse. Soft lining is a must to maintain the sweater-like feel to the Chanel-inspired jacket.

If you would like to make something really special, pipe all jacket edges with satin piping. Knitted trim will then be applied by hand to the jacket. The combination of knitted trim next to the satin piping is quite striking. Piping is optional, of course.

Before trim application, run a small hand stitch ¼ inch from finished edge around the neck and front edges between the lining and the edge of the garment. This small hand-stitch bonds the fashion fabric and lining together, preventing lining from rolling to the outside—necessary since there is no facing.

Trim is applied around the entire jacket sleeves and top of pockets. Purchase slightly more to allow for shrinkage and mitering on corners. Preshrink trim by merely holding an iron which gives out plenty of steam ½ inch away from trim. This process allows trim to relax.

To prevent trim from ravelling on starting end, machine sew with small stitches through one thickness of braid. Cut excess trim away beyond line of stitching, creating a clean edge. Press under ¼ inch of trim on the end. Begin trim at side seam, aligning edge of trim with edge of garment. Miter trim at corners (see page 205). Trim away excess trim under miter only if you feel your machine-sewing is strong enough to prevent the braid from ravelling. Most miters on knitted braid may be flattened into oblivion with a good press and pound with a clapper.

Braid can be shaped on curves with an iron if necessary. For hand-stitching braid to garment,

strengthen thread by running through beeswax. Do not pull thread too tight as you attach each side of the braid to the garment. Braid should float on the surface, but be well attached. Hand stitches can be ¼ to ½ inch apart.

If your goal is Chanel-inspired, gold buttons are a must. A well stocked button department may even have a few inscribed with a lion's head or two C's—Chanel trademarks.

Since this jacket is not overly constructed, good shape is maintained with a string of weighted gold chain. Attach chain 1 inch above finished hem from center front to center front.

Hand buttonholes on top and faced or bound buttonholes through the lining give the most authentic result for the Chanel-inspired jacket (see page 152). If you prefer to do machine buttonholes, make buttonholes *before* trim is attached. Try buttonhole twist thread or shiny rayon thread on the top of the machine, using an "N" needle, and regular thread on the bobbin.

For more information on Chanel-inspired clothing, Barbara Kelly's class at the Sewing Workshop in San Francisco is very informative. Also, Claire Shaeffer has written an article on the subject published in issue 23 of *Threads* magazine.

The Art of Pressing

Good pressing can turn a mediocre-looking garment into a beautiful one if the presser knows how to handle her tools: the iron, a presscloth, a tailor's ham, and most important, the tailor's clapper.

The clapper, an essential for serious sewers, is a 9 by 3-inch block of hardwood with rounded edges. It can be purchased in most notions departments.

Many a construction mistake has been steamed and flattened into obscurity. An accomplished seamstress is as good with the iron as she is with the sewing machine.

Some fabrics shrink with the use of steam; others shine if pressed on the right side without a press cloth. Press a sample piece of fabric to discover any idiosyncrasies. (Use little or no dampness on silks.)

Construction pressing is the pressing you do as you are making the garment. After a seam is sewn, press the seam closed on both sides. This will get rid of any ripples. Now press the seam open.

Never put more weight than the weight of the iron on the underside. Too much pressure on the wrong side of the garment leaves seam imprints on the right side. If your fabric is temperamental and the seam imprint shows on the right side, slip 1-inch strips of brown paper between the seam allowances and the garment when pressing.

Before pressing on right side of garment, try a sample piece of fabric. If pressing directly on the right side of a garment causes a shine or flattening effect, cover garment with press cloth and use steam for a good press (no steam on silk, please). The right side can take more pressure than the wrong one.

Napped fabrics take special consideration. To avoid flattening the nap, always keep the right side down against a needle board during pressing. June Tailor's Velvaboard, 8 by 34 inches, is excellent for napped fabrics.

I have found June Tailor's Bristled Pressing Cloth (available in notions departments) especially helpful in making tailored jackets in velvet. It allows you to press lapels on the right side.

Areas that need shaping, such as collars, the bust and sleeve caps, should be pressed over a tailor's ham, also obtainable in notions departments. Pressing on the ham retains the shape of curved and three-dimensional details.

Now for the real finishing touch. Most garments made at home lack the sharp, crisp edges of their counterparts in the stores. The industry uses 12-pound steam irons to achieve that look.

To get the maximum effect from the tailor's clapper, press the area to be flattened with a dampened press cloth. Holding the iron in your right hand and the clapper in your left, press the clapper against the fabric as you lift the iron off. Hold the clapper against the fabric for about five seconds, to hold in steam and flatten the surface.

Use the clapper on pockets, collars, tab fronts, waistbands, lapels—virtually any area of detail. But never use a clapper on seams because it will bring out an imprint of the seam allowance.

Lace, braid and trim can all be blocked into shape before applying by hand to the garment.

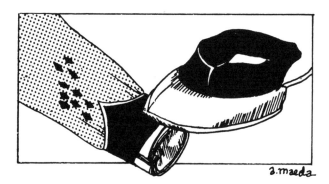

To press a cuff, insert a rolled-up magazine into the sleeve, press with steam, and pound with a clapper.

Blocking Shape Into Pants

Here is a pants-pressing trick used by tailors to gain a close fit through the derriere without destroying the hang of the garment. Famous pants designer Leonora Schulhoff gives us this trick.

After the pants pieces have been cut out, mark the front and back creaselines clearly. You are now ready to shrink in fullness along the creaseline and stretch the fabric along the seamlines.

Whenever a fabric is pressed along the fold, the fabric tends to stretch. Pressing a crease in pants after they have been constructed can actually stretch the creaseline at the fold and cause the pants to hang improperly. This shrink-and-stretch technique will eliminate all that.

Before assembling pants, fold each of the four pant pieces right side out along the creaseline. Set a soft crease with a press-and-lift motion, working from hem to waistline.

Holding the cut edges of the pants taut, start stretching and ironing at the same time along the seam edges of the pants.

This will cause the creaseline fold to wrinkle a bit. Using a steam iron with plenty of steam and employing a press-and-lift motion, steam fullness out. Repeat this process if necessary until a distinct curve is formed. Then assemble pants as pattern indicates.

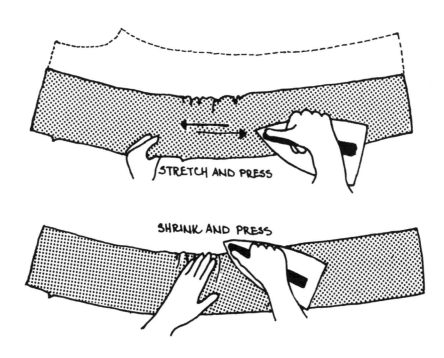

Organizing Your Work Space

Ideally, we would all like a separate sewing area, a place where we could leave everything out and ready for whenever a few hours sewing is possible. For most of us, this is a dream. Everything has to be put away between work times.

Two or three medium to large cardboard boxes can make the task a lot faster. Put the current project in one box. Another box can be used for interfacing, zippers, buttons, trim, thread. The third box should be used solely for sewing tools. A handyman's tool box is perfect for this. I will mention a few tools I consider essential.

A tailor's clapper: A clapper is a small piece of hardwood used to flatten certain details of a garment, such as collars, lapels, pockets, tabs, waistbands, cuffs.

To use a clapper, press the detail with plenty of steam. Immediately after removing the iron, press down hard with the tailor's clapper. The clapper holds the steam in the fabric, flattening the area. Never use a clapper on seams or hems, or an imprint will form on the right side.

A point turner has saved many collars from frayed ends, caused by pushing the point out with scissors. Point turners come in wood and plastic. A point turner enables you to get a sharp corner without tearing the fabric. Use it in the same way you would the points of the scissors, only without the disastrous results.

A tailor's ham is a cloth-covered item shaped exactly like a ham, filled with sawdust. A ham is a pressing aid used to shape certain areas when pressing a garment.

Press darts over the ham instead of a flat ironing board and the garment will mold better to the shape of the body. Mold a collar or lapel over the ham, press, and you will notice a better roll.

Good scissors are essential. If your scissors are dull, either get them sharpened or throw them out. You don't need that sort of aggravation in your life. Wipe the blades occasionally with a cloth to remove the lint.

And you need a seam ripper. In fact, you need two. If you need to rip something out, you are usually experiencing some anxiety and your eyesight may be affected. Not finding the ripper adds to the annoyance.

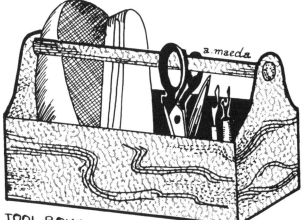

TOOL BOX: TAILOR'S HAM, CLAPPER SHARP SCISSORS, POINT TURNER, SEAM RIPPERS.

A magnetic seam guide is a must if your machine is metal and not plastic. This little magnet is placed $5/8$ inch to the right of the needle. It acts as a fence while you are sewing. You can push the fabric against it and get perfect $5/8$-inch seams.

Of course, you need a tape measure and a ruler for measuring things. I like the fashion ruler, which has one straight side for measuring grainlines and one curved side, which aids in making alterations. Everything I mention can be found in the notions department.

Beeswax in a holder is essential for strengthening the thread for handwork like sewing on buttons and hooks. Simply run your double thread through the beeswax. The wax makes the thread much stronger and also keeps the thread from knotting.

Do not use beeswax on your thread for handhemming. The wax makes the thread too thick and the hem is no longer invisible.

Organizing Your Work Space

A new item that I have found especially useful is the needle sorter. Singer Select-O-Pac® is a small wheel with slots for different sized sewing machine needles. This is great if you change needles often. If I am making a silk blouse, I am using a size 60/8 needle. To hem a pair of jeans, I need a size 100/16. After you take the small needle out of the machine, what do you do with it? Chances of your remembering the size later are slim. The needle sorter does all of the remembering for you.

The toolbox needs some Scotch tape, waxed chalk, and air-erasable felt-tip pens for making alterations. A good steam iron and press cloth might also be kept in the box. I use cheesecloth for a press cloth, as it is excellent for holding moisture. Stacy's Clean & Glide® Iron Cleaner is a must.

If you sew with velour, velvet, or corduroy, you need a needle board. This is a small board with stiff needles protruding every ⅛ inch. When pressing napped fabrics, place the right side of the fabric against the needles. You can then press and pound with the tailor's clapper without crushing the nap.

You will add more tools that fit your needs, and having them all in one place saves a lot of time.

■ Store patterns in large manila envelopes with the pattern taped to the outside. This eliminates trying to cram them back into the original envelope.

■ To keep the foot pedal from moving around on the floor when you are sewing, tape it to the floor with masking tape.

Care and Feeding of Your Sewing Machine

There is nothing more annoying than a sewing machine so jammed with knotted threads that the fabric gets stuck under the presser foot.

To fix, lift up the presser foot and hold the fabric lightly but firmly. At the same time, turn the balance wheel (the large wheel found at the right end of the machine) forward and backward in small turns. This will release your fabric.

Now here's where the light touch comes in. Open up your bobbin case and study the extra threads, and perhaps the knots. By cutting these threads you will only leave the ends lodged—often where you can't reach them.

Take one of the threads in your fingers and pull lightly at the same time that you are moving the balance wheel forward and backward. You will find that the extra threads will all come out in one piece. Rethread your bobbin and you are ready to sew again.

A very noisy sewing machine can be caused by two things: a dull or bent needle and/or lack of proper oiling.

Try changing the needle first. Man-made fabrics dull both scissors and sewing needles, so you may find it necessary to change the needle more often.

Sewing machines rarely need oil more than once a year with once-a-week use. Oil sparingly in all the holes, using sewing machine oil. The bobbin workings may need to be oiled more frequently. Keep lint out of the feed dog and keep moving parts oiled.

Adjusting the tension should not be necessary for every fabric. Looping can be caused by a dull needle, incorrect threading, or merely missing a thread guide. Check threading first and put in a new needle before touching the tension.

■ Using the correct sewing machine needle is essential to eliminate frequent thread-breaking.

■ When changing thread, do not simply pull the spool away from the machine. This can mess up the tension. Clip thread at spools and pull out remaining thread through the needle. This process will prevent needless tension repairs.

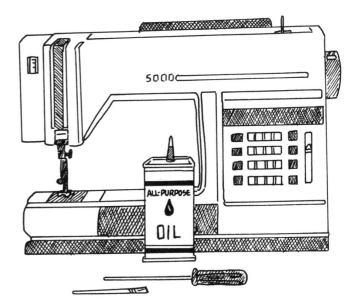

Leftover tapestry from upholstery sofa *inspired this fitted Style pattern. Lightweight interfacing—fusible knitted tricot—is used on front and side fronts, eliminating interfacing altogether on facing due to stability and body of tapestry fabric (see page 8 in* **More Power Sewing**). *Since fabric leftovers were used, pattern match is impossible, camouflaged by corded seams (see page 212). Mismatched antique buttons using button loops as closure provide the finishing touch.*

Always keep an eye out for interesting fabric. This well styled top is made from **African mudcloth** using a Burda pattern. Decorative braid on bias loops form closures for buttons from Worldly Goods (see Sources for address). Asymmetrical closing in this overshirt makes an excellent tummy camouflage. For button loop closure (see page 150).

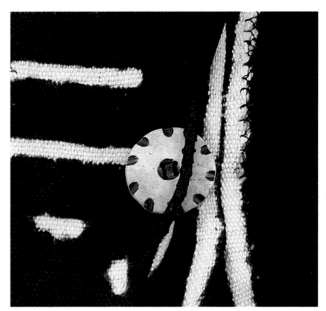

2. **Straight sheath dress** with dolman sleeves is made from a Vogue pattern in wool crepe (see page 144 in **More Power Sewing** for crepe tips). Back neckline was changed to mirror front neckline (instructions for beading on page 217).

1. **Cocoon styled opera coat** with dolman sleeves is made from a McCall's pattern in a crushed rayon velvet with antique lace trim (see page 82 for velvet tips). Shoulder to sleeve seam embellishment added using bridal tulle for stuffing.

Rayon jacquard jacket is cut with double front to keep facing in place and give support to a weak fabric (see **More Power Sewing**, page 10). Entire front is interfaced with fusible knit tricot. Jacket is made from a Vogue pattern. Hem is eliminated on Burda skirt by cutting skirt double, facing bottom edge with second skirt piece. Beaded appliques, seed and bugle beads trim hemline on skirt (see pages 200-202 in **More Power Sewing**).

Organize
Your Time

No matter how much you love to sew, time seems to be at a premium. It is mandatory to get organized to complete your projects in a reasonable time period.

Much time can be wasted shopping. Fabric-shop for outfits rather than separates. When buying the fabric for a skirt, choose the fabric for the blouse and jacket at the same time. This will eliminate making separates that are wonderful but go with nothing you currently have in your wardrobe.

If possible, start with accessories, such as shoes and purse—before the fabric purchase. I find it is far easier to match fabric to accessories than vice versa.

Before you leave the fabric store, buy interfacing, stay tape, zipper, buttons, and any other needed notions. This saves a return trip.

Cut out and mark two or three garments at once. Consider using pattern weights rather than pins. Mark with snips center front, center back, and fold-lines so that constant reference to pattern is unnecessary. Cut out and apply interfacing wherever needed *before* you begin sewing.

Read through the pattern and think through the garment before sewing. You may have read about a method that will be faster and more professional than that indicated in the pattern instructions.

Try to anticipate any problems you may have before you begin sewing and figure out solutions before rather than after poor results.

Use the "clothesline method" for sewing as much as possible. Sew two shoulder seams in one continuous stitch. Snip between the two shoulders. Machine-knot at the beginning and end of all seams to eliminate bulky backstitching or time-consuming tying of threads.

Hang garment pieces on a hanger between sewing times. This eliminates a great deal of pressing.

Set aside blocks of time if possible. Miracles can occur in three uninterrupted hours. If the phone is the culprit, take it off the hook. If a large block of time is impossible, think small.

As Marcy Tilton from the Sewing Workshop in San Francisco says, "You can set a sleeve in 20 minutes. Get up a half hour earlier. Use the nicest part of the day for your favorite activity."

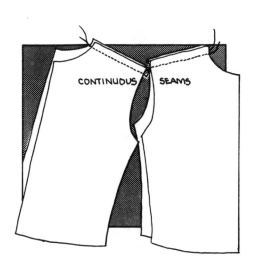

Work Around Your Small-Fry

"What do you do with your children when you sew?" I had 7-month-old twins, a boy of 2½ and an 11-year-old girl, when I was asked this question. So I had naturally given it quite a bit of thought. After a lot of experimentation, I found some solutions.

Advance preparation is the key. In addition to having your sewing area organized, have the machine threaded and the garment cut out. Because most cutting involves alterations, concentration is a must. This is best accomplished without distraction, so wait until babies are asleep.

Before you begin sewing, round up everything you think you will need for four hours: diapers, bottles (two more than you think you need), pacifiers, rattles, teething rings. For older children, bring crackers and fruit that can be used as bribes for good behavior. Make sure a cup is nearby. Someone will need a drink within the first 5 minutes. Put all of these items in a basket you carry to the site. This saves ten separate trips upstairs.

Next to my sewing area, I have a covered foam mat where I lay the babies and a low table for the 2-year-old to play on with toys I let him use only when I am sewing—three small cars, one little bag of marbles, a book, a package of picture postcards, a stuffed bear.

If the children are older, puzzles are great. Set a kitchen timer for 15 minutes as incentive for each of you to work quietly on your own. Every 30 minutes, sit down for ten minutes to read a story, help with a project, or roughhouse a bit. Set the timer for your 10 minutes of together play. When the bell goes off, tell the children it is time for each of you to go back to work.

After playtime and your sewing time is over, put all of the toys back in a plastic bag in the closet near the machine. The important thing to remember is that the contents of this bag are only used when you are sewing. When you finish sewing for the day, round everything up and put it out of sight until the next time.

It is not easy to sew with small children around, but it can be done. If you accomplish only half of what you had hoped, don't get annoyed. Be happy with what you did get done rather than what you didn't and do the same thing tomorrow.

Stop Making Clothes Children Hate

As a mother of young children, I know well the frustration of finding a wonderful pattern, choosing the fabric, spending far too much time on construction, and having the outfit worn only once to please Mommy. How can we get out of this self-defeating cycle of making clothes our children hate?

The secret lies in taking a well planned shopping trip to a store that offers a big selection. Really listen to what the child says while examining clothes. Take a notebook. Make notations of the child's favorite colors, choice of prints, fabrics themselves.

Buy things that look too time-consuming to make. Number one in that category is pants with a fly front. Don't rule out the possibility that making school clothes could be easy. My son's favorite shirt is a plain black sweatshirt to which I appliqued fake fur trim in shapes he cut out himself. Most children love sweatshirts. Buy several plain ones in assorted colors. Let the child decide on the decoration.

For girls, body-conscious knit miniskirts, stirrup pants or leggings combined with oversized tops are a big hit. Keep proportion in mind; children don't want to look fat, either. Big tops need skinny bottoms for the look to make it in a girl's eyes.

Comfort and ease in dressing are other key points in children's eyes. Pull-on pants and tops will always be more popular than button versions. Soft fabrics rate high marks. If you are uncertain about sizing, compare the pattern to one of their favorites by flat pattern measurement. You are more likely to get a fit that's at least in the ball game.

Are the pants you make for your children too big in the seat? Try cutting 4 fronts instead—a perfect solution for skinny bodies.

Marketing Your Skills

Many excellent amateur seamstresses who are spending eight hours a day at a job they don't enjoy have asked me how to turn their sewing hobby into a career.

The most profitable businesses are those that fill a specific need. For example, San Francisco is full of restaurants, each one trying to establish a unique identity in a very competitive area. One entrepreneur contacted several restaurants and made arrangements to sew vests, cummerbunds and aprons especially for each establishment.

Another sewing hobbyist started a menswear line specializing in a silky, sexy T-shirt for men. Find the need and fill it.

When you have decided what item you will make, make it up many times, perfecting it and cutting down sewing time as much as possible while retaining quality. Sit down and decide on possible outlets for the item. Ask friends. Keep written notes.

Make several samples of your product. If you don't have the confidence to sell the product yourself, find someone who does. Offer a commission; ten to twelve percent of the wholesale price is about standard.

Deciding on the selling price can be tricky. Make up the item, timing yourself to the minute, with no interruptions. Figure out how much your time is worth. Add to this figure the cost of materials. Then add in the salesman's commission, if you have one. Most stores will charge their customers twice what they are paying you for the product. Will the product sell at this price?

Once your samples are made and you have established your wholesale cost, you are ready to begin selling. Take orders and give an honest estimate of the delivery date—and keep to it. Stores know the best times for selling an item and count on you to deliver on time. If you are going to be late, at least have the courtesy to call.

Now suppose your orders get too big for you to fill. You will have to hire other people to cut and sew for you. Most garment factories have fluctuating periods of productivity. A small factory would probably welcome the work of a relatively small order if it could be done during a slow time. Look in the Yellow Pages under "Dresses—Manufacturers" and "Sewing—

Contract." Call a few and discuss your needs. Most will be happy to talk to you, and if they cannot do the work, often they will recommend someone who can.

To make a profit in this competitive arena, you will need to find wholesale and retail sources for the items you need. The directory for the Los Angeles area is TALA Westcoast Directory, 110 East Ninth St., Suite C 765, Los Angeles, Ca 90070 (213) 627-6173. The directory for the New York area is the Fashion Resource Directory, Fairchild Publications, 7 West 34th Street, New York, NY 10001 (1-800-247-6622).

Professional dressmaking has some very distinct advantages as a career. It is a business that can be operated from the home; therefore it can be combined successfully with the rearing of young children. Commuting time is eliminated. Being your own boss, you can work at your own pace and set your own schedule.

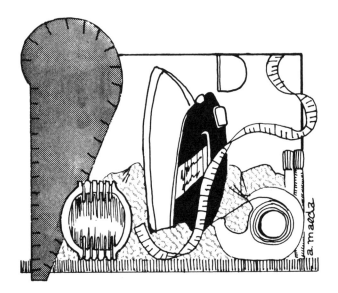

Marketing Your Skills

A good dressmaker can earn about $10 an hour—more if he or she specializes.

Several factors can help determine whether dressmaking would be successful for you. Since you work at your own pace, you must be motivated and organized to make maximum use of your sewing time. Scheduling periods of undisturbed sewing time is the best idea.

Coming across as a competent professional has a number of facets:

• Your personal appearance should be attractive and well put together.

• Your work area should be organized and uncluttered.

• A portfolio of your work should be available for viewing by prospective customers.

If your sewing skills are somewhat limited, under no circumstances should you take on a project that is beyond your ability. If the result is not professional, it will kill your reputation.

It is far better to specialize in the areas you do well. For example, specialize in men's and women's shirts. Practice collars and sleeve plackets until they are flawless. Charge a flat fee per shirt.

One seamstress specialized in putting up hems. She worked in a large office, carried four hem style samples in her purse and marked hems at lunch hour. She charged high fees but guaranteed 48-hour service.

Another successful woman specializing in silk ties gave away 20 of her ties to men she considered well dressed and visible in the business world. Her ties were outstanding. Undoubtedly they were noticed. In a few weeks she called her 20 contacts and asked if they would like to order any ties and if they knew other men who would like to see her samples. She sold a lot of ties.

The approach to dressmaking can be made from many angles, but it should be rewarding.

Informative interviews with designers, dressmakers, and a sales rep as well as lots of valuable information for anyone starting a business in this field is available in my video, *Marketing What You Make—Video #11.*

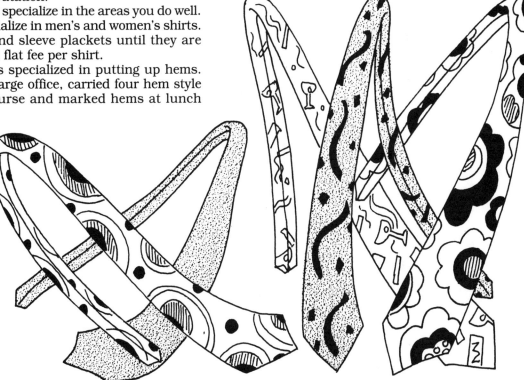

Reverse Applique

If you like uneven surfaces, asymmetrical lines and/or textural fabric, you will find reverse applique appealing. Well-known California designer Jean Caciedo is, in my opinion, the absolute master of this technique. Her felted wool vests and coats make their way to wearable art establishments such as Obiyko in San Francisco and Julies in New York. Caciedo is adept at repositioning seams to form a canvas for her designs. Meltons, felted wools, and leather make good canvas choices for this technique.

If you don't think of yourself as artistic, think geometric forms. Most of us can either draw or trace a circle, square or rectangle. Letters of the alphabet or shapes from nature such as leaves or shells make simple shapes which can be used for applique forms.

Cut desired shapes from thin cardboard no thicker than the back of a standard writing tablet. Cut cardboard shapes exactly as they will appear on the garment. Applique fabric works best if its weight is similar to the weight of the fashion fabric. For example, when making a melton wool vest, I used contrasting color melton wool for appliques. If the applique fabric is lighter weight, consider doubling or using press-on interfacing on the back side to give more stability.

For reverse applique, work is done from the wrong side of the garment. Decide desired placement of motif on garment. Cover this area with applique fabric which is cut about an inch larger than template in all directions. Place the right side of the applique fabric on the wrong side of the fashion fabric. Position template. Since pins will distort template, tape template and applique fabric to the wrong side of the fashion fabric. Since you are working on the wrong side of the garment, position motif the mirror image of what you ultimately want. This is especially important with lettering. In an attempt to get the word "NO," I got the word "ON" with the "N" backwards. Work backwards on lettering. Tape into place. Go to a mirror to check. This is how it will read on the outside of the garment. Allow at least ⅝ inch spacing between each letter for topstitching.

Using template as a guide for sewing, sew around template with a straight stitch. If you are sewing on the cardboard, you are sewing too fast. Make certain to machine knot or tie off threads at beginning and

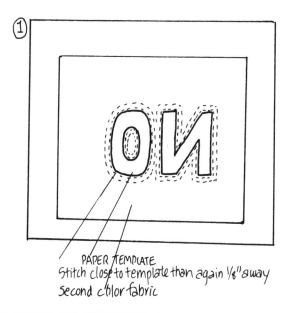

PAPER TEMPLATE
Stitch close to template than again ⅛" away
second color fabric

CUT
close to
stitching

Reverse Applique

end of all stitching. A second row of stitching ¼ inch to the outside of the template gives added definition to the reverse applique.

From the WRONG side of the garment, trim away excess applique fabric close to the second row of stitching. From the RIGHT side of the fabric, within the applique design, make a slight clip with sharp scissors on the fashion fabric. Do not go in too deep with scissor points. The goal is to trim away the top layer of fabric within the motif so that the applique fabric shows through. Trim top fashion fabric away to the initial stitching line, revealing the applique fabric.

Close to the stitching, rub fingernail back and forth, forcing all stray threads to stand up and be clipped off. Your reverse applique is now finished.

If your fashion fabric has a tendency to ravel, in my opinion a poor fabric choice for reverse applique, the applique can then be finished with a satin stitch, a dense narrow zigzag, width 3 mm., length 0.6, tension 2. Use rayon thread, Sulky or Madeira, and a machine embroidery needle. Satin stitch, while giving a finish to the outside of the motif, cuts down on the dimensional qualities of reverse applique, making it appear flatter, more like regular applique work.

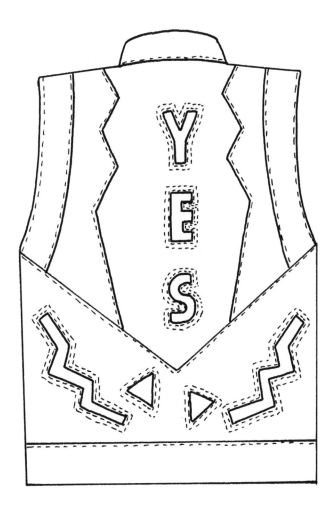

Cutwork

You may be familiar with cutwork on tablecloths and pillowcases. A white or black linen shirt becomes very special with cutwork. Until I met Michelle Pullen, cutwork and applique designer from Australia, I was intimidated by cutwork. Now I love it. Try the following on your next linen blouse.

Before you begin, you will need: iron-on design transfers; fabric stabilizer in sheet form, such as Stitch and Tear or, in liquid form, Perfect Sew Fabric Stabilizer; machine embroidery needle by Madeira; shiny rayon thread—Madeira and Sulky are my favorites; water soluble disappearing fabric—called "magic fabric" in Australia. Fashion fabric must be preshrunk before you begin.

Perfect Sew Fabric Stabilizer is a relatively new product which makes both cutwork and applique a much simpler process. Since this product dissolves in water, tedious time spent cutting fabric stabilizer out between sewing lines is eliminated. If your design is small, it becomes difficult to get the stabilizer to tear away from small design elements. If this is not available in stores near you, try mail-order notions—Clotilde or Nancy's—listed in Sources. Liquid stabilizer beefs up the fabric enough so that machine stitching will not bunch up the fabric.

Wet fashion fabric thoroughly with liquid fabric stabilizer, only in area where design will be applied. Saturate thoroughly. This product feels thick and gooey. It can be poured on or brushed on. Let air dry or use a hair dryer to speed up the process. Using this product will save time later.

If using fabric stabilizer by the sheet, such as Stitch and Tear, cut a piece slightly larger than design. Press onto the wrong side of the fabric. One stabilizer, liquid or by the sheet—not both—is needed to give the fashion fabric support so that it will not bunch up during decorative sewing.

Place design transfer against the right side of the fabric. With a hot iron, press over design paper. Lift paper up carefully to make sure design has transferred to fabric. If you are working on a fabric such as black linen, tracing paper and wheel will transfer the design with greater visibility.

With regular thread and straight stitch length 1.5 mm, sew around all shapes. Save time—do not cut threads between designs. Sew slowly in this step; designs are defined but not reshaped later. Backstitch or machine knot at beginning and end. Use small sharp stitches to cut out designated design shape. On shapes which have been cut out, an additional step is necessary. Switch stitch to zigzag width of 2 mm and stitch length of 1 mm. Zigzag around cut-out shapes. Zigzag goes over original straight stitch, into cut-out. Trim any fraying fabric or threads from the inside of cut-out.

Cut a piece of Solvy—"magic fabric"—large enough for design area. Pin Solvy behind work you are doing, on the wrong side of the fabric.

Change machine needle to a machine embroidery needle. Thread shiny rayon thread on top only, not on bobbin. This same thread can be used in outline stitching of design elements as well. If your machine is capable of satin stitch, use this stitch. If not, a dense zigzag can be used. Experiment on a scrap to get the length, width and tension correct. Start with zigzag width 3 mm and stitch length 1 mm. Decrease upper tension between the range of 4 and 1. Decrease stitch length and tension until the result is an even dense flat stitch. My preference is zigzag 3 mm, stitch length of 0.4 mm, tension 2.

To finish corners go over again

This   not this

■ Michelle Pullen's cutwork patterns are available from Stretch and Sew (see Sources).

■ Cut a piece of Solvy—"magic fabric"—large enough for design area. Pin Solvy behind work you are doing, on the wrong side of the fabric.

Cutwork

Start shiny dense zigzag or satin stitch on outside edges of design, working inward. When turning a corner, leave needle in down position on the outside of the corner. Turn; the next stitches should sew over corner again. If needle is left in down position on inside of a corner, a gap in stitches will result. Always sew over where you started a few stitches to seal thread ends.

Slow down. Be careful to stop and start decorative stitching on straight stitching lines which indicate pattern. If you sew too fast, you will miss the turns. Clip off excess threads.

Tear off Solvy. If you have used a fabric stabilizer such as Stitch and Tear, you must now tear off this stabilizer from the back of the fabric around and between design elements. A seam ripper can help, but use carefully to avoid cutting through fashion fabric.

If you have used the liquid fabric stabilizer, merely tear off the excess Solvy and rinse in warm water. Excess Solvy and the Perfect Sew Fabric Stabilizer are removed at the same time. Aren't you glad you preshrank the fabric?

Transfer design
Outline with one line of stitching
ZigZag stitch
Cut out fabric

Scorch and Stain Removal

We all know the old sayings "Never sew across an unpressed seam" and "Press as you sew." What the old sayings do not mention is what to do when you scorch the fabric. This is no joke when it happens, and with so many new fabrics requiring different iron temperatures, scorching has become a fairly common occurrence.

When pressing a new fabric, try pressing a sample before applying the iron to the garment. Thus, scorch-and-shine lessons may be learned with less serious consequences.

To remove scorch marks, alternate applications of ammonia, detergent, and water. Rinse area well before re-pressing. If this treatment fails, mix a few drops of ammonia with one tablespoon of peroxide. Rub mixture into the stain. Rinse well. For wools, it may be necessary to sand the scorched area with very fine sandpaper.

A fabric may develop a shine from ironing without a press cloth. To remove the shine, make a solution of hot vinegar and water or ammonia and water. Rub into the fabric. Rinse well.

To remove grease marks on washable fabrics, pour cleaning fluid through the stain. For dry-clean-only fabrics try trichlorocthane. For ball point pen marks, spray polyester fabric with hair spray. Marks will often disappear. If this fails, try a spot remover. Pencil marks may sometimes be removed with an eraser or by alternate treatments of ammonia and detergent. To remove paint, rub detergent into the stain and rinse. If the spot remains, rub turpentine into the area. Rinse well.

Mildew should be treated as soon as possible with alternating applications of detergent and rubbing alcohol. Expose to sunlight. For grass stains, try rubbing with detergent first. If stain remains, rub with one part alcohol and two parts water. If stain persists, use chlorine or peroxide bleach.

Food and drink stains are common and fairly easy to remove. To remove stains of alcoholic beverages from a dry-cleanable garment, rub with water and cornstarch. For a washable garment, soak first in cold water and then warm sudsy water. If stain persists, combine two tablespoons of hydrogen peroxide to one gallon of water. Soak for one-half hour and

rinse well. For coffee and tea stains, pour boiling water through the stain from a three-foot height.

For fruit and berry stains, apply white vinegar and rinse well. To remove milk stains, soak in cool water and detergent for washable fabrics or sponge with cleaning fluid for dry cleanable fabrics.

Chewing gum is a real stubborn one. Apply ice and pry gum from surface with a knife. Soak gummed area in cleaning fluid.

For perspiration stains, sponge a fresh stain with ammonia. Restore an old stained area with white vinegar. Rinse well.

The main drawback in owning real suede or leather garments is having to dry-clean them. If a leather garment is really quite soiled, professional dry cleaning may be necessary. However, many stains can be removed at home.

For protection against water and stains, spray your new leather garment with All Protector, which keeps spots from setting in.

A high-gloss leather is more difficult to keep looking new than a natural finish and may show spots

Scorch and Stain Removal

and streaks if worn in rain or snow.

If you get caught in the rain while wearing a smooth leather garment, the leather will probably stiffen up a bit after it dries. To return the garment to its original supple condition, rub Cadillac Lotion Reconditioner into it. These products are available in good quality leather clothing shops.

If you get a grease spot on smooth leather, here's what you can do. Purchase a paste of mink oil from a shoemaker. Apply a small amount to a soft cloth such as an old T-shirt. Rub the cloth over the bristles of a soft brush, distributing the mink oil evenly. Go over the entire garment with the brush, blending into the grease mark. Try a sample on a hidden part of the garment first. This drastic measure works, although it deepens the color.

Suede is easier to care for. If you spill wine on it, clean spot with a water-soaked cloth, using a blot-and-lift motion. If you notice a grease mark, apply corn meal or baking powder to absorb the grease. Brush carefully with a medium-bristle brush.

Chandler's Shoe Stores puts out a product called Dry Clean®, which takes out ballpoint pen marks. To remove body oils from suede at the neck, cuff, and elbow areas, try a product called Nu Buck®.

To remove a food spot from suede, rub in corn meal and let dry overnight or sand lightly on the spot with a very fine grade of sandpaper.

Before using any of the above treatments, always try the solution on an unseen part of the garment to check for color fastness and general reaction.

FAST REWARDING PROJECTS

■ Measure out curtain lengths with chalk on the entire piece of curtain fabric before you cut the first length. Either you or the clerk may have misfigured measurements. Knowing you are an inch or so short allows you the flexibility of refiguring cut lengths. Stealing a little bit from headings or hem might eliminate another trip to the fabric store. Before hemming curtains, hang one panel on the rod to check length. Rods or hem depth may need adjustment. It's much easier to change the hem on one panel than eight.

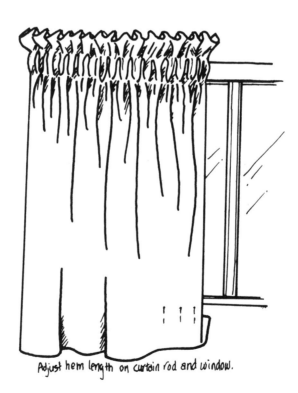

Adjust hem length on curtain rod and window.

Pleated Pants

Haul out that old piece of polyester that will never drape right or really look like silk. If you have 3¼ yards, this fabric is a perfect candidate for a pair of pleated palazzo pants. You need a good full pant pattern to begin with.

Tape each pant leg on a piece of paper that is at least 7 inches wider than the pattern piece on both inner and outer leg seam. Lengthen or shorten crotch length and do all the alterations you usually do at waistline seam, such as cutting off ½ inch at center back front tapering to zero at side for a sway back, or adding ¼ to ½ inch at center front tapering to zero at side seam for tummy. Lengthen or shorten pant leg, allowing for a 1 inch hem.

The pleating process eats up about half of your fabric, therefore extra fabric must be added, not only at side seams, but inner leg seams as well . On inner leg seam, add 3 inches past cutting line on inner leg front and 3¾ inches past cutting line on inner leg back. Most full leg patterns have some curve to the inner leg seam; pleated pants must have straighter inner leg and side seams, but some curve at inner leg is still necessary. Therefore, while 3 inches is added at front crotch point and 3¾ inches is added at back crotch point, the amount decreases by half as it goes to the bottom of the leg, or inner leg becomes too full and uncomfortable in the wearing.

Now flat pattern measure the pattern at the hipline on front and back legs. Double this amount to determine how much this pattern has at the hip. My pattern, size 12, measured 10¾ on the front and 11¾ on the back. Added together, each whole leg measures 22½. Multiplied by 2, this equals 45 inches flat-pattern measure at hip.

Now take your hip measurement and multiply this by 2. This is the amount the cut peices must measure before they go to the pleating company. My hip measures 38 inches, times 2 equals 76 inches. Compare your hip times 2 to the flat pattern measurement amount on pattern. Example: A flat pattern measurement of 22½, multiplied times 2, equals 45 inches, compared to a hip of 38 multiplied times 2 equals 76 inches. The difference between the two is 31 inches. Divided by half, 15½ inches is the amount between the front and back legs at side seams.

Pleating works best with as few seams as possible, therefore side seams can be eliminated by joining front and back legs at side with a 15½ addition (per example) in between at hip. Pin front and back pieces with parallel grainlines.

Due to the fact that side seams were eliminated, it is now necessary to cut pants on the crosswise grain, which is preferable since cutting cross grain eliminates puckered seams on polyester. Always cut off the selvages, since they tend to shrink later and draw up the seam.

After the pants have been cut out, overlock all edges except for pant bottoms. Go to the iron and press up a ½ inch hem fold. This is not easy because polyester needs high heat for a press. Turn up a ½ inch hem fold. This is not easy because polyester needs high heat for a press. Turn up another ½ inch to enclose hem's raw edge, and topstitch hem in place. Press hem flat. If you own a large press, this step is easy because 100 pounds of pressure easily flattens this hem in polyester.

Send to a pleating company (see Sources) and have pleated in a 2 to 1 ration, ¼ inch pleat on top, ⅛ inch on underside. have pleating direction reversed on each side of the pants. When the pants come back from the pleating company, run an ease line around the waist to hold pleats in place before attaching the waistband. To sew seams in pleated fabric, pull pleats away for the seam allowance. Sew seam. Pleats will return and cover sewn seam.

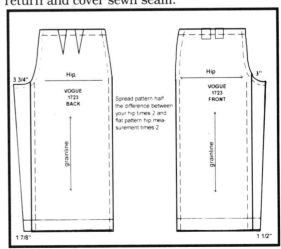

Kimono Wraps

At a fashion show on minimalistic styling, the winner made a pattern for an outside wrap that can only be described as a cross between a cocoon and a kimono. The whole outfit was a sensation and definitely a crowd-pleaser for the 300 spectators watching an annual sewing competition given at In Material, a fabric shop in Palo Alto, CA.

After the judging, the winner slipped off the wrap and demonstrated the ease of making the garment, which requires just 2 yards of fabric and less than 2 hours of construction time.

First, purchase 2 yards of a 54- to 60-inch-wide material that drapes well, plus another ¼ yard of contrasting or compatible fabric to be used as bias trim around the wrap. A version of this wrap was made in a rust wool jersey, using black wool jersey for the bias trim. Wool jersey is an excellent choice for this wrap. However, an Austrian knit would be suitable for summer and could be used as a bathing suit cover-up.

Fold the 2 yards of fabric in half crosswise so that the selvages match with right sides together. Sew two seams. Along the folded edge, cut two slits 6 inches long close to the newly sewn seam. This will make a 12-inch armhole which will later be finished with a bias strip. Through one fabric thickness—which we will now designate as the front—cut a slit 17 inches long in the center of the front piece.

Cut a strip from the contrasting fabric 18 inches long and 4 inches wide. Fold under raw edges ½ inch all around and press. Place the wrong side of the strip against the wrong side of the front in the center 2 inches above the slash. Topstitch lengthwise edges into place and then sew two rows of lengthwise stitching parallel to the topstitching, ½ inch away from the first stitching. This forms two channels into which you will insert a drawstring to draw up the fabric as tightly as possible to create the drape effect in the back.

Finish the armholes and all raw edges with bias binding, which is usually easier to apply if you round the corners in the center front. Pound bias binding flat.

Since the construction for this wrap is so unusual, many are afraid to try it. Follow the directions exactly and make up a miniature doll-size version to get confidence.

Slip on by letting the placket with drawstring fall to the back and putting your hands through armholes.

This is a wonderful solution to the problem of which coat to wear over evening kimonos at night—the style is compatible and the wool jersey provides warmth.

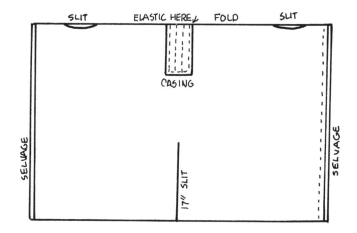

Scarf Dimensions

If you love scarves but are dismayed at the high price of those in the stores, why not start making them? Even someone who never sews can make a scarf. You don't even have to know how to operate a sewing machine. If you can do a running stitch by hand, you are capable of making a magnificent scarf for yourself.

Choice of fabric is the critical thing. Most people tend to choose fabric that is too stiff. Only a very soft fabric will drape well enough to make a flattering scarf or shawl. Cotton and rayon challis make beautiful scarves, but ironing is definitely required.

Wool challis is my first choice because it is soft to the touch, drapes well, and does not need ironing. You can also make beautiful silk scarves.

Fabric designed especially for scarves is available in some stores. This fabric is designed in large squares with a border on all four sides. Fabric is purchased by the panel rather than by the yard.

Many other fabrics make excellent scarves, shawls, and stoles. If you are in love with a fabric with questionable drapability, an oblong scarf cut on the bias might work. Anything on the bias drapes better than the same fabric on the straight grain.

Now for cutting dimensions. If you have a favorite scarf, chances are its dimensions are flattering on you. Measure that one. For a square scarf, the size varies with the size of the wearer. A very small woman will look best in a 36-inch square; an average woman in a 42- to 45-inch square; and a large woman in a 58- to 60-inch square. Experiment a little to find the ideal size for you.

Oblong scarves also vary in size. A short woman will look best in a scarf 13 by 45 inches, whereas a tall woman would look better in an oblong piece 13 by 60 inches. Once again, experiment with scrap fabric before you cut.

When making oblong scarves, you may need to buy the fabric 60 inches long—if the fabric is less than 60 inches wide—to get enough for a flattering length. In this case, make another one for a friend with the leftover fabric.

To make sure you are cutting precisely on the grain, pull threads lengthwise and crosswise. Cut along pulled line (Illustration 1).

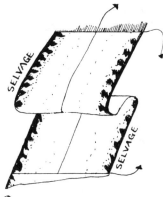

① PULL OUT CROSSWISE AND LENGTHWISE THREAD FOR STRAIGHT GUIDELINE.

② MACHINE STITCH BELOW SELF FRINGE.

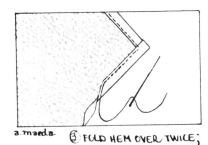

a. maeda

③ FOLD HEM OVER TWICE; HAND STITCH OR MACHINE STITCH EDGES.

To finish the ends, you have two choices. You can fringe the scarf all around by pulling threads (1½- to 2-inch fringe looks great). If the scarf is going to be washed, run a machine stitch next to your last line of unravelling or the threads will continue to unravel (Illustration 2).

The second choice is to hand-roll the edge, turning under ⅛ to ¼ inch once, and then once again. A small running stitch by hand or a machine stitch will hold the hem in place (Illustration 3).

Demonstrated on *Power Sewing* Video #1: *Fear of Sewing.*

Measure for Curtains

Let's face it: Window coverings turn living space into a home. The simplest curtains make a world of difference. Make them yourself and you save a bundle, although in most cases the choice is between make them yourself or do without, because they are so expensive.

To determine finished width, measure from the outside edges of the woodwork across the window. This measurement will also be used to buy a rod which is capable of extending to this width. To determine finished length, measure from the top of where the rod will be to the bottom of the window sill or to the floor, if you want full-length curtains. Shrinkage (1 inch per yard) needs to be added only if you plan to wash the curtains. Fabric, by its very nature, hangs slightly away from the windows, using up 1 inch in length termed "loft."

To *figure cut lengths* for yardage, use this formula: finished length, plus 4½ inches (rod casing and heading allowance), plus 2½ inches (hem allowance), plus 1 inch (loft), plus shrinkage (1 inch per yard shrinkage—only if you plan to wash the curtains) equals the cut length. (See Example 1, next column)

For gathered curtains, determine the number of cut lengths needed by the amount of fullness desired. For adequate fullness, double the finished width of the window. For luxurious fullness, triple the finished width or use a fullness somewhere in between determined by the width of the fabric you are using. For example, if your finished window width measures 37½ inches and your fabric measures 45 inches, two fabric widths will be sufficient to cover the window.

To *figure yardage*, multiply the cut lengths times the number of widths needed. Add 5 inches more for every two tie backs needed and 4 inches to straighten fabric ends before cutting. For example: a cut length of 68 inches times 2 widths equals 136 inches plus 5 inches for tie backs, plus 4 inches to straighten fabric equals 145 inches. Divide 145 inches by 36 inches (number of inches per yard) and obtain 4 yards. (See Example 2, next column.)

Ask a clerk to measure twice to be certain to cut the correct yardage.

Decorative flat sheets are often an economical route for attractive curtains for large windows at an affordable price. The finished size of a flat, twin sheet is 66 inches by 96 inches, a full sheet is 81 inches by 96 inches, a queen sheet is 91 inches by 102 inches, and a king sheet is 108 inches by 102 inches. Since the top and bottom hems must be cut off the sheets before using, figure sheet length to be 5 inches shorter than the sheet lengths given above.

Example 1

Finished length	60"
Casing and heading allowance	+ 4½"
Hem allowance	+ 2½"
Loft	+ 1"
Shrinkage (1" per yard)	+ ___"
(only if you plan to wash the curtains)	
Cut length	68"

Example 2

Cut Length	68"
Number of fabric widths	x 2
	136"
Tie backs	+ 5"
Straighten fabric	+ 4"
	145"

Divide by 36 inches for yardage: 4 yards plus 1 inch

Make Curtains

Before cutting, straighten ends of fabric by making a clip 2 inches from newly-cut end. Try to tear fabric across. If the fabric will not tear, pull a thread across. If thread breaks, pick up another one next to it (Illustration 1). Cut along pulled thread. Straightening fabric ends insures curtains which hang straight on the window.

If the window is very wide, you may need to join fabric widths. These are the cut lengths you figured. To do a really first-class job, cut off the selvages. Turn under ½ inch to wrong side of fabric. Press. Turn another 1 inch to wrong side. Machine-stitch close to hem fold (Illustration 2). But, if the selvage edges look finished enough for your taste, side hems are not necessary.

lot of curtains. Before hemming, slip one of the curtain panels on a rod and hang it at the window. Fold up intended 2½ inch hem. Is the curtain too short, too long? Before the hem is sewn, you can decide to make it shorter or longer. If curtain seems too short, the hem can be made narrower. If the curtain is too short, hem can be made narrower. If you like the length of the curtain with 2½ inches folded under, proceed as planned.

On the bottom edge of the curtain, press ½ inch to the wrong side, then press 2 inches to wrong side to form curtain hem allowance. Machine stitch close to the ½ inch hem fold.

To make tie backs, fold a 5 inch strip of fabric in half lengthwise. Sew one long side. Turn right-side

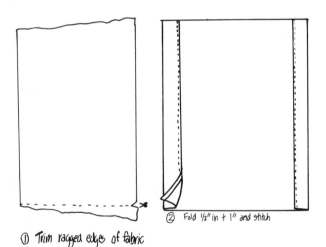

① Trim ragged edges of fabric

② Fold ½" in + 1" and stitch

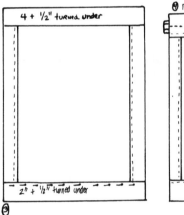

4 + ½" turned under

2" + ½" turned under

③

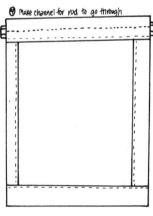

④ Make channel for rod to go through

On top edge of curtain, press ½ inch to wrong side and then 4 inches to wrong side to form heading allowance and rod casing (Illustration 3). Sew close to hem fold. Parallel to this row of stitching, sew another row halfway in between the top of the curtain and the row of hem stitching. This row of stitching forms the channel for the curtain rod. Leave ends open so that rod can be inserted (Illustration 4).

Take this advice from a person who has made a

out. Press. Cut in half. Tie around curtain to determine desired length of tie backs. Turn raw edges and sew by hand, or merely tie in place, positioning so that raw edges fall behind the curtains.

Clutch Bag

You can make a clutch bag in surprisingly little time and come out with a very good product. Marcy Tilton perfected this one, and the results are impressive.

Decide which two or three colors will be the focus of your summer wardrobe and incorporate these into a purse. This is a good way to use up fabric scraps if you have some great ones.

For spring, a version was made with ⅜ yard of cream linen, ½ yard of pearl gray linen for the lining and contrasting band and ⅛-yard salmon linen for piping, ⅜-yard polyester fleece, and a 14-inch zipper.

Cut two pieces 11 by 15 inches of the outside purse fabric. two pieces 11 by 15 inches of the lining fabric. two pieces 15 by 6 inches of contrasting band fabric (which may be the same as the lining), two pieces 15 by 3 inches of piping fabric and two tabs 3 by 2 inches for zipper, and two pieces 11 by 15 inches of polyester fleece.

Place one layer of the outside purse fabric on top of one layer of polyester fleece right side up. On top of this, place one layer of the contrasting band. Press 15- by 3-inch strips in half lengthwise. Place this strip between the outside purse fabric and the contrasting band.

Turn under the raw edge of the contrasting band ½ inch over the piping strip. Topstitch the contrasting band, the piping, the outside fabric, and the fleece into place. Hand-baste outside edges together (Illustration 1).

Place the right side of the lining fabric against the right side of the outside purse fabric. Stitch around all sides, leaving a 3-inch opening on the side. Hand-walk the machine two stitches at the corners for easy turning (Illustration 2). Trim seam to ¼ inch, clip corners, and turn right side out. Hand-stitch opening closed. Press with steam. Pound edges flat with the use of a tailor's clapper. You have now made one side of the purse. Repeat the process to make the other half.

Use one 3- by 2-inch piece to make each tab. Sew three sides with small stitches using a ¼-inch seam, leaving one 2-inch end open. Turn tab right side out.

Fold under ½ inch at raw edge. Press and pound flat. Slip one tab onto each end of zipper and topstitch into place (Illustration 3).

Place two sides of purse with right sides up and top of purse facing each other. Lay zipper over tops of purse. Pin zipper. Topstitch zipper onto purse, sewing very close to the outside edge of the zipper (Illustration 4).

For a quilted effect, do some decorative topstitching on contrasting piece at the top of the purse.

Placing the lining sides of the purse together, sew the body of the purse together ½ inch from the edge (Illustration 5). Sew as close to the top of the zipper as your machine permits. A small opening will never be noticed.

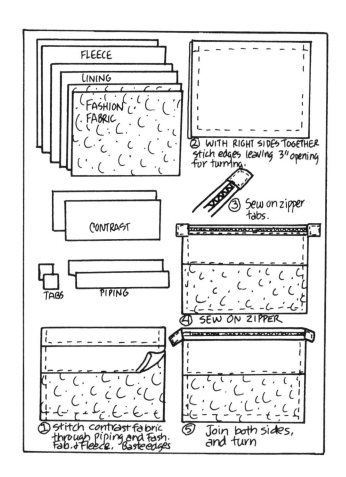

Silk Camisole

The silk camisole is great for spring and summer. It can be worn under an open jacket or blouse, or worn just as is with a skirt for evening or warm days.

If the camisole pattern you are using is not cut on the bias, draw a new grainline for bias and cut the camisole on the bias. The straps and facings should also be cut on the bias. Bias conforms better to the body shape. Interfacing should be eliminated except when used with very stretchy or weak fabrics (Illustration 1).

If you have broad shoulders, you might move the strap placement out toward the armhole ¾ inch. This gives the illusion of well-proportioned shoulders. A narrow-shouldered individual might move the strap placement toward the center front ½ to 1 inch. This will keep the straps from slipping off the shoulder.

A great trick for turning the straps right side out is to sew a line of stitches on the end of the strap through a single thickness. Now, place right sides together and sew the strap ¼ to ⅜ inch from the fold using a narrow zigzag stitch. Use of the zigzag stitch keeps the threads from popping when the strap is being turned right side out. Cut a small hole near the end stitching from the fold, but not quite to the vertical stitch. Insert a bobby pin through the loop of fabric you have formed. Push the bobby pin down through the strap, turning the strap right side out in the process (Illustration 2).

Try on garment to check strap length. Sew the straps to the camisole. Sew the front facing to the front camisole, and the back facing to the back camisole. Trim and understitch the facings. Press and pound the facings into place with a tailor's clapper to flatten. Now, pin the camisole together at the side seams. Fit the camisole according to your taste and baste the side seams. Press the seams open and try the camisole on before sewing permanently. Make adjustments as needed. Sew the seams permanently and anchor the facings at the underarm seam by sewing in the well of the seam from the right side of the camisole (Illustration 3).

① PLACE ALL PIECES ON BIAS

② Insert Bobby Pin to turn straps

③ sew facing to bodice in well of seam.

Well Fitting T-shirts

Most T-shirts or patterns for knits only are cut without darts and with front and back the same length at the side seams. On a full-busted woman, a straight T-shirt pulls up at center front and stands away from the body.

To build curves into this straight form, cut the pattern horizontally in the bust area and insert a $\frac{1}{2}$-inch piece of tissue. Build out a $\frac{1}{4}$-inch curve to the side in the same area (Illustration 1).

Run an easeline over this area at the side seam. Press with steam to flatten any look of gathers (Illustration 2).

Now you are ready to join the front and back at the side seams. You will see that even with the $\frac{1}{2}$-inch addition. they match.

If you are making a sleeveless garment in T-shirt or woven fabric and you would like to avoid a gap at the front armhole, run an easeline on the front and the front facing in the armhole area from the underarm seam to 1 inch above the front notch (Illustration 3).

Ease each piece separately. Press flat with steam. Join the garment and the facing. You will find that the ease pulls the garment closer to the body.

Always use the greatest stretch of the knit going around the body (Illustration 4).

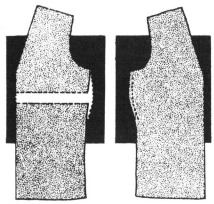

① SPREAD PATTERN AT BUST, FRONT ONLY. ADD 1/4" TO SIDE SEAM.

② EASE SIDE AND STEAM IRON TO FLATTEN.

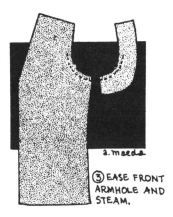

a. maeda

③ EASE FRONT ARMHOLE AND STEAM.

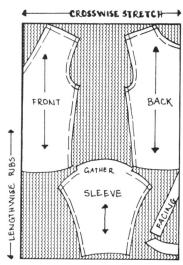

④ STRETCH SHOULD GO ACROSS BODY.

Leotards

Making your own leotard may seem ridiculous; but if you are on a regular exercise program, you will need three leotards unless you want to do laundry daily. Very few store-bought leotards show much imagination.

If the leotard or bathing suit patterns from normal sources do not excite you, remember Stretch and Sew and Kwik Sew Patterns. Other pattern companies advertise in the back of *Sew News*.

Good two-way stretch fabric is needed for exercise garments. Preshrink fabric. Rotary cutters make cutting a breeze. Polyester thread will be the strongest. Double-sew all seams, two rows of stitching right next to each other for greater endurance to stress. Use a size 1 zigzag and a medium- to small-length stitch with a ballpoint needle (Schmetz Suk ball point). If you have an elastic foot, use it when applying elastic.

Interfacing is not necessary, but use stay tape if the front is a low V-neck, scoop, or wrap style to keep the neck from gaping (Illustration 1).

If you are going to all the trouble to make your own leotard, have some fun with the design. Insert a seam wherever you want by drawing in a style line. Make an "X" on either side of the line to remind yourself to add seam allowances when you cut out. Insert piping in seam or merely change colors altogether (Illustrations 2-3).

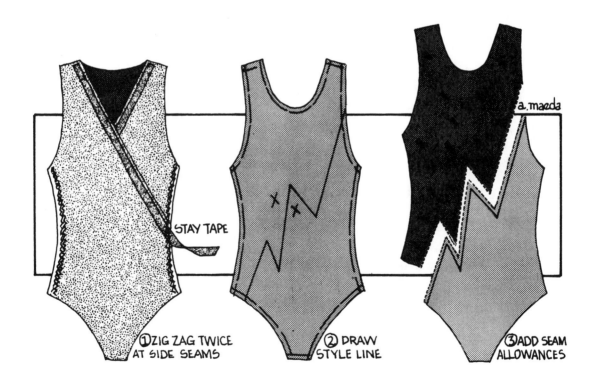

STAY TAPE

① ZIG ZAG TWICE AT SIDE SEAMS   ② DRAW STYLE LINE   ③ ADD SEAM ALLOWANCES

a. maeda

Oval and Circular Tablecloths

Starter households often inherit the big round or oval table that nobody wants. If you've received a table like the one I inherited, you'll want to cover it fast. Surprisingly enough, once a tablecloth is made, the eyesore turns into an attractive piece of furniture.

To measure for a circular tablecloth, first measure the diameter of the table (the distance from edge to edge across the center of the table). Then measure the distance from the tabletop to the floor. Double the floor-to-tabletop measurement and add this to the diameter. Call this the "total diameter" (Illustration 1).

To measure for an oval tablecloth, tape newspapers together. Make a pattern of the tabletop by tracing the outside edge of the table onto the paper. Cut away excess paper. Measure the distance from the tabletop to the floor. Add twice this measurement to the length and width of the oval table. The result is a total width and total length measurement.

Most fabrics are not wide enough to make an oval or circular tablecloth without being pieced together. Two or three fabric widths may be needed depending on the "total diameter" of the circle or the total width of the oval. For example, if your total diameter of the circle or total width of the oval is 101 inches and your fabric is only 45 inches wide, you will need three widths (Illustration 2). If your fabric is 60 inches wide, only two widths are needed. If only two widths are needed, split one width in half lengthwise, and join half widths on either side of the full fabric width used in the center (Illustration 3). This avoids a seamline across the top of the table.

To arrive at the total amount of fabric needed, multiply the number of widths needed times the total diameter of the round or total length of the oval.

After joining fabric widths, to cut a circular cloth, fold the pieced fabric once and then once again into quarters. Cut a piece of string and tie one end to a pencil. Take the total diameter of the cloth you wish to make, plus a 1 inch hem allowance, and divide it in half. This is the radius of the circle. Make a knot in the string this distance from the pencil. Pin the knot securely with a safety pin at the corner where everything is folded. Hold the knot down with

one hand and draw a quarter circle with the pencil with the other hand. Cut along traced marking (Illustration 4).

To cut an oval cloth, piece fabric widths. Spread fabric out in a single thickness on floor. Place newspaper patterns (the shape of the oval top) in the center of the fabric. All around the oval pattern, measure the distance from the tabletop to the floor. Mark. Add a 1 inch hem allowance all around. Join markings and cut along this line (Illustration 5).

To hem tablecloth, thread "fusible thread" on bobbin only. Regular thread goes on the top of the machine. Machine stitch ⅜ inch from edge of fabric with right side of fabric up. Sewing closer to fabric edge sometimes causes fabric to stretch or pull down into the bobbin. Trim ¼ inch of excess fabric away from outside edge, ⅛ inch away from machine stitching. If you don't have fusible thread, simply do the pressing process without it.

Take tablecloth to ironing surface. Press ¼ inch hem to the wrong side of the fabric all around cloth. Let iron rest on fabric long enough for the fusible thread to melt, holding crease in place, but don't scorch. Roll hem over again to enclose raw hem edge. Press. Machine stitch with regular thread on top and bobbin. If you want to trim cloth in fringe, subtract width of fringe all around cloth before you begin hem process.

Sheets now come in such a variety of patterns that it is likely you can find one that will make a good tablecloth. King-size sheets are usually large enough to make a cloth without piecing. Unfortunately, if the fabric combination has any polyester, soil release can be a problem. However, it's not a problem if the cloth is merely decorative. One hundred percent cotton is a better choice for a cloth you will use for dining. Velour makes a beautiful tablecloth which needs no ironing. Smaller rounds or squares in patterned fabric can be made to drape over the center of the velour, cutting ironing and cleaning to a minimum.

Oval and Circular Tablecloths

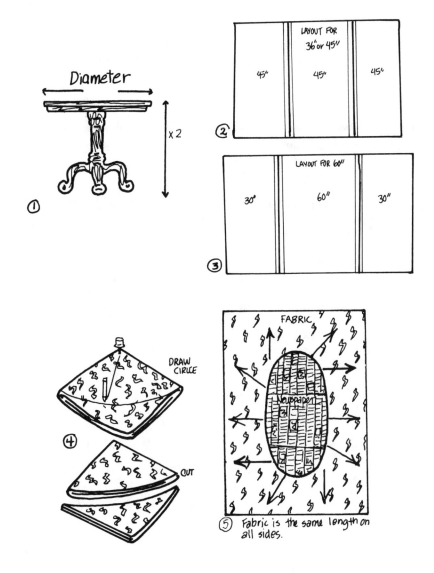

Diameter

× 2

①

② LAYOUT FOR 36" or 45"

45"   45"   45"

③ LAYOUT FOR 60"

30"   60"   30"

④ DRAW CIRCLE   CUT

⑤ FABRIC   Newspaper

Fabric is the same length on all sides.

Napkins

A set of cloth napkins makes a wonderful gift for any occasion. While you are at it, make an extra set for yourself. The investment is minimal: one yard of fabric makes four napkins, and little sewing skill is needed.

While most purchased napkins measure 15 inches, why not make slightly oversized dinner napkins of 18 inches? Larger napkins give guests a feeling of opulence.

For a four napkin set of 18-inch-square napkins, use 1 yard of 45-inch wide fabric. For a four napkin set of 15-inch-square napkins, use 7/8 of a yard of 45-inch wide fabric. The same length of 54-inch wide fabric will yield six napkins.

In order to have napkins which are perfectly square, it is necessary to straighten the ends of the fabric before cutting. To straighten the ends (those cut at the fabric store, the opposite direction of the selvages) choose a thread which you can pull across the width of the fabric. This thread may break as you pull. Simply choose one right next to it and continue across. Cut fabric along pulled thread line. Cut fabric into napkin squares and you are ready to begin.

How about napkins without sewing? Gail Brown, author of *Quick Napkins*, came up with this one. Purchase one 15-yard roll of Fusible Transfer web in 3/4 inch width, enough for seven 18 inch napkins. Purchase more web if you are doing more napkins. If rolled web is unavailable, purchase web yardage and cut your own strips. On wrong side, fuse with iron 3/4 inch strips to two opposite edges of napkin. Remove web paper and finger press 3/8 inch hem (half width of web). Press in place. Repeat for remaining two sides of napkins. These edges will remain fused through washing. Any loose threads may be clipped.

If you own a serger you can switch to the narrow foot. Shorten stitch length, and create a rolled hem as it sews. For a neater edge, allow the serger to cut off 1/8 inch as it sews. Serge all sides allowing the knife to cut off the serger thread from the previous side. Cut off the last thread and seal with Fray Check.

Napkins in specialty shops are often made on a straight-stitch machine. Fill bobbin with fusible thread. Use regular thread on top of machine. Using a straight stitch, roll the right side of the fabric and sew 1/4 inch from the raw edge of napkin. On a flat surface, press down 1/4 inch to the wrong side. Enclose raw napkin edge by rolling in another 1/4 inch fold. Machine stitch pressed hem in place. If your machine has a difficult time starting at the napkin corner, start machine sewing in the center and sew to the corner.

Large Absorbent Bibs

A good project for a beginner is a child's bib. Do not waste your time on little nonsense bibs; make large absorbent bibs that are fun for a child to wear and attractive for a parent to look at.

Many fabric stores are selling printed panels with trucks, flowers, and numbers on them. The fabric is sold by the panel, which provides six to eight rectangles about 10 by 11 inches that make perfect bibs.

For the back side of the bib, use terry cloth sold by the yard or recycle a few towels that no longer look new.

Cut the terry cloth the same shape as the printed panel. Pin with wrong sides together. Machine-baste the outside edges, rounding corners (Illustration 1). Trim excess fabric ⅛ inch away from basted edge. Cut a small neckline curve at the top of the bib about

① BASTE FABRIC TO TERRY

② TRIM OUT NECKLINE

③ START BIAS AT BACK

④ MAKE TIES FROM BIAS

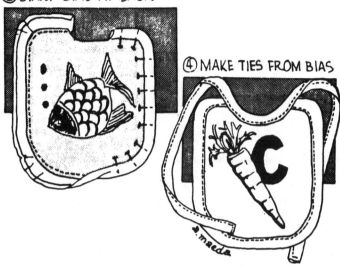

2½ inches long and ½ inch deep at the center (Illustration 2).

While you are at the fabric store, purchase some wide bias tape in stripes or polka dots or make your own about 2½ inches wide. Starting at the outside edge of the neck, place the right side of the bias against back of bib. Sew seam at ¼ inch.

Wrap bias around seam toward front of bib, folding under ¼ inch of the bias. Pin into place. Topstitch the folded side of the bias onto the front side of the bib (Illustration 3).

To create ties and finish the neck, let 12 inches of bias extend on either side of neck. Sew as described above. Finish tie ends by folding in raw edges. Topstitch into place (Illustration 4).

Make a dozen of these bibs. Then you will have baby gifts whenever you need them.

Scrunchy

Keeping pace with inflation are scrunchies, those popular elasticized fabric hair ties. While scrunchies in nice fabric used to sell for $5 to $6, they are now priced between $8 and $11. Considering the minuscule amount of both fabric and time scrunchies take to make, perhaps you and I are in the wrong business.

Chiffon or georgette make beautiful scrunchies which do not wrinkle. Buy $\frac{1}{4}$ yard (9 inches) of 44–45 inch wide fabric or $\frac{1}{2}$ yard of narrower fabric which can be pieced to create a rectangle 45 inches long by 9 inches wide. Fold fabric in half lengthwise and sew seam along lengthwise edge, leaving one inch free on each edge of the long seam. Do not sew ends. Press seam open. Turn tube right-side out. Press again with seam on one side, fold on the other side of long strip.

The scrunchy fabric must now be joined at the ends to form a circle. Because you left one inch free on each end of the long seam, it is now possible to join the ends of the strip together. Right sides together, pin the ends of the fabric strip to form a circle. Before sewing, check to see that the strip is not twisted.

My favorite elastic for pulling in fullness is Talon's polyester oval elastic. Cut a length of elastic 12 inches long. Fasten one end of the elastic to a bodkin or a safety pin. Insert elastic into the sewn circle through the opening left when you didn't stitch the last inch on each end of the long seam. As the elastic goes around the circle, the fabric will draw up into the circle.

When the first end of the elastic has gone around the circle and comes out the opening, you are ready to join the two ends of the elastic. Using a square knot, left over right and right over left, knot the elastic so that each end of the elastic extends two inches past the knot.

Before finishing the scrunchy, try it on your hair. If your hair is very thick you may decide to knot leaving only a one inch extension on each end. If you prefer the scrunchy to go around the pony tail only once, you may decide to knot leaving three inches extended on each end. The formula for two inch extensions is used in the ones sold commercially, which double wrap.

Cut off the ends of the elastic. Hand sew the small opening in the scrunchy closed with a hand sewing needle and thread.

Scrunchies are a great way to use up scraps. If you don't mind the smaller scrunchy version, they can be made with scraps 5 inches by 20 inches. In addition to having fun yourself, children love this project. At age 11, my daughter Monique made three for friends and two for her older sister. The scrunchies were a great hit.

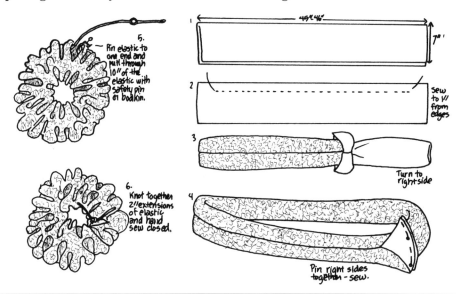

Shortening Trousers

Although pant length alterations on men's trousers are usually free with purchase, the return trip to pick them up is often a hassle. Even a non-sewer without a sewing machine can put up a hem in trousers. Let's see how.

Unless you have experience in marking pants length on the body, perhaps the best method for determining pants length is by comparison to another pair of hemmed trousers from the closet.

Laying the trousers side-by-side, compare side seams, marking the finished length onto the unhemmed pant. Now compare the inner leg seam lengths as well, marking the finished pant length. Compare the two markings. If they are not the same, determine a point halfway between the two to use as the finished length. From my experience, inner leg seam comparison is the most reliable since different pant styles ride the body differently at the waist.

After the finished length is determined, 2 inches will be added for hem allowance. Mark 2 inches from the finished length toward the pant bottom. Measure this distance from the pant bottom. This measurement determines the amount to cut off from the bottom of the pants. Measure and mark the cutting line from the pant bottom. Use a ruler to connect chalk markings. Cut off excess length with pinking shears, if available. Since menswear fabrics rarely ravel, pinking shears are optional; regular scissors will do the job. If the fabric seems likely to ravel, zigzag or overlock raw edge, or dab raw edge of fabric with Fray Check, a fabric sealant found in the notions department of fabric stores.

After excess length has been cut off, mark finished length at regular intervals 2 inches from newly cut bottom. Fold hem allowance to the wrong side. Hand-baste in place. Press well with steam.

To hand-hem with invisible stitch results, pick up one thread from the garment, move forward $1/4$ inch and pick up one thread from the hem. The secret to an invisible hem is to make sure you don't pull the thread too tight. Make a knot every 4 inches to prevent entire hem from falling out if you catch your heel.

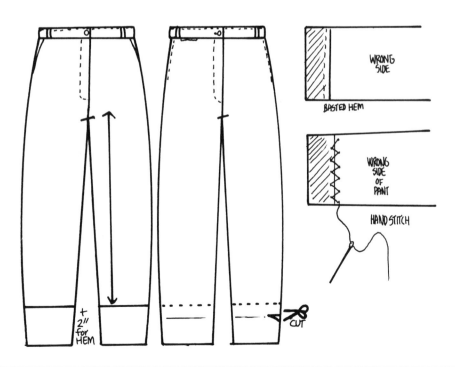

Demonstrated on *Power Sewing* Video #1: *Fear of Sewing.*

Duvet Covers

Even a novice can make a duvet cover. Think of a duvet or comforter cover like a giant bag with an end closure and you will feel less intimidated. Since the purpose of a duvet cover is to keep the comforter clean, choose soft, washable fabric which feels good to the skin. A duvet cover made with two sheets is easiest, but fashion fabric can be used as well. Preshrink both fabric and sheets in washer and dryer to avoid disappointing shrinkage later.

Measure the comforter to be covered, adding $1\frac{1}{2}$ inches to the width and $3\frac{3}{4}$ inches to the length for seaming. If you are using sheets, check sheet dimensions on the package to determine what size to buy. Two complementary sheets make a more interesting duvet cover than the same sheet on both sides; let your personal preference dictate.

If you are using fashion fabrics, fabric will have to be pieced to get enough width to cover the comforter. Consider one fabric for the center and another fabric cut in half lengthwise to form borders on each side.

Do not cut final width (duvet dimension plus $1\frac{1}{2}$ inches for seams) until after the fabrics are pieced. To determine how much fabric to buy, decide how many fabric widths plus seam allowances it will take to cover the width of the comforter plus $1\frac{1}{2}$ inch seams. Measure the length of the comforter plus $3\frac{1}{2}$ inches for seams and multiply times the number of fabric widths needed. This calculation is for one side of the duvet. Double if both sides are the same. For a cozy duvet, consider flannel for the underside. Don't forget to preshrink.

Because the cover will be repeatedly washed, French seams (enclosed seams) are used to join pieces for the duvet. Place wrong sides of fabric together. Sew a $1/4$ inch seam along two long sides and top. To reduce bulk, clip over corner seam allowances close to stitching. Turn fabric wrong sides out. Enclose raw edges of seam allowances. Sew seam at $3/8$ inch.

On open end, press under 1 inch seam allowance. Enclose this edge by pressing under 1 inch seam allowance again. Sew close to folded edge. Duvet cover may be closed with large, heavy-duty snaps at intervals no larger than 9 inches, or use velcro.

To close with velcro, purchase a length of $3/4$ inch width velcro to measure the width of the duvet. Topstitch velcro strips to the inside of the hemmed open end of the bag. Anchor all sides of the velcro with stitching.

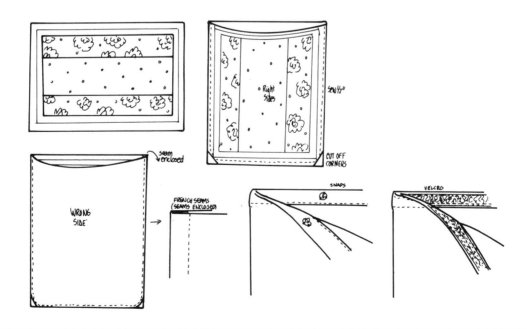

Pillow Shams

Pillow shams are easy and fast since they don't require a zipper. With one twin-bed flat sheet you can make two pillow shams.

Measure length and width of your pillow. Multiply times two. If you like a soft, pliable pillow, add 1 inch to these measurements in both directions. For a crisp looking pillow, use exact measurements.

Cut off the hemmed edge at top of sheet. Cut or tear 3½ inch strips on the lengthwise edges, using the selvage as a finish. Seam these together in one long strip. Zigzag over thin string to gather the ruffle. Pull the string and a ruffle forms (Illustration 1).

Cut one piece of fabric the size of your pillow cover as determined above for sham front. Cut two pieces desired width of the pillow plus half the desired length plus 4 inches. These two pieces form the back with an opening to slip the pillow through. Hem one crosswise end on each one of these two pieces by turning under ½ inch edge once and then turn 1 inch hem. This method hides the raw edge.

Overlap one over the other until shape matches pillow sham front. Machine-baste together the two pieces that form the back (Illustration 2).

Place the right side of gathered ruffle against right side of pillow sham front. Push in a few extra gathers at the corners so there will be ample fullness when the pillow is turned.

Machine-baste ruffle to front (Illustration 3). Place right sides of the pillow sham back and front together and stitch over basted seam joining ruffle to front (Illustration 4).

Trim off corners ¼ inch away from stitching line. Turn pillow cover right side out through lapped opening on back. Insert pillow. Admire results!

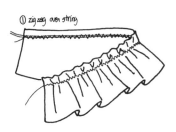

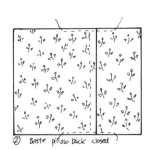

Corded Covered Pillows

Custom covered pillows are a great way to pull a room together or fill in the gaps in a new apartment.

If you can't find muslin-covered pillows in the size you want, consider purchasing covered pillows found in a discount store, bed pillows or large, oversized squares, which can be easily covered.

Uncovered cord comes in a variety of widths in the ribbon and braid department of most sewing stores. If you plan to wash the pillow, the cord must be preshrunk. Do not put the loose cord in the washing machine since it will tangle. Simply fill a basin with warm water and soak the cord for a few moments. Squeeze out excess water and hang to dry. If you are planning to wash the pillows, preshrink all fabric, except the stuffing, before you cut out the pillow. If you are not planning to wash the pillows you can skip preshrinking both the cord and the fabric.

Measure the pillow from seam to seam (Illustration 1). Cut the top pillow fabric exactly the size of the pillow. Do not add seam allowances unless the pillow you are covering is firm. In that case, add seam allowance of $\frac{5}{8}$ inch all around the pillow. The fabric should fit snugly over the pillow.

If you are planning to cord the pillow, it is much easier to insert a zipper on the backside of the pillow, rather than trying to insert a zipper in a corded seam. Cut the back pillow fabric the size of the pillow in one direction and $1\frac{1}{2}$ inch larger in the other direction, to allow for seam allowance (Illustration 2). Make a vertical cut in the center of the longer side. Seam newly cut edges, basting in the area of the zipper. Insert a zipper 2 inches shorter than pillow measurement.

After zipper insertion, check top and bottom pillow cover pieces to make sure they are the same size. Trim so that they are identical. Round the corners slightly, using the first corner you round off as a pattern for the other three (Illustration 3). Cording works better when corners are slightly rounded.

The fabric strips that cover the cord can be cross-grain if using a knit, or bias if using a woven. These grains allow the cord to go around corners without wrinkling. Unless you are using very wide cord, 2-inch-wide strips should be sufficient. Seam the strips in one long strip. Press seams open. Wrap this fabric around the cord (Illustration 4). Pin into place.

Using a zipper foot, enclose cord with fabric strip. With raw edges together, pin covered cord in place on front side of pillow, letting both ends of cord go out into the seam allowance (Illustration 5).

Before joining back side of pillow cover, unzip the zipper. Place the two pieces of pillow fabric, right sides together. Pin these two pieces together with the side of the pillow with cording attached facing up. Sew the two pieces together using the stitching line that attached the cording as a guide. This will ensure the tight fit of the cord (Illustration 6).

Turn the pillow cover right side out through the open zipper. Insert pillow. Reward yourself with a nap on the pillow.

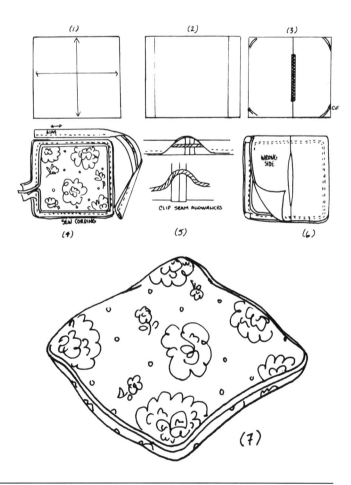

Christmas Stockings

Christmas stockings make a great gift for a special friend, new family member; or maybe your own stocking is not big enough. This project is fun, fast, and very impressive as a gift.

To make a pattern for a Christmas stocking, trace with chalk one you like the shape and size of. After tracing, add ⅝ inch seam allowance all around the shape with chalk (Illustration 1). Cut your pattern, including seam allowances, out of of a piece of brown paper or newspaper.

Take the pattern to the fabric store in search of great fabric. Choose fabric with body that's not prone to ravelling. Don't worry about cutting the stocking on the grain, just buy enough to cut two shapes to form the front and back of the stocking. Two different fabrics can be used as well. If your fabric lacks body, purchase interfacing which can be pressed on and used as a stiffener. Measure the top edge of the stocking. Purchase three or four trims to sew across the stocking, such as braid, ribbon, rick-rack, or lace. You can trim both sides of the stocking or just the front if trim is expensive.

At home, place fabric right sides together and cut out two stocking shapes including seam allowances. Remove paper pattern. Press on interfacing, if necessary, to give extra body. To form the finished edge on the top edge of the stocking, turn down ⅝ inch to the wrong side of each stocking. Machine stitch in place (Illustration 2). On the right side of the stocking, arrange trim in a pleasing way. One row of trim can cover hem stitching. Change top thread to match color of each trim. Sew into place (Illustration 3).

Place right sides of stocking together and sew all sides at ⅝ inch except for top hemmed edge. Clip corners. Form a loop with excess trim. Attach in back corner of stocking with small machine stitches (Illustration 4).

Turn right side out. Admire your results.

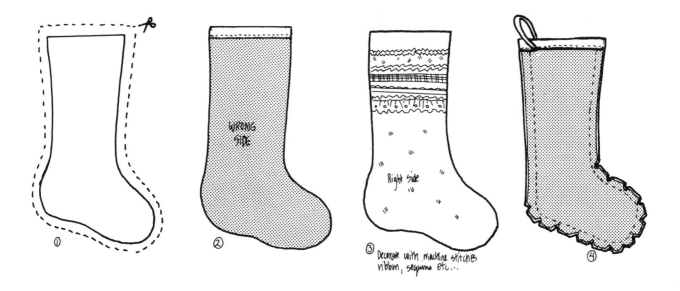

① ②

③ Decorate with machine stitches ribbon, sequins etc...

④

How to Choose Upholstery Fabric

PIN CROSSWISE AND LENGTHWISE.

a. maeda

Choosing fabric to reupholster a sofa or chair can be an agonizing experience because of both the money and time involved. This process can be simplified if you begin your fabric search with definite ideas of what will work for you.

Limit your fabric choice to fabrics which will wear well. Pull the fabric in all directions to see if the fabric will hold its shape. Hold the fabric up to the light. Tightly woven fabrics wear and hold their shape better than loosely woven ones. Loosely woven fabrics pull away at the seams, making seamlines more visible and threads prone to catch on shoe buckles, purses and even sharp corners of magazines.

Check the fabric content. Wool and cotton are strong and sturdy and release soil when spot cleaned. Nylon and acrylics are durable fabrics but have some ten-dency to pill and snag. Polyester has the same durable qualities with slightly more resistance to pilling. Olefin is a good fabric choice in areas where sun fading might be a problem. Rayon and acetate, while soft to the touch, do not wear well. Silk and linen are strong fibers which give a textural feeling but tend to be expensive.

Bring paint, carpet, wallpaper, and fabric samples of other furniture with you to the fabric store when you shop. Do not rely on your color memory. On printed fabrics, check dye set by rubbing the right side of the fabric together.

Keep the size of the furniture piece in mind if choosing a print. A large print will make a small chair seem out of proportion. Consider buying a half yard of material, bringing it home, and living with it for awhile before making it a part of your life.

Hire Upholstery Work

DO YOURSELF A FAVOR. HIRE THIS OUT!

Day to Evening Fashion Transitions

If you're working 9 to 5, with an invitation for dinner or a cocktail party at 6, do you: (a) Drag your party clothes to work and try to redo yourself in the ladies room; (b) Wear your best outfit to work, look inappropriate for the office, and get the clothes wrinkled as the day progresses; or (c) Tuck a few snappy accessories in your bag, and freshen your daytime look into a sensational evening one?

It takes only a few well chosen accessories to boost a daytime outfit and change the mood to evening. What can you wear to work that also works for evening? Start with a simple daytime outfit, a wool jersey dress or wool crepe or jersey pants and matching top in basic black. There are many fast and easy patterns in figure flattering styles to sew up simply. Look for a pattern with few pattern pieces which can be made in an evening. Let the beauty and drapeability of the fabric and simplicity of design create a background for stunning accessories.

"Having a little black dress is the best idea for a working woman," says Vicki Hastings of The Sewing Fashion Council. "You can make a simple, sophisticated dress in a few evenings. Then at 5 o'clock, workday pumps and jewelry can be stashed in a desk drawer and replaced with heels and some simple-to-sew but smashing hairbows, belts, jackets or even this season's chic hats."

Adding accessories to the top half of the body draws attention upwards to the face. Glittery earrings, a lace collar, fancy hairbow or evening hat sparkles up your look from basic to brilliant. Another quick-change trick: Change only your top. Sew an easy, glamorous shoulder-baring evening blouse to pair with a basic work skirt or dress pants. Sweep your hair back, add a hair accessory, sparkly earrings, a beaded belt, and you are ready to go.

This quick and easy changeover can take you through a cocktail or dinner party with a minimum of fuss and planning. For a bit more evening glamour, you can make a tailored evening jacket in brocade or velvet.

When entertaining at home, the casual and comfortable elegance of a silky, flowing top and easy-to-wear pants outfit can be stitched up in a flash. Try soft, pretty colors for spring in wool jersey or crepe. If you are a messy cook, make your at-home entertaining outfit in Austrian cotton knit. Build your look around an eye-catching piece of jewelry.

■ "If a woman rebels against high heeled shoes, she should take care to do it in a very smart hat."
—George Bernard Shaw.

Holiday Dressing

a. maeda

How about switching your priorities this season? Make a holiday outfit for yourself now before you even begin the endless hours of Santa's workshop. One of the best gifts you could give your family is you in a festive mood looking radiant.

Everyone goes to at least one dressy occasion during the year. If you suspect you won't be invited to one, consider having a small dinner party yourself and ask the guests to dress up.

Dressing up puts everyone in a festive mood. You may have such a good time; your small dinner party will become an annual event.

Planning for holiday glamour can be fun if you allow enough time to assemble the elements required to make the outfit spectacular.

If lace has always been one of your favorites, consider making a black lace dress or a blouse to go with a pair of wool crepe pants. Wool crepe is a good fabric choice for dressy pants since it has a soft drape as well as an interesting texture. Wool crepe is noted for shrinkage so preshrink fabric at the dry cleaners before cutting. Search out lace that is soft with shots of metallic, which will show up better at night.

Another fabric choice for a dress is rayon or silk velvet. These velvets drape far softer than polyester or cotton velvets and are more flattering. Top this with a jacket in quilted metallic, sequins, or shiny satin in a hot color and you have created a real show stopper.

If a less formal approach to dressing up is more your style, consider making soft pants, a shell, and a loose kimono in a three-color palette of wool jerseys. Use a spectacular piece of jewelry as the focal point.

For a very dressy occasion check out what is available in the department stores. Look to readywear for style trends and fabric ideas. If you have your heart set on strapless, purchase a good strapless merry widow right away so that the garment can be fitted around it.

Getting ready for the holidays can be a particularly busy time for the home sewer. Rather than returning with shopping bags full of gifts; the home sewer returns with shopping bags full of supplies and a head full of ideas of things to make and ways to spruce up the house for holiday festivities. When a party invitation arrives, she feels distressed by the "nothing to wear syndrome" and often has no time to buy or make anything suitable.

Holiday Dressing

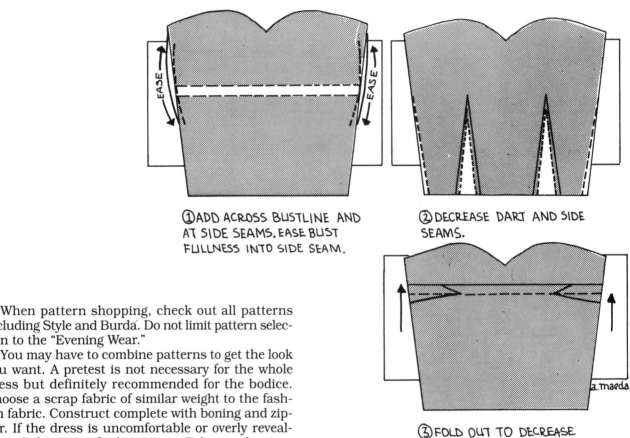

① ADD ACROSS BUSTLINE AND AT SIDE SEAMS. EASE BUST FULLNESS INTO SIDE SEAM.

② DECREASE DART AND SIDE SEAMS.

a.maeda

③ FOLD OUT TO DECREASE DART.

When pattern shopping, check out all patterns including Style and Burda. Do not limit pattern selection to the "Evening Wear."

You may have to combine patterns to get the look you want. A pretest is not necessary for the whole dress but definitely recommended for the bodice. Choose a scrap fabric of similar weight to the fashion fabric. Construct complete with boning and zipper. If the dress is uncomfortable or overly revealing, it's better to find out now. Polyester boning, available at the notions department, is a must for strapless or any well-fitted bodice. Grosgrain ribbon makes an excellent casing for boning. Round off both ends of boning with scissors and nail file to avoid fabric punctures. If the bust is large, build out the bust area a bit by adding onto the pattern ½ inch horizontally across the bust and curving the side seam at the bust area out slightly by ¼ inch.

This addition makes the front bodice ½ inch longer when joining the side seams. Run an easeline for 5 inches in the bust area before joining the side seam. Press gently to flatten but not remove the ease. Join the side seams.

For the small bust, large darts will create too much fullness and make the individual look even more flat-chested. For vertical darts, decrease the size of the dart and remove the excess at the side seam. For horizontal darts, fold out ½ inch horizontally through the darts. Sew in remainder of dart, which will be smaller by ½ inch.

To give the skirt the desired amount of fullness, consider combining netting and tulle. Several layers are often necessary for desired fullness. Bulk can be eliminated at the seam by gathering one or more layers of tulle onto the support layer 1 inch lower than the finished seam. If the netting is scratchy, consider using rayon taffeta as the support layer for the tulle.

Holiday Dressing

TOPSTITCH GATHERED RUFFLE B ON TOP OF A. THEN GATHER A.

A
B

a. maeda

CIRCULAR FLOUNCE OR GATHERED RUFFLE IS EQUAL TO SKIRT.

The taffeta will be kinder to the legs. Horsehair braid can give extra support to the outer and underskirt. Zigzag the horsehair braid to the skirt bottom with right sides together. Turn braid under toward the wrong side of the skirt. Sew in place.

To provide skirt fullness you have two options: a flounce which provides fullness without gathers; and a gathered skirt—straight grain or bias. For a flounce,

the inside of the flounce circle must measure precisely to the piece to which it will be added. Successful gathers depend very much on the fabric.

Experiment with samples. "Gather 25 inches to 10 inches, 50 inches to 10 inches, and decide what look you want," says Bobbie Carr. A bias ruffle will be less bulky than a straight grain ruffle.

Holiday Dressing

Nighttime is an opportunity to really pull out the stops with both makeup and jewelry. Daytime makeup can fade you out at night; go for darker eyes and lips. Jewelry adds the sparkle to make an outfit festive. Look for jewelry that catches the light. It's no wonder rhinestones have been popular for so many years. Consider investing in one fabulous fake piece. Bracelets are especially appropriate for evening since they are feminine and make noise.

Don't forget to do something festive with your hair. Casual daytime hairstyles are inappropriate and will distract from your look. Long hair can be pulled back with combs, barrettes, and loose ribbons. Short hair is more problematic. Consider wearing a beautiful flower (real or silk—no plastic, please) or covering your hair in a turban. Make one in related fabric or wool jersey, add a spectacular pin on the side.

Hose should be color related but slightly sheer—it's sexier. Consider a pair with a few rhinestones on the side. Patterned hose are usually too busy for evening and may compete with other elements in your attire—keep leg looks simple.

For the final touches, don't forget a small evening bag and beautiful soft gloves. Don't leave your coat decision until the last minute. Make time for a facial or massage the day of your special event and your most important asset—your face—will be radiant.

■ When making a bustier, always run the lengthwise grain around the body to prevent stretching.

How Not to Look Your Age

Being over 60 is no excuse for not looking your best. Women who once took great pride in their appearance often give up, making little or no effort as they age. Let's look at some options.

• If your hair has gotten thin, treat yourself to a couple of new hats. Vogue patterns offer several good ones.

• You don't need a whole new wardrobe to be in fashion. A scarf, earrings or shoes in the season's "fashion" color picks up your whole look.

• Experiment with the new skirt length. Long skirts are flattering to all figures.

• Don't be afraid of color. Beige and grey unless well accessorized with color can fade you into the woodwork.

• If your waist is large, belt at the waist only under a jacket. A looser belt worn at a slant over high hip is usually more flattering.

• If you have been wearing the same hairstyle for 10 years, make an appointment for a consultation at a salon you do not visit regularly. Short straight hair or long hair worn in a loose french twist is usually more flattering than the wash and wear permed "do."

• Avoid tiny florals. Is "Betty Crocker home in the kitchen look" really the way you see yourself?

• Do use eye makeup remover at night. Clumped mascara has always been tacky.

• Flesh tone hose should be the exception. Match shoe, hose and skirt color for a taller more put together look.

• Avoid the decorated sweatshirt, pull-on pant look. Although this look is very popular, it is rarely flattering on a mature woman.

• Don't always wear sensible shoes. Well cut flats can be comfortable and feminine.

• Because you wore a size 12 once doesn't mean you still do. Clothes which are too tight add weight by showing off rolls from the back.

• Do wear makeup. A little blusher, lipstick and mascara do wonders over 40.

• Be careful of too many rings. Too many of anything devalues each.

• If you have worn the same glasses for 10 years, go to an optician and see what's available. Glasses have changed greatly in the past 5 years. Do spend the extra money on lenses without the definite bifocal line.

• Don't always go for the small pearl earring or tiny hoop. Large, more distinctive earrings draw attention to the face.

• When skirt lengths go up, opt for pants. Unless the short skirt is paired with opaque tights and a flat shoe, mini skirts and an older face are incompatible, no matter how good your legs are.

• As women age, their coloring often changes. Treat yourself to a makeup lesson and learn how to make the most of what you have.

• Invest in a good quality tote, a better substitute for a flight bag.

• Tight waistbands make the tummy protrude. Make or shop for slightly elasticized waistbands.

• Do make a ⅞ length lightweight coat in tweed which can go over everything. This piece can pull your look together when you are in a hurry.

• If your hair is white or grey, avoid the cotton candy look with blue and purple hair rinses.

• Do try to be less critical of yourself and others. A positive spirit is your number one asset.

• Don't give up. Spunky souls have more fun and live longer.

Index

Sources

DISCONTINUED PATTERNS

From domestic pattern companies can usually be purchased up to a year after the pattern is taken out of the book. Discontinued Burda are unavailable.

CONTACT THE FOLLOWING:

Vogue and Butterick—800-221-2670
McCalls—212-880-2624
Simplicity, Style and New Look—800-223-1664

AMERICAN SEWING GUILD

If you would like to connect with other sewers in your area, the American Sewing Guild is a nonprofit organization which provides sewing information through lectures, classes and newsletters. To find the chapter nearest you contact: ASG, National Headquarters, P.O. Box 50936, Indianapolis, IN 46250.

Sources

American Sewing Guild, National Headquarters, PO Box 8476, Medford, OR 97504-0476; (503) 772-4059.

Bay Area Tailor Supply, 8000 Capwell Dr. #A, Oakland, CA 94621; 1-800-359-0400.

Beaded Clothing Techniques by Therese Spears (price: $6.75 ppd.), Promenade, Box 2092, Boulder, CO 80306. Fax 303-440-9116.

Bee Lee Company, Box 36108, Dallas TX 75235-1108; (214) 351-2091. Source for snaps and western trim; free catalog.

Burda Patterns: 1-800-241-6887 to find the nearest source.

Carr, Bobbie, PO Box 32120, San Jose, CA 95127; (408) 929-1651. Sewing tool and book catalogue as well as source for videos produced by Bobbie Carr.

Cinema Leathers, 1663 Blake Ave., Los Angeles, CA 90031; (213) 222-0073. Mail order leather and suede skins.

Clotilde, Inc., PO Box 22312, Ft. Lauderdale, FL 33335; 1-800-761-8655. Mail order notion supplies.

C.R. Crafts, Box 8, Dept. 12, Leland, IA 50453; (515) 567-3652. Bear and doll patterns, kits, and supplies. Catalogue: $2.

Crosby Creations, East 124 Sinto Ave., Spokane, WA 99202, 1-800-842-8445. Travel bags for sewing machines and supplies.

Daisy Kingdom, 134 NW 8th Ave., Portland, OR 97209. Mail order nursery ensembles, dress kits, craft kits, and outdoor fabrics. Catalogue $2 ppd.

Dharma Trading Co.; 1-800-542-5227. Great source for fabric paints; free catalogue.

Donna Salyers' Fabulous Furs, 700 Madison Ave., Covington, KY 41011; 1-800-848-4650. Free brochure.

Erickson, Lois, PO Box 5222, Salem, OR 97304, Books on wearable art.

Fouché (Shermaine) Patterns, 2121 Bryant St., San Francisco, CA 94107. Free brochure.

Garden of Beadin, PO Box 1535, Redway, CA 95560; (707) 923-9120. Mail order beads and findings. Catalogue $2.

Geisreiter, Andrea/*Travel Handbook,* PO Box 22934, Sacramento, CA 95822.

Ghee's, 106 E. Kings Hwy., Suite 205, Shreveport, LA 71104. Handbag patterns and findings.

Great Fit Patterns, 2229 NE Burnside, Suite 305, Gresham, OR 97030; (503) 665-3125. Patterns for large sizes. Catalogue $1.

Green Pepper, Inc., 3918 W. 1st St., Eugene, OR 97402. Mail order outdoor fabrics. Catalogue $2 ppd.

Horizon Leather Corp., 38 W. 32nd St., New York, NY 10001; (212) 564-1886. Leather and suede skins.

Islander School of Fashion Arts, Inc., PO Box 66, Grants Pass, OR 97526. 1-800-944-0213. Distributor of Margaret Islander's sewing videos.

Kwik Sew Patterns, 3000 Washington Ave., N., Minneapolis, MN 55411-1699. Home catalogue $5 ppd.

Nancy's Notions, PO Box 683, 333 Beichl Ave., Beaver Dam, WI 83916. Mail order notions.

Neue Mode Patterns, 1-800-862-8586.

Ornament, PO Box 35029, Los Angeles, CA 90035. Magazine for jewelers or anyone interested in embellishment.

Paco Despacio, Buttonsmith, PO Box 261, Cave Junction, OR 97523. Write, sending fabric sample, for information.

Practicality Press, 95 Fifth Ave., San Francisco, CA 94118; 1-800-845-7474. *Power Sewing* books and videos.

Rain Shed, 707 NW 11th St., Corvallis, OR 97330. Mail order outdoor fabrics. Catalogue $1 ppd.

Ranita Corp./Sure Fit Designs, PO Box 5567, Eugene, OR 97405; (503) 344-0422. Free brochure.

Revelli Design, 1850 Union St., San Francisco, CA 94123; (415) 673-6313. Color, style and design books, videos, and kits. Free catalogue.

Ruddy, Kathy, 10207 Marine View Dr., Everett, WA 98204. Producers of *Generic Serger* Video.

San Francisco Pleating Co., 425 2nd. St., San Francisco, CA 94107; (415) 982-3003.

Sew News, Box 3134, Harlan, IA 51537; 1-800-289-6397. Monthly fashion and information sewing magazine. $23.98 for 12 issues ppd.

Sewing Machine Exchange, 1131 Mission St., San Francisco, CA 94103; (415) 621-9877. Source of Naimoto industrial iron, costs approx. $400.

Sewing Workshop, 2010 Balboa St., San Francisco, CA 94121; (415) 221-SEWS.

Shaeffer, Claire, PO Box 157, Palm Springs, CA 92263. Source for *Fabric Resource Guide.*

Stretch and Sew Patterns, 19725 40th Ave. West, Lynnwood, WA 98036; (206) 774-9678. Catalogue $3.50.

Tailor, June, Inc., PO Box 208, Richfield, WI 53076. Mail order pressing supply and information source.

Tandy Leather Co., Box 2934, Ft. Worth, TX 76113. Mail order leather and suede skins. Catalogue $2.

Tex-Mar Publications/*Silks and Satins, Couture Action Knits,* #57-10220 Dunoon Dr., Richmond, B.C. Canada V7A 1V6; (604) 277-3231.

Threads Magazine, Taunton Press, Box 355, Newton, CT 06470-9955; 1-800-283-7252

Tire Silk Thread/Things Japanese, 9805 NE 116th St., Suite 7160, Kirkland, WA 98033

Treadleart, 25834-1 Narbonne Ave., Lomita, CA 90717; 1-800-327-4222. Mail order thread and machine supplies.

Update Newsletters, PO Box 5026, Harlan, IA 51537; 1-800-444-0454. *Sewing Update* is published bimonthly for $24 per year; *Serger Update* is published monthly for $48 per year. Also in-depth booklets available by subject for $3.95 ppd. per booklet. Send for list of titles.

Worldly Goods, 848 Camino de Pueblo Bernalillo, NM 87004; (505) 867-1303. Catalogue available, please call.

POWER SEWING PRODUCTS

☐ **POWER SEWING book: New Ways To Make Fine Clothes Fast**
A method which combines the step-by-step time saving techniques used in the ready-to-wear industry with the fitting and finishing techniques used in couture houses. For professional results found in ready-to-wear, you must use ready-to-wear techniques.
Hard cased, spiral bound   ISBN: 1-880630-13-3   **$29.95**

☐ **MORE POWER SEWING book: Masters' Techniques for the Sewing Connoisseur**
More Power Sewing is the second step in the Power Sewing formula, providing behind the scene tips on inner structure, pattern refinements, embellishment and finishing techniques used in better ready-to-wear or fine quality "made to measure."
Hard cased, spiral bound   ISBN: 1-880630-14-1   **$29.95**

☐ **FEAR OF SEWING book: For the Novice**
written for the non-sewer or would-be sewer intimidated by the sewing machine. Learn simple survival skills for hemming pants and skirts, fixing zippers and sewing on buttons, then see sewing as a hobby.
ISBN: 1-880630-15-X   **$7.95**

Do you have difficulty either remembering what you saw in a demonstration or visualizing a technique you read about? Sewing videos with camera close-ups and step by step instructions are the answer – instant replay – like sitting right next to the teacher. Available in VHS, BETA and PAL.

☐ **VIDEO #1 *FEAR OF SEWING***
How to thread and operate any sewing machine plus skirt and trouser hems, sewing on a button and much more.
82 minutes   ISBN: 1-880630-03-6   **$24.95**

☐ **VIDEO #2 PATTERN SIZING AND ALTERATION** *(formerly Pattern Smarts)*
End fitting frustration by getting the facts on which patterns run large, small, and true to size plus an easy method to determine pattern alterations.
63 minutes   ISBN: 1-880630-04-4   **$24.95**

☐ **VIDEO #3 FITTING SOLUTIONS**
See sixteen women representing a wide array of fitting challenges. See pattern alterations and final garments.
63 minutes   ISBN: 1-880630-05-2   **$24.95**

☐ **VIDEO #4 FOOLPROOF PANTS FITTING** *(formerly Class Act I)*
Secrets of European fit are revealed with this foolproof method for perfect fit, eliminating guesswork, altering the pattern before you cut.
75 minutes   ISBN: 1-880630-06-0   **$24.95**

☐ **VIDEO #5 CONSTRUCTION DIFFICULTIES** *(formerly Design Details)*
Perfect to overcome obstacles found in garment construction: fly fronts, difficult seams, sleeve vents, lapels, shoulder pads and grainline changes to flatter the figure.
120 minutes   ISBN: 1-880630-07-9   **$24.95**

☐ **VIDEO #6 EASY LININGS**
Learn lining shortcuts used in the industry which cut lining time by two thirds. Jacket, vest and pants are covered.
75 minutes   ISBN: 1-880630-08-7   **$24.95**

☐ **VIDEO #7 HASSLE-FREE DESIGNER JACKETS**(formerly Troubleshooting 1)
Learn interfacing choices for a wide variety of fabrics as well as world-class welt pockets and handling difficult fabrics at the machine and press.
62 minutes   ISBN: 1-880630-09-5   **$24.95**

☐ **VIDEO #8 EMBELLISHMENT** *(formerly Troubleshooting 3)*
Learn embellishment techniques for multiple piping, braid application, layered trim plus hand and machine beading.
78 minutes   ISBN: 1-880630-10-9   **$24.95**

☐ **VIDEO #9 COMMERCIAL PATTERN REFINEMENTS**(formerly Troubleshooting 2)
Refine the pattern to eliminate shoulders which ride to the back, sleeves which wrinkle, armhole stabilization for silk and tips for good looking buttonholes.
59 minutes   ISBN: 1-880630-11-7   **$24.95**

☐ **VIDEO #10 FEARLESS SERGING**
Learn to use your serger to its full potential, adjusting tension knobs and varying thread type to achieve a variety of decorative effects.
51 minutes   ISBN: 1-880630-12-5   **$24.95**

☐ **VIDEO #11 MARKETING WHAT YOU MAKE**
Get the nitty gritty on determining your market, pricing items, sewing contractors and making your first sales - from informative interviews with a designer, a sales rep and a dressmaker.
59 minutes   ISBN: 1-880630-16-8   **$24.95**

☐ **VIDEO #12 HANDWOVEN AND QUILTED GARMENTS**
Learn construction and finishing for garments in handwoven or quilted fabric. Learn suitable interfacings, seam treatments, neckline facing and hem finishes, as well as lining and closure tips.
128 minutes   ISBN: 1-880630-17-6   **$24.95**

PASS IT ON
Many of us have been sewing a long time. This hobby has brought us pleasure and satisfaction. Many schools have eliminated sewing from their curriculum. While few have time to teach someone to sew, you can turn someone on to this wonderful craft. Send them a *Fear of Sewing* book and video - only $27.95 for the combination.

☐ **COMBINATION *FEAR OF SEWING* BOOK AND VIDEO**   **$27.95**

Available in stores everywhere